Hiking Trails in the Mid-Atlantic States

Hiking Trails in the Mid-Atlantic States

by Edward B. Garvey

CONTEMPORARY SPORTS BOOKS
CHICAGO

Hiking Trails in the Mid-Atlantic States
© Edward B. Garvey 1976
All rights reserved
Printed in U.S.A.
International Standard Book Number 0-915498-21-9
Library of Congress Catalog Card Number: 75-41634

Published by arrangement
Greatlakes Living Press

Cover design by Joseph Mistak, Jr.
Cover photograph by Ron Nielsen
Other design by Dale and Lynn Beda

On opposite page is mountain wilderness country typical of much of that found in the regions covered by this book. Pictured here is Bear Rocks, a favorite scenic overlook in the Dolly Sods National Wilderness Area east of the Canaan Valley State Park in West Virginia. Noted for its glacial bogs and arctic tundra, Dolly Sods is popular with cross-country skiers who enjoy the wide, flat Alpine plateau reaches. The area's newly granted wilderness designation has brought hikers and backpackers flocking into the vicinity. [Photo by Gerald S. Ratliff, West Virginia Department of Commerce.]

CONTENTS

Chapter 11

Pennsylvania

Chapter 12

Delaware

Chapter 13

New Jersey

Appendix I

Appendix II

Appendix III

Scouting The Mid-Atlantic States

In March 1975 I was approached by Keith Ray and Mike Michaelson of Greatlakes Living Press to write this book. The proposition came at an opportune time. In 1969 I had retired from government service with the National Science Foundation, hiked the 2,000 mile Appalachian Trail the following year, written my book, *Appalachian Hiker,* and traveled extensively in 1971 in Europe with my family. Returning home late in the year, I went to work for Appalachian Outfitters, a chain of wilderness outfitting stores in Virginia, Maryland and North Carolina. It looked like I would lead a pleasant life, working 40 weeks a year with 12 weeks off for hiking, writing, and doing whatever retirees are prone to do.

But this routine was interrupted when I received, in late 1972, an opportunity to participate in an Outdoor Recreation Exhibit in Yugoslavia. That was followed by another in Yugoslavia, then two long assignments in the Soviet Union — I visited Moscow and Eastern Siberia. The final exhibit was in Hungary in September, 1974. So now I was back in the United States, and instead of putting up and taking down backpacking tents and cooking freeze dried foods at overseas exhibits I found myself doing about the same things at the Appalachian Outfitter store in Oakton, Virginia.

By then I was infected with this business of going to other places, doing different things and then writing books or articles about my experience. And along came the invitation to write this book. To complete the assignment I saw that I would have to visit the far reaches of the six mid-Atlantic states. I would see old friends, make new ones, and get in hundreds of miles of hiking in my beloved Appalachians. All of it under the guise of work!

In April, 1975, the second hiking book in the Greatlakes series *Hiking Trails in the Southern Mountains*, was published. The area covered western Oklahoma to northeastern Virginia, a tremendous distance for the two authors, Glenda Daniel and Jerry Sullivan to travel. I felt that my job would be much easier, since I lived in one of the mid-Atlantic

Landowner Nelson Hay [with child and dog but sans shoes] relaxes with trail patrolman Tim Abel. The Appalachian Trail crosses Hay's front lawn near Three Springs Shelter, Virginia.

states — Virginia — and had hiked in all of them except Delaware. Pretty nearly everything worked out as planned except that the ratio of automobile driving to hiking was not entirely to my liking.

It seems safe to say that the U.S. Forest Service maintains more miles of hiking trails then does any other single U.S. institution. In 1967 during Congressional hearings on what later became the National Trails System Act, Orville L. Freeman, then Secretary of Agriculture, stated that the Forest Service maintained more than 100,000 miles of hiking trails. Hence, anyone writing a book on hiking trails in an area that includes national forests, is well advised to first develop descriptions of the national forest trails and to build upon that base. That's exactly what Sullivan and Daniel did in the Southern Mountains book, and that is what I have done here in Virginia, West Virginia and to a lesser extent in Pennsylvania.

Not only are the foot trails in forest woodlands under the Forest Service's jurisdiction, but the Service has a good inventory of those trails, their distances and where they begin and end. Unfortunately, not all the

Memories of the Big Blue work trip of August, 1975—David and Steven Showalter, Mark Andrews and work-trip leader, Jeff Smith, work at trail clearing near Berkeley Springs, West Virginia.

trails that appear on their records still exist on the ground. One must be selective as to which trails to describe and attempt to verify the facts with Forest Service personnel at the district ranger level.

Personnel who manned the four national forests within the six mid-Atlantic states were most helpful in providing trail data and reviewing my writeups of those trails. All of the trail descriptions in this book, Forest Service, or otherwise, have been reviewed for accuracy by some knowledgeable person at the local level.

I have attempted throughout to focus attention on the tremendous role played by the volunteer hiking clubs and those of their members who establish the hiking trails, paint blaze them, erect signs, prepare the guidebooks and maps and carry on the year in and year out maintenance of both trails and trailside shelters. They are members of a great unofficial fraternity and I have met many of their members in this country and in Yugoslavia, and Austria. They and the private landowners who permit hiking trails to cross their property are the real heros of the trail movement.

Finally, a few words about these six mid-Atlantic states. It's a beautiful section of the United States of America, comprised of wide sandy ocean beaches, rolling Piedmont, the great agricultural valleys between the mountains, and lastly the Appalachians — "the friendly mountains" — as they are often called, with their tremendous acreages of hardwood timber, clear cold water gushing from thousands of springs and mountain streams, and their gorgeous displays of spring flowers. Truly it is a delightful area in which to plan a hiking trip.

Preparations for the Hike

This chapter and the four succeeding chapters contain information on a variety of basic subjects and conditions that the hiker should at least be familiar with. Entire books and long and comprehensive articles have been written on each of these subjects, but this book is primarily about hiking trails; hence we have not gone too deeply into these other basic matters. An appendix lists the names of books which supply more detailed information on these subjects.

Purchase of Equipment: In 1974 I developed an article specifically for the 1974 Yearbook of the United States Department of Agriculture. The yearbook was entitled *Shoppers Guide* and my article on the shopping for backpacking gear is reproduced in condensed form on page 9, with updated prices.

Backpacking ranks 18th in popularity among outdoor sports and it is rapidly gaining in popularity. Within the past three years some half dozen new backpacking and wilderness and camping magazines have hit the newsstands. The number of stores that cater to the backpackers' needs have increased greatly.

Suppose that you have an adventuresome spirit and that you are young in years, anywhere from 10 to 70, and want to take up backpacking.

Oh, you think 70 is a bit too old? Perish the thought! The legendary Grandma Gatewood took up the gentle pastime of backpacking at age 65 and hiked the 2,000-mile Appalachian Trail. She did it again at age 67 and again in her early 70's.

So let's suppose you have accepted an invitation to participate in a three-day backpacking trip. There is one little problem. You have no equipment. What should you buy and how much should you spend?

I know of one man who, in three nights of intensive shopping, purchased $1,000 of backpacking equipment for himself and two very young sons. That's one extreme.

Grandma Gatewood's cash outlay for equipment was the price of a pair of Ked basketball shoes plus the cost of one yard of blue denim cloth which she fashioned into a bag with a drawstring at one end. That's the other extreme.

Hopefully, your tastes and your pocketbook will put you somewhere between these extremes.

If you do not have access to an outdoor store you must resort to catalogs. Check outdoor magazines at your local library or newsstand and send for catalogs.

Some nationally known outdoor merchandisers via catalogs are L.L. Bean of Freeport, Maine; Holubars of Boulder, Col.; and the well-known cooperative of Seattle, Wash., Recreational Equipment, Inc. ("REI").

Now for some basic advice on your shopping procedure and then we will proceed to a discussion of what things you should buy and the price you should pay.

Do not let a salesman, a magazine advertisement, or even a fellow hiker convince you that you *must* buy the XYZ backpack, Model 3J; or the ABC sleeping bag, Model 12W. Don't believe it!

Since 1971 I have been affiliated with a small chain of outdoor stores in the Virginia, Maryland, and North Carolina area. This permits me to see and examine new products coming into the market. I also get feedback from both store employees and customers who use the products.

Competition is keen in the manufacture and distribution of backpacking gear, and a variety of competing makes and models are available that will fulfill your needs. Your decision should be based on the advice of the salesman and fellow hikers, your own appraisal of the article being purchased, and that very important consideration — how much you wish to spend.

If you are dealing with a salesman, and if you are green as grass in the knowledge of backpacking gear, inform the salesman of that fact. And if you have a definite limit on how much you can spend for a certain item, inform the salesman of that also. Any salesman worth his salt will be appreciative of both situations.

Nutritional food buying emphasizes the "Basic Four." Backpacking also has its basic four, these being in order of importance: 1) hiking shoes, 2) the backpack, 3) sleeping gear, and 4) shelter.

Selection of hiking shoes should be your first concern. Even a one-day hike can be misery without comfortable, good fitting, well broken-in shoes.

Today's hikers prefer a shoe that is six inches high, is made of leather, and has thick sturdy composition soles. Within this framework you could purchase shoes that weigh from 2½ lbs per pair to over 5 lbs per pair (for a size 10 shoe). The cost could range from $20 to $50.

If you are just getting into back-packing, I would suggest (using size 10 as an indicator again) a pair of shoes that weigh in the 3 to 4 lb range and that would cost somewhere between $28 and $34.

Take plenty of time in getting your shoes fitted. Wear the type of socks (usually a thin inner pair and a thick outer pair) that you will wear while hiking. Insist on a roomy fit to allow for the swelling that comes from carrying a 30 to 40 lb pack hour after hour. Break the shoes in thoroughly on short walks before going on any extended hike.

In purchasing a backpack you will find an almost bewildering array of makes, styles, and materials to choose from.

Over the past 20 years, the backpacking fraternity has come to prefer a combination aluminum frame to which is attached a pack of heavy duty nylon taffeta or cordura nylon with various side pockets and compartments to permit quick access to any desired article. The backpacking frame must have both shoulder straps and a waist strap, the latter strap being of such design as to permit much of the weight of the pack to rest on the sturdy hip bones rather than on the more fragile shoulder bones.

Backpacks that meet these general requirements can be purchased at costs ranging from $25 to $90. Cubic inch capacity may range from 1,500 to 6,000.

For growing youngsters and for adults who feel they may make only occasional use of their packs, I would recommend a pack and frame combination costing in the $25 to $30 range and having a cubic inch capacity of perhaps 2,000 to 2,500.

If you've already had your initiation into backpacking and know that it's going to be your thing, then I would suggest a pack and frame combination in the $45 to $60 range with a capacity from 2,500 to 4,000 cubic inches.

Two other items to consider are waterproofing and padded hip belts. There are waterproof backpacks and those made with no waterproofing. You can get valid arguments either way.

If you buy a non-waterproof bag and you are hiking in wet weather areas you will wish to buy a waterproof cover of some type for your pack.

A padded hip belt is a belt approximately one-half inch thick and four inches wide that distributes the weight of your pack more comfortably over a wider area of your hips than does the conventional inch-wide belt. It adds $6 to $8 to the cost of your backback.

The sleeping bag can be made or bought in a variety of fabrics and with a variety of filler material.

You can make a simple sleeping bag from a single blanket by sewing it so that it is closed on three sides. The bags that you buy at an outdoor store, however, are generally made with nylon ripstop or taffeta cloth and filled with either goose down, duck down, or a synthetic material such as Dacron II.

Goose down is generally considered the warmest ounce for ounce, and duck down is rated as 85 percent as effective as goose down.

Synthetic fills such as Dacron II do not enjoy wide popularity but a small and growing segment of the backpacking fraternity thinks the synthetic fills are superior to anything on the market. For one thing they generally are cheaper than goose and duck down.

Also, the synthetics are bulkier and firmer, the firmness being an asset in that you need less protection between you and the ground than when the highly compressible down filling is used. Bags with synthetic fill are also easier to clean.

In considering how warm a sleeping bag to buy and how much to pay, you first must decide in what months of the year you plan to use it. Perhaps 80 percent of all sleeping bag use in the United States occurs between April 1 and October 31.

If you anticipate that all of your backpacking will be done in temperatures above 20°F you can purchase a lighter weight, less expensive bag than you would otherwise need.

Presuming you are one of the 80 percent hiking in the warmer months, a bag with 2 lbs of goose down or its equivalent should be more than sufficient. Such a bag may cost from $40 to $80.

If you are buying a bag at an outdoor store, ask to try it on for size. A bag that is two inches too short is *much* too short! When buying a bag costing from $40 to $100 you have every right to try it on for size.

There are mummy type bags, barrel bags, and full rectangular bags. The mummy type bag is tapered to fit the body, is the lightest to carry, and the easiest to keep warm. But some people find the mummy bag too confining.

Two accessories to the sleeping bag are the ground cloth and mattress. The ground cloth can be an inexpensive piece of clear plastic (costing, say, 80 cents) about 6 ft by 8 ft in size. Or you can buy a piece of waterproof nylon — easier to handle but more expensive — for about $11. A few backpackers require no mattress whatever, but most of us want some type of protection between the sleeping bag and the ground (in addition to the razor thin groundcloth).

Veteran backpackers have progressed from air mattresses to foam pads to the present-day preference for either Valera or Ensolite (trade names of two types of closed cell insulation). Of the two I prefer the Ensolite as it is softer and easier to roll up into a small bundle.

The Ensolite does not absorb water and it provides excellent protection against cold. It comes in various thicknesses and sizes. For warm weather camping I use a piece 20 in x 40 in that is a fourth of an inch thick (cost, $3). For temperatures that are below 30°F, I would use a piece approximately 21 in x 56 in and three-eighths of an inch thick, costing $6.

This brings us to the fourth and last of our basic four, the tent or other emergency shelter.

A very inexpensive shelter is the plastic tube tent. A tube tent for one person costs $1.50. Next on the list of inexpensive shelters is an 8 ft x 10 ft waterproof nylon tarp with grommets which cost $17. This can be used as a tent or a ground cloth or partially as both.

From here we move into bona fide tents, those ingenious little homes on your back that are made from colorful ripstop or taffeta nylon, with sewn-in floors, and mosquito netting. One- and two-man tents weighing from 3 to 5 lbs can be purchased for as low as $25, and they range up to $170.

Space does not permit detailed descriptions of the other items you will need for backpacking.

But I have prepared a price chart showing at 1976 prices what you might expect to pay.

Start slowly and shop carefully. That's half the fun! And hopefully, one day you will have completed all your purchasing, and your hiking shoes will have been thoroughly broken-in and waterproofed. You and your friends will reach the trailhead where the hike is to begin. You square your shoulders, take a final cinch on the waistband of your pack, and you're on your way.

BACKPACKING PRICE CHART

(1976 Prices)

ITEM	GOOD	BETTER	BEST
HIKING SHOES	$0-$18	$35	$50
BACKPACK	$25	$40	$50-$90
SLEEPING GEAR	$30	$60	$100
SHELTER OR TENT	$2-$15	$30-$80	$110-$170
STOVE	$0-$3	$12-$15	$12-$25
COOKING AND EATING GEAR	$0-$2	$7-$10	$18-$25
RAIN GEAR	$1-$2	$12-$16	$25-$40
HIKING CLOTHES	$0-$15	$30-$50	$70-$150
MISCELLANEOUS First Aid Kit, Cord, Flashlight, Matches, Compass, Toilet Articles	$6-$8	$14-$16	$20-$25
ROUGH TOTAL	$95	$290	$550

Conditioning: Before going on any extended hiking trip, it is wise to take a few shakedown hikes both to test the condition and capacity of your own body and to test the equipment you have purchased. If you have purchased a tent, practice putting it up and taking it down at home. A hastily selected campsite on the trail with the sun rapidly fading is *not* the time and place to try to acquire such skills. The same goes for a gasoline stove. Practice the operation at home, so that you feel like an old pro when you set up that stove in the woods, pour in the preheating fuel, and shortly hear the steady roar and watch its dancing blue flame.

If you have not hiked before and are unsure of where to go and what to do, it would be wise to hike with others to acquire some necessary experience. Many of the metropolitan areas have Sunday hikes sponsored by various hiking clubs. Look in the leisure sports section of your newspaper around Tuesday or Wednesday of each week to find out what hikes are scheduled, who the leaders are, and other particulars. Newcomers are always welcome. Or you might just telephone the newspaper and talk to one of the leisure sports writers to obtain information on hiking clubs and scheduled hikes. One last suggestion: look in the yellow pages of the phone book under Camping Equipment and telephone one of the outdoor stores to obtain information. An appendix to this book lists names and addresses of hiking organizations in the six mid-Atlantic states.

Should you join a hiking club if there is one in your locality? By all means! Frequently the trails over which you hike and the trailside shelters you use are available because of the efforts of the hiking organization. If you use these facilities it seems only fair that you support the organization that makes these things possible. Furthermore, you will more than likely find yourself enjoying the company of people who are enthusiastic about the very activity you are about to undertake and enjoy.

Hazards of the Trail

In this chapter we will discuss just a few of the more common hazards a hiker may encounter in the mid-Atlantic states — such things as insects, snakes, bears, and unprotected water supplies.

Water

> *"In the Blue Ridge Mountains we had the purest, coldest,*
> *and best water on earth."*

The words were spoken by George T. Corbin on or about 1969 as a group of five of us walked with him on a six-mile hike down Nicholson Hollow in Shenandoah National Park. Two of the group were carrying tape recorders and we were asking the 80-year-old Corbin questions about life in the hollow where he had been born and raised. A little later, Park Service Ranger Paul Lee asked, "Mr. Corbin, what was the most frequent cause of death among the mountain people?" Unhesitatingly George replied, "Typhoid Fever."

Since typhoid fever is generally transmitted by water it would seem that there was a glaring inconsistency in Corbin's statement. Not necessarily so. Blue Ridge spring water is cold. The spring water at the Corbin cabin has a temperature of 42-44°F in mid-summer. As to taste, I will agree that it's the best-tasting water I have ever drunk. As to purity, well, no one that I know has contracted typhoid in recent years from drinking water in the Shenandoah National Park. But Corbin was speaking about an era when there were more than 400 families living in the area along with their livestock and other domestic animals, and even the purest of water supplies can become quickly contaminated under such conditions.

Item: The danger of typhoid is always present in unprotected water sources. To mitigate that danger, get a *typhoid shot.* Why take a dangerous chance when protection is so easy to obtain?

Remember, State Boards of Health will not test or render any report on water samples taken from an unprotected water source. "Unprotected" means from an open spring or stream or cistern. Any time you drink water from such unprotected sources you do so at your own risk. At the more commonly used springs in Shenandoah National Park for example, there are signs reading *"Unprotected Water Source. Recommend Boiling Or Use Of Purification Tablets."* The water is so good in the Park and the chance for contamination so slight that most of us drink it just as it comes out of the ground. But each of us does so at his own risk.

Generally speaking, how great is the risk? In my 1970 hike of the Appalachian Trail, I drank from unprotected water sources perhaps six times a day for 158 days. I boiled or purified the water on perhaps five occasions. I should have done it one more time because I came down with a severe case of dysentery that lasted almost a week before I could shake it off. I attributed it to impure water. A good point to remember: generally, if the water source is near a dwelling or around pastures, avoid it.

If you're uncertain of the water and you wish to purify it, how do you do so? Bob Burrell, a microbiologist (also a hiker and a canoeist), writing in the book *Hiking Guide to Western Pennsylvania*, cites four ways, tested under laboratory conditions that are equally effective in purifying water:

1. Boil for at least one minute.
2. Place eight drops of a 2.5% iodine solution in a quart of water and let stand 10 minutes.
3. Place one Halazone (R) tablet in a pint of water, and let stand for 30 minutes after it has thoroughly dissolved.
4. Add 16 drops of fresh household "Clorox" to a quart of water and let stand for 10 minutes.

But in correspondence with Burrell he amplified his conclusions by stating that, while the latter three methods were equally effective in killing all disease producing *bacteria* in the water, it is uncertain as to how effective they would be in killing some of the enteroviruses, such as those that cause hepatitis. He therefore concluded that to be fully safe, one should boil the water. So there you have the pros and cons and you are on your own as to how safe you wish to be on your drinking water.

Insects — Not too much of a problem in these states, mostly mosquitos, noseeums (tiny black flies) and deer flies. By all means carry insect repellant and a large bandana kerchief, the latter for both head and neck protection from the small flies that have a pronounced fondness for ears and eyes. Woodticks present a problem in the early spring months. If they reach the point where they have become imbedded in your skin, a drop of alcohol or gasoline will generally cause them to disengage.

Domestic Dogs — Time and again people, even those in the small mountain villages, would express tremendous concern for the hikers' welfare because of the danger of bears and snakes. Neither of these critters gave me too much concern, but domestic dogs, that's another story. Each year hikers get bitten by dogs. There seems to be something about a hiker and that pack that infuriates them. In dog territory, carry a staff If they keep pestering reach for a stone, real or imaginary. That scares most of them. Where dogs are really a problem, carry a small squirt can of "HALT." The stuff doesn't seem to hurt the dogs but they suddenly lose interest in attacking.

BEARS — In wilderness areas, where hunting is permitted, they will avoid you. In national parks where they are protected, and especially where they have developed the habit of raiding garbage cans and receiving handouts from tourists, they become a menace. In such areas be certain to remove all food from your pack and tent and suspend the food sack by a rope from a tree. Be sure the suspended food is at least eight feet off the ground, preferably a bit higher. Bears are good climbers so hang the food in such a manner that the bear cannot reach it by climbing the tree.

SNAKES — The fear of poisonous snakes is one of the principal reasons why many people are reluctant to hike or camp out where such snakes are known to exist. But first let us put the danger of snake bite in its proper perspective. Some 6,680 people are bitten by poisonous snakes each year in the entire United States. Of this number about 14 or 15 die, less than ¼ of 1%. The authority for these statistics is *Emergency Medicine* magazine, July, 1969. Compare this to the 45,000 or so people who die each year from automobile accidents.

Statistically you are much safer hiking in the woods, even where there are poisonous snakes, than you are driving on the highways. The two poisonous snakes that frequent the mid-Atlantic states are the copperhead and the rattle snake. You should learn to identify these two snakes — and there is ample literature available — because in the rare, rare event you or one of your party is bitten by one of them the doctor will need to know what type of snake did the biting so that the proper antivenin can be selected. The rattlesnake generally (but not always) assists in the identification by sounding his buzzer. And I might say that if you are hiking and one of these rascals buzzes you at close range (as one did me on the Appalachian Trail hike) it will cause you to jump right out of your boot tops! The buzz is an unmistakeable, insistent noise that leaves no doubt as to what will happen if you ignore it.

I have not carried a snake bite kit for years. This is a calculated risk, perhaps, but there is a growing number of people who think that a snake bite kit in the hands of the untrained person is more dangerous than the bite. And how does one get training on cutting through someone's flesh to just the proper depth? *Patient Care* magazine, May, 1972, contains excellent instructions. What follows is a condensed report of the article's instructions on getting the patient to a doctor.

Get the patient to the doctor quickly. Those who obtain treatment within two hours after being bitten stand a very good chance of recovery. If there are enough people in the party, carry the patient out on a litter. If that is not feasible, have the patient walk slowly, but avoid running. Place a tourniquet about two-five inches above the wound. Don't make it so tight that it constricts the blood flow in the arteries. Loosen the tourniquet slightly as swelling appears but do not remove it.

NETTLES AND POISON IVY— Both these plants appear in profusion in the mid-Atlantic states. Learn to identify them, but especially the poison ivy. The stinging nettles are irritating and will pierce right through your trousers. Fortunately the sting lasts only a few moments.

Poison ivy is an entirely different matter. Even a mild case can cause much discomfort for about two weeks. And a really bad case can almost totally incapacitate a person for days, though such cases are quite rare. Any part of the plant can do the damage, the leaf, berries, bark, or roots. And unlike stinging nettles, which sting immediately on contact, the poison ivy causes no discomfort upon contact.

In a day or so, if the infection is mild, you will discern a number of tiny pimple-like blisters which will ooze water and can itch furiously. If the infection is a severe one, angry looking red patches will appear; they will slowly become larger blisters from which water will occasionally seep forth.

If this sounds like the voice of experience talking, it is! For the voice of experience was once incapacitated for two weeks with the lower part of his body covered with corn starch and swathed in loosely tied old baby diapers until those huge blisters dried up.

In my scouting trip for this book I encountered one of the lushest growths of poison ivy I have ever seen, this one in western Pennsylvania. Small wonder that I strongly advise people hiking in the mid-Atlantic states to wear long trousers for protection from insects and from poison ivy. There are many lotions on the market that alleviate the itching, but only time — ten days to two weeks — really cures it. So learn to recognize poison ivy in all its forms, as a shrub, a trailing vine, or as a climber. And it's a terrific climber, very much like a grape vine, only the poison ivy vine, as it matures puts forth dark hair. So if you see a climbing vine, thick as your wrist covered with darkish hair, watch out! It's poison ivy . . . *Rhus.toxicodendron,* the *numero uno* of poisonous plants in the eastern states.

SORE FEET—Sore feet should not occur on the hiking trail. But they do, frequently, much too frequently. The most likely culprit is the owner of a new pair of hiking boots who has failed to either obtain a proper fit or to break in the boot properly. Thousands of words of warning have been written on this subject, but hikers continue to ignore them so let's consider what to do when sore feet begin to develop during the hike.

At the first indication of soreness — *Stop*. Even if you are with a large group of other hikers — *stop*. A quick first aid remedy at this point will avoid longer and more frequent pauses later on. If you have stopped soon enough there should be no blister, just a red spot where a blister is hoping to be born! Apply two half-inch or three-quarter-inch width pieces of adhesive tape in the form of an "X" on the sore spot. Put socks and boots on and resume hiking. If you delay your stop until a blister has already formed then a different remedy is in order. Select a piece of

Spruce Knob, elevation 4861 feet, contains many miles of developed hiking and backpacking trails—besides campgrounds, a lake and good surfaced access roads. Here, two backpackers rest atop one of the boulders that dot the mountain slopes. [Photo by Gerald S. Ratliff, West Virginia Department of Commerce.]

moleskin big enough to cover the blister and some of the surrounding area. Cut out a hole in the moleskin the size of the blister. Apply the patch so that the blister is protected but not covered by the moleskin. Again, put on socks and shoes and resume hiking.

CHAFING—Chafing is second only to ill fitting shoes as a source of discomfort on long distance hiking. Chafing is primarily a hot weather ailment from skin rubbing against skin with a big assist from perspiration. It occurs chiefly in the crotch and buttock areas but again it can occur any place where skin rubs against skin, or where clothes or equipment rubs against skin. Powders are quite effective in relieving discomfort — corn starch, baby powders, or a medicated powder such as Ammens. One experienced hiker maintains that relief can be obtained from Vaseline. As with sore feet, early treatment is important.

HYPOTHERMIA—The word "hypothermia" seems to have entered into our vocabulary in only the past few years. My 1963 *Webster's Collegiate Dictionary* doesn't even include the word. I have hitherto avoided its use, because I somehow felt that someone had coined a five syllable word to describe something that could more simply be described by such words as "freezing", "frostbite," or "exposure." But it's not quite like that. Hypothermia is considered to be the *only* word that accurately describes the rapid collapse of the human body due to the chilling of the inner core. Two aspects of this killer were surprising to me: (1) It occurs most often in temperatures of 30 to 50 degrees, and (2) it is the number one killer of outdoor recreationists.

Outdoor books are increasingly devoting space to hypothermia; the 20th Appalachian Trail Conference meeting at Boone, North Carolina, in June, 1975 had as one of its workshops "Dangers of Hypothermia and How the Hiker May Protect Himself". Space permits only a brief coverage here.

Principal contributing factors to hypothermia dangers are wind, exhaustion and getting wet. Have rain gear that will keep out water under windy conditions (this eliminates most types of ponchos). When weather is wet, cold, and windy, wool clothing is your best bet. Carry a tight, storm proof tent. Make camp early in the day. Don't push yourself too far. In planning your trip, think hypothermia. Let people know where you're going and when you expect to be back. Three people rescued from the 4,860 foot Spruce Knob in 1975 were overdue at home. A telephone call to the Forest Service office in Petersburg, West Virginia, prompted a snowmobile rescue trip. So let family or friends know where you are going, when you expect to be back, and where to telephone in case you do not return on schedule.

Do some more reading on the subject. A little leaflet given me by the Forest Service called *Four Lines of Defense Against Hypothermia* is useful. Single copies may be obtained free by sending stamped self-addressed envelope to the Appalachian Trail Conference, P.O. Box 236, Harpers Ferry, West Virginia 25425.

Map and Compass

Throughout this book we have shown at least one map, and sometimes two or three, for each trail we have described. They will assist the hiker in determining the location of the beginning and ending points of the hike. The maps will also inform the hiker what physical features he will encounter while hiking — i.e., mountains, streams, lakes, roads, or other trails. Some of the maps are topographic, with contour lines showing elevations which permit the skilled map reader to figure out how steeply or how gently the trail leads up to or descends from the higher points of elevation.

The most frequent map reference made throughout the book is the reference to the topographic maps of the U.S. Geological Survey. For simplicity we have referred to these maps as "U.S.G.S. Quads." The U.S. Geological Survey (USGS) is an agency of the Federal Government that prepares a variety of maps for many purposes. We are concerned with topographic maps, which the USGS defines as "a graphic representation of selected manmade and natural features of a part of the earth's surface plotted to a definite scale. The distinguishing characteristic of a topographic map is the portrayal of the shape and elevation of the terrain."

USGS maps are available from a number of retail outlets throughout the country. They are also available from the USGS itself, both from over-the-counter sources and by mail from two big central warehouses. Maps of areas east of the Mississippi River should be ordered from the U.S. Geological Survey, 1200 South Eads St., Arlington, Virginia 22202. For maps west of the Mississippi, order from USGS, Federal Center, Denver, Colorado 80225. In Washington, D.C. area *over-the-counter purchases only* may be made from:

1028 General Services Building, 19th & F Streets, NW, Washington, D.C. or from Room 1C402, U.S.G.S. National Center, Reston, Virginia

As a first step you might write to the USGS at either Arlington, Virginia, or Denver and ask for the free "Index to Topographic Maps of _____ (name of state)." Also ask for the free booklet "Topographic

Maps." The index map is a harvest of map information by itself. I have before me the index map for Virginia. It is a 22 x 30-inch affair showing on one side an outline map of Virginia and appearing on the map in its proper location is the name of every 7½ minute and 15 minute quadrangle map of the state. In the lower left corner appears the following: "The number of published maps shown on this index is 823 as of January, 1975."

For my home county, Fairfax, there are perhaps six or seven quadrangle maps listed. For the particular part of the county in which I live, I find that the "Falls Church 1956-65 (71PR)" map is the one I would order. The 71PR symbol means that the map was photo-revised in 1971. On the reverse side of the index map appears much more information. There is a listing and description of various types of maps available for Virginia — the three special maps of the Shenandoah National Park, a map of the Appalachian Region, maps of the Colonial National Monument, Virginia (Yorktown Battlefield and environs). There is also a listing of all maps covering National Parks and Monuments, descriptions of various U.S. maps, and finally of all libraries in the state where there are reference files of USGSmaps plus a listing of names and addresses of all retail dealers within the state.

The map scale is generally shown as a ratio — e.g., 1:24,000 or 1/24,000. This means that one inch of the map equals 24,000 inches (or 2000 feet) on the ground. Or stated another way, 2½ inches equals 1 mile. Perhaps 75% of all the USGS quads in the six mid-Atlantic states are available at this scale, and this is considered a large-scale map, large enough so that hiking trails and contour lines can be easily identified. A map of this scale is also known as a 7½ minute quadrangle or quad. On smaller scale maps, 1:62,5000, 1 inch equals nearly 1 mile. This is also known as a 15 minute quad. Hiking trails can be identified on this smaller scale map, but it's difficult, and trying to check elevations by way of the contour lines is even more difficult on this small scale. All of this is explained in more detail in the little booklet "Topographic Maps" which you will receive free from USGS. The booklet has copious illustrations in color, using the same colors and symbols that are used on the topographic maps (topos).

The reference to "15 minute quads" or "7.5 minutes quads" requires a bit of explanation. This tells you how big a portion of the earth's surface is portrayed on the map. A 15 minute quad covers 15 minutes of latitude and longitude, printed at a scale of 1:62,5000. The 7.5 minute quads cover but 7.5 minutes of longitude and latitude but since they are printed on the same size sheet of paper the scale is larger and much easier to read.

Most of the symbols used on these maps represent a physical entity that you will find on the ground, a lake, stream, mountain or whatever. Of course, you won't find any contour lines on the ground, but this symbol enables the map reader to determine the elevation of the terrain over which he will hike.

The 7½ minute quads are 22″ x 26″ in size and since you may need a number of them for a hike of a weeks duration, it can become somewhat of a problem as to how to store them in the pack and yet have them available for ready reference. Veteran hiker Norman Greist of North Haven, Connecticut, uses the following method. If his hike requires the use of four 7.5 minute quads, Greist traces in with a colored marker the exact route that he plans to hike. Then with scissors he cuts an 8″ wide piece out of the big map which has in its center the route of the trail, plus approximately four inches on either side. He then glues all his 8″ pieces end to end on a single roll of brown wrapping paper, rolls it up, and puts the whole thing in his pack. The maps are protected by the wrapping paper; the roll can be removed from pack at any time and promptly opened up to the proper spot for examination. *Caution:* Before doing any cutting be certain to copy on to the abbreviated map the "North" arrow and the angle of declination of the compass. Without such information the convenient 8″ wide map loses much of its value, and you are liable to find yourself lost!

Another convenient way to carry a map is to fold or refold it so that the immediate area in which you are hiking is exposed. Then put the map in a plastic case that has clear see-through plastic. Some of these map cases are designed with cloth carrying straps that permit fastening them to your belt.

In ordering the USGS quad maps be certain to provide three pieces of information — name of quad, name of state, and the scale. Example: Hackensack, New Jersey, 7½ minutes. If you order an index map from USGS you will receive an order blank on which all the maps and their scales are listed and the buyer need only indicate the number of each map desired. The quad maps sold for 75 cents each in December, 1975.

In addition to the USGS quads, there are many other maps we have made reference to in this book, principally U.S. Forest Service maps and maps issued by hiking organizations. The latter generally show trail routes and location of trailside shelters in much more prominent fashion than do the general purpose USGS and Forest Service maps. For most of my hiking in the Appalachians and in the Alps I have relied on maps prepared by hiking club organizations and have found them to be quite satisfactory.

We must also discuss the compass and how the compass is used with respect to the map. Those who have gone through Boy or Girl Scout ranks are taught the use of the compass early in the program. The compass has a moveable needle with one end, generally colored red, that points to magnetic north. Magnetic north is not exactly the same as true north and the difference on the map is referred to as the angle of declination. In our six mid-Atlantic states this difference is only about 5% so you can forget it for all practical purposes. Just remember that your compass points *generally north*.-Many of the hiking club maps do not attempt to make the distinction.

Compasses show directions in two ways — by degrees (from 0° to 360°) and by the abbreviations for North, South, East, and West and for the points in between. To orient compass to map, put the map flat on the ground and lay the compass on top of it. Hold the compass firm and keep turning the map around until the North arrow on the compass points in the same direction as the North line on the map. If the map has two North lines, line up your compass with the one labeled "MN" (magnetic north). Once you've done that, move the compass over to the exact point where you are at present. Take a reading, either by direction point, e.g. NW, or by degrees, e.g. 315° to the spot on the map that you want to go to. Take compass in hand and sight in that same NW or 315° direction and pick out some prominent landmark on that sighting. Upon[1] reaching that landmark, take another reading on your 315° course, etc. I've oversimplified somewhat but this is basically the system. Two books on the market that explain this in detail with illustrations are *Be Expert With Map & Compass* (Bjorn Kjellstrom), published by Charles Scribner's Sons and *Orienteering* (John Disley), published by Stackpole Press. Both books were selling for $3.95 in December, 1975.

Who should carry a compass? Just about anyone who is hiking or vacationing in forested or mountainous areas with which he is not *intimately* acquainted. In the wooded Appalachians it is amazingly easy to become lost. Once your are out of sight and out of earshot of the familiar landmarks, all the trees and shrubs suddenly look totally *unfamiliar*. People who most frequently get lost are not the backpackers but those who just wander off from a known spot and cannot find their way back. What makes these cases so tragic is that frequently the person involved may be wearing only light clothes and is ill equipped for the exposure he may face before being found.

When hiking or camping in unfamiliar areas it is wise to fix firmly in your mind a landmark, a road, or trail that you can always head for in case you do become lost. Suppose that you are walking on a prominent hiking trail that runs north-south and you make a camp at a point 50 yards to the west of that trail. If you stray too far from your camp area and those trees suddenly take on that unfamiliar look, you know that all you need to do is to walk straight east until you pick up that north-south trail. You may not know whether to go north or south when you reach that trail but you must check it out either way until you are back at your campground.

There is a little known book that came on the market in 1974. It is entitled *Celestial Navigation For The Simpleminded* and has clear simple directions for using the sun, moon, shadows and other objects to ascertain directions without use of the compass. It was written especially for car drivers, hikers, hunters, backpackers, campers and other outdoorsmen. It is at present available only from the author, Bill Thomas, whose experiences as an airplane pilot, avid mountaineer, and amateur astro-

High on the flanks of Spruce Knob, backpackers find the deep mountain valleys filled with morning mist as they climb the highest peak in West Virginia. [Photo by Gerald S. Ratliff, West Virginia Department of Commerce.]

nomer (to name a few of his pursuits) make him well qualified to write such a book. Cost in December, 1975 was $1.25, available by mail from William C. Thomas, Jr., 5906 North 19th St., Arlington, Virginia 22205.

The Appalachians

The Appalachian Mountains begin in eastern Alabama, enter into northern Georgia, continue in a northeasterly direction through western North Carolina and eastern Tennessee, and on into Virginia. Here they split; the Blue Ridge, the more easterly segment comes within 60 miles of Washington, D.C., and extends almost to Harrisburg, Pennsylvania. The more westerly group, known as the Alleghenys, extends through the most westerly part of Virginia and eastern West Virginia and marches on into western Pennsylvania. North of Pennsylvania, the Appalachians continue their northeasterly course extending throughout the New England states and into Canada terminating at the Gaspe Peninsula.

The Appalachian Trail, which has its southern terminus at Springer Mountain in North Georgia, clings tenaciously to the crest of the Blue Ridge until, near Harrisburg, Pennsylvania, the Blue Ridge disappears. The Trail then continues its northward course through other parts of the Appalachians, the Kittatinny Mountains, the Berkshires, the Green Mountains, the White Mountains and to its terminous at Katahdin in Central Maine. All of these mountains segments are part of the Appalachians.

In that wonderful book entitled simply *The Appalachians,* naturalist Maurice Brooks lets you explore these mountains with him, from Alabama to the Gaspe Peninsula. With color and black and white pictures, drawings by the Darlings, and in simple straightforward prose he literally dissects the mountains, explaining everything from bird life on the tallest tree in the highest mountain to reptile life in the deepest limestone cave. Writing in a first person conversational style, he digresses occasionally as most of us do in informal conversation. In his discussion of flowers and woody plants he is reminded of the various types of wild honey produced from such flowers and from there he takes off on a discussion of bee trees.

His description of the Canaan Valley and the pronunciation of the word "Canaan" struck a responsive chord. Forest Service District Ranger

Contrary to the more stereotyped images of strip-mined wastelands and tarpaper shacks, West Virginia contains much of the last unspoiled wilderness in the Eastern United States. Vast mountain regions spread out for miles across the state where the only vague hints of civilization may come in the jet airplane contrails in the sky. This view looks down the crest of North Mountain from the North Mountain Firetower in the Seneca Rocks-Smoke Hole Recreation area. [Photo by Gerald S. Ratliff, West Virginia Department of Commerce.]

Harry Mahoney had suggested trails that I might hike in that area (West Virginia-Cheat Ranger District), and had gone so far as to tell me how the word was pronounced. I had toyed with the idea of informing my readers of its pronunciation also. It's a Biblical word, but in West Virginia its pronounced "Kuh-NANE." Brooks goes about it by spelling it phonetically as Ka-nane, "with the accent on the second syllable and the second 'a' given its long sound." If you do hike trails in this area you should now certainly be able to pronounce the name of the area as the local people do.

Valley land within the Appalachians is highly prized as agricultural land and intensively farmed. Possibly because of this reason, the hiking trails in the mid-Atlantic states tend to be concentrated in the mountain areas. Thus, perhaps three-fourths of all the trails in this book are so located. The valley trails quite frequently involve some road walking and expose the hiker to more evidences of "civilization." Some hikers may find this objectionable, but most long distance hikers welcome an occasional break where they can walk along wooded rural roads and even into small towns.

The height of the mountains in our six-state Appalachians area varies considerably. In the extreme southwest part of Virginia we have the two 5000 footers — Mt. Rogers at 5729 and Whitetop at 5520. West Virginia lists ten mountains in the 4600-4800 foot elevation, but generally our hiking trails in the mountains of these two states is about 2500-4500 feet in elevations. As we leave the two Virginias, the elevations continue to drop, seldom exceeding 3000 feet, most frequently being at the 1500-2000 foot level. But don't underestimate the Appalachians even when the elevation seems somewhat unimpressive. The few that have hiked both the 2000 mile Appalachian Trail and the 2300 mile Pacific Crest Trail (California, Oregon, Washington) rate the Appalachian Trail as the more difficult because it has so much up and down hiking.

The flora of the Appalachians is one of its greatest charms. The early European explorer-botanists were amazed at the variety and beauty of the trees, woody plants, and flowers found in the new continent. And, Springtime in the Appalachians is spectacular. As a Midwesterner, transplanted to the mid-Atlantic states in 1943, I continue to marvel at the sheer beauty of the springtime flowers and woody plants — the rhododendron, the wild azaleas, the mountain laurel. On May 12, 1970, in southwestern Virginia I had walked through six miles of trillium of various hues and in my book I designated that day as "trillium day." The next day I walked through miles of wild azalea. The air was heavy with their delicate fragrance and I designated that day as "wild azalea day." In May, 1975, I received a postcard written from a trailside shelter in North Carolina. It was signed by six hikers of the Appalachian Trail — just to let me know that they, too, were celebrating "trillium day!"

Probably the most spectacular display put on by the southern Appalachians each year in May and June is that of the Catawba rhododendron, the big woody plants that grow from 10 to 20 feet high and have fist-sized flowers that range in hue from pink to purple. While the most popular display is that on Roan Mountain, Tennessee, the mountains in West Virginia and in southwestern Virginia also have impressive displays of this beautiful plant.

The final chapter in Brook's book on the Appalachians deals with animal life. The establishment of the eastern national forests, the national parks and the state parks and forests throughout the Appalachians has resulted in a gradual increase in the big game animals. In southwestern Virginia a herd of elk was established some years ago and seems to be thriving. Black bear and deer have returned, and there are some who believe that the deer population in the Appalachians is larger now than when the white man came to America. Among the game birds, the ruffed grouse is the most popular. Show me the man who doesn't jump a bit when one of these birds takes off suddenly like a fighter plane starting out and up at full throttle. When hiking in early May if you examine the spot from which the grouse began her flight, you will frequently find a clutch of 10 to 15 eggs. Three weeks later you begin seeing grouse hens with baby chicks and frequently the mother will charge you — dragging her "broken" wing in an effort to lure you away from her endangered chicks. If you ignore the mother and carefully examine the area in which she first began her charge, you just may spot some of the chicks, which freeze to the ground and blend in almost perfectly with the surroundings.

The Appalachian Trail

*"The story of the Appalachian Trail has been
many times told; it cannot be told too often."*

The above quotation is from the book, *The Appalachians*, by Maurice Brooks, which we cited in the previous chapter. And indeed the story of the Trail does need to be told often. Each year a new body of young hikers — and thousands who are not so young — arrive on the scene eager for a place to test or acquire their hiking skills. And what better place than on this granddaddy of all long distance marked hiking trails. Secondly, the Appalachian Trail is in trouble. Approximately 800 miles of the Trail is still in private ownership and there is a continuing encroachment of mountain top ski developments, mountain top summer home developments; and roads, radio and television towers threaten to squeeze the Trail right off the map.

*"If enough good people don't know about a beautiful place,
chances are it won't be a beautiful place very long."*

Ansel Adams

We need to tell the Appalachian Trail Story again, and again, and again, so that enough good people know about it to insure the permanent protection of this marvelous wilderness trail.

It is quite difficult on a project as big as a 2000-mile foot trail, to determine just who it was that conceived the idea for the trail. Not so in this case. Benton MacKaye first conceived the idea in the year 1900, but it was not until 21 years later that he was prevailed upon to put his ideas into print. His article "The Appalachian Trail, a Project in Regional Planning" appeared in the October, 1921 issue of the *Journal of the American Institute of Architects*. The idea caught the public fancy. Meetings were held; organizations formed. The first meeting of the newly formed Appalachian Trail Conference was held in Washington, D.C., in 1925. The project languished for a short time but was rescued by Arthur Perkins, a retired lawyer of Hartford, Connecticut, who became Chairman of the Conference in 1926. Perkins, and Myron H. Avery, who succeeded him, pushed the project until the last mile of trail was completed in 1937. It was a tremendous undertaking just to establish a feasible route, then to mark it, clear the trail, erect signs, measure the entire route and to develop guide books.

Clearly, the above is the briefest of brief histories. The entire history of the Trail appears in ATC Publication 5, "The Appalachian Trail." The history section of this publication occupies 16 pages of small print, and anyone who reads this history will marvel that people like the Perkins and Averys and those who helped them could have accomplished so much in so short a time.

One further observation on history. Two men who attended that first organization meeting of the Appalachian Trail Conference in 1925, are still living. Benton MacKaye, age 96, lives in Shirley Center, Massachusetts, and continues to display a keen interest in the affairs of the Trail. The other man, Paul Fink, of Tennessee attended the 50th anniversary meeting of the Conference at Boone, North Carolina in June, 1975 and recalled events of that historic first meeting a half-century earlier. [Note: During the course of publishing this book, word was received that Benton MacKaye died on December 11, 1975].

Today there are 36 hiking club organizations that maintain assigned sections of the 2000-mile trail. In many cases the maintenance work is shared with the national forest or national park through which the trail passes. Today, as in 1925, the Appalachian Trail Conference is the coordinating organization for the entire trail. During the first 40 years of its existence, the Conference had no paid employees and rarely were its volunteer employees even reimbursed for out-of-pocket expenses. Today the Conference has a paid Executive Director. He and a small staff are headquartered in historic Harpers Ferry, West Virginia, a scant two miles from where the Trail crosses the Potomac River. The Conference has 10,000 members who pay annual dues. There are perhaps another 100,000 people who are members of hiking clubs and other affiliated organizations. Little financial support is received from these organizations. The principal source of revenue for the Conference comes from the annual dues of the individual members. Those who desire to preserve the Appalachian Trail are urged to become Conference members.

We will not devote an undue amount of space to the Appalachian Trail in this book for two reasons. First, one of the purposes of this book is to alert the hiking public to the existence of many other trails in the six mid-Atlantic states. Second, there is already a wealth of literature describing the Appalachian Trail, most of it published by the Conference itself, and other literature has been published through commercial channels. These are listed elsewhere in this book. The Trail goes through five of the six mid-Atlantic states. The route is shown on the map that appears at the beginning of each state chapter, and there is a short narrative at the beginning of each state chapter on the Trail that passes through it. And that's all. For additional information, write to the Con-

Several steep hiking trails wind around the massive outcroppings known as Seneca Rocks near Mouth-of-Seneca, West Virginia. Nestled in the Spruce Knob-Seneca Rocks National Recreation Area, spots like this afford good viewing and resting locations. [Photo by Gerald S. Ratliff, West Virginia Department of Commerce.]

ference or obtain one of the other books dealing with the Trail: Appalachian Trail Conference, P.O. Box 236, Harpers Ferry, West Virginia
25425; telephone: 304/535-6331.

Please enclose 25 cents to cover the cost of the information packet
that will be sent to you.

A few words are in order on the role of the Federal and State Govern-
ments in the protection of the Appalachian Trail. In the early 1960's,
Conference officials became increasingly aware of the encroachments
upon the Trail and sought Federal legislation to protect it. Eventually
that legislation was obtained. The National Trails System Act, Public
Law 90-543, was signed into law by President Lyndon B. Johnson on
October 2, 1968. Under the law the Department of Interior (National
Park Service) and the Department of Agriculture (Forest Service) were
assigned responsibilities for acquiring the Appalachian Trail right-of-way.
The fourteen states through which the Trail passes along its entire route
were given two years to acquire the right-of-way, after which the Federal
Government (National Park Service) was authorized to begin right-of-
way acquisition.

What has happened? The fourteen states have moved very, very
slowly. Some have done nothing. Maryland has perhaps the best record
to date and is systematically purchasing tracts of land over which the
Trail passes. Two of the trail clubs (and there may be others) have, from
their limited funds, made land purchases or obtained easements (i.e.,
permanent, recorded, rights-of-way) from land owners. The U.S. Forest
Service has, with little fanfare, purchased enough parcels of land to protect 77 miles of the Trail. It has protected another 24 miles by relocation.
That is, by moving the Trail off of roads and private land and relocating
it upon Government-owned land. And what of the National Park Service, the agency that has primary responsibility for the Appalachian
Trail? During these seven years, the Park Service has acquired not one
acre of land or obtained one single easement! Trail enthusiasts are concerned. The House and Senate Committees that have jurisdiction over
trail legislation are concerned. As this book goes to press, we are informed that the House Committee on National Parks and Recreation has
scheduled oversight hearings on the National Trails System Act (i.e.,
hearings in which a government agency is asked to make an accounting
of its progress with respect to a particular law for which it has responsibility).

This problem will be with us for many years. Those who are concerned about the plight of the Appalachian Trail are urged to express
their views in writing to their Congressmen and Senators.

State Forests, State Parks, State Game Lands

All, or almost all, of the fifty states have one or more state forests, one or more state parks, or one or more parcels of state game lands. Several states have scores of parks, scores of forests, and a hundred or more parcels of state game lands. Frequently the length of any one trail within a state park, forest, or game land parcel is not significant enough to single out for attention in a book of this nature. But the aggregate mileage of short and medium distance hiking trails within a particular park, forest, or game land may be rather impressive if the hiker uses the many interconnecting pathways. In Douthat State Park, Virginia, for example, there are hundreds of miles of trail route, counting the many linking paths.

Not all people who enjoy hiking find it necessary to carry tent, sleeping bag, and cooking equipment and to clear a space in the out-of-doors for their home-away-from-home for each night of their trip. There are many among my hiking acquaintances who, rather than burden themselves with heavy backpacking equipment, prefer to travel light and to expend the extra energy by hiking more miles, seeing more, and spending the night in a comfortable bed in a motel, travel trailer or at a car camper tent in a public campground. For such people, "day-hikers" if you will, the type of trail provided by the state park, forest, or game land is a source of tremendous enjoyment. For each of the six states covered in this book, we give the name and address of the organization which provides information, literature, and maps on the state parks, state forests, and state game lands within a particular state. A word of caution — literature and maps cost money, so don't request mountains of literature from various sources when prudence dictates that pamphlets from but a few is all that your vacation plans will permit.

We have described the hiking opportunities in a few of the state parks, forests, and game lands. Almost all of these state-owned areas have hiking trails of some sort. When you are in such areas, inquire of the ranger, the forester, the clerk or whoever is manning the office. He can often direct you to a relevant map or sometimes to a writeup of the hiking trails in the area.

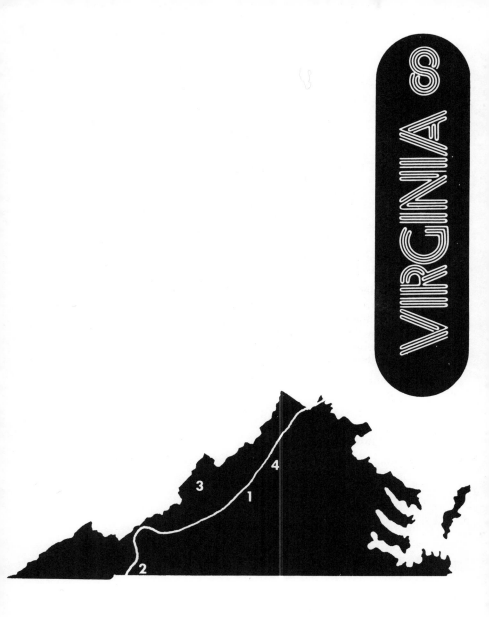

1. APPALACHIAN TRAIL
2. JEFFERSON NATIONAL FOREST
3. GEORGE WASHINGTON NATIONAL FOREST
4. SHENANDOAH NATIONAL PARK

VIRGINIA

To obtain the Official Highway Map and for information on attractions and events, visit, write, or call the:

VIRGINIA STATE TRAVEL SERVICE
Department of Conservation and Economic Development
    Richmond 23219, 6 North Sixth Street, phone 804-770-4484
    New York 10020, 11 Rockefeller Plaza, phone 212-245-3080
    Washington 20006, 906 17th St., N.W.,
        phone 202-293-5350

For information on State Parks, write to:

Division of Parks
1201 State Office Building
Capitol Square
Richmond, VA 23219

For information on Game Lands and Inland Fisheries write to:

Commission of Game and Inland Fisheries
4010 W. Broad Street
Richmond, VA 23230

For information on State Forests, write to:

Division of Forestry
Box 3758
Charlottesville, VA 22903
Telephone: 804-977-6555

Appalachian Trail

Almost 500 miles, or one-fourth, of the entire Appalachian Trail follows the crest of the Blue Ridge mountains of Virginia. Part of the time the Trail straddles the Virginia-West Virginia line and at times it actually leaves the Old Dominion and wanders over into Wild Wonderful West Virginia. The fact that part of the Trail lies in West Virginia is a bit of information that I completely omitted from my book *Appalachian Hiker,* an oversight of which I have been reminded by my West Virginia friends. Unfortunately, some of the Appalachian Trail Conference maps (in ATC Publications 5 and 17) also show the Trail coming close to, but not entering, West Virginia.

The Appalachian Trail crosses over from Tennessee into southwestern Virginia near the friendly little town of Damascus. From here the Trail promptly proceeds to Virginia's two highest mountains — Whitetop (5530 feet) and Mt. Rogers (5729 feet), continues northward through the Jefferson National Forest, goes through another friendly hikers' town, Pearisburg, reclimbs the mountain outside of Pearisburg and makes its first brief trip into West Virginia. From there it swings back east into Virginia, goes to the north of Roanoake, climbs the mountain and plays hide and seek with the Blue Ridge Parkway as the Trail wends its way north to the James River. At the James the Trail leaves Jefferson National Forest, within whose friendly boundaries it has meandered for 250 miles. The 28 trailside shelters, well equipped and well maintained, plus the beauty of the mountains through which the Trail passes, make this 250 miles an especially pleasant segment. There are tremendous rhododendron displays throughout the Jefferson during late May and early June.

At the James River, the Trail drops to its lowest elevation (750 feet) since it began down in Georgia. It now enters the George Washington National Forest and continues in that Forest for 78 miles until reaching the Shenandoah National Park. This is a rugged and beautiful 78-mile stretch marked by a series of mountains in the 3500-4100 foot elevation range that are divided by river gorges. The hiker begins at the James River (elevation 750) and climbs within a few miles to 3550 feet. Further north, the hiker descends into the Tye River Gap (elevation 900 feet) and begins a strenuous 3000 foot climb to the summit of Three Ridges. Seven trailside shelters dot this 78 mile stretch.

At U.S. Route 250 (I-64), the Trail leaves the George Washington National Forest, enters the Shenandoah National Park and intersects the Skyline Drive some 25 times on its 94-mile course through the Park. The 17 shelters along the Appalachian Trail within the Park have been declared out-of-bounds for overnight use by Park regulation, but the footway itself is, by consensus, considered to be the best designed and best maintained of any similar length of footway in the 2000-mile long trail.

Backpackers must obtain permits on entering the Park.

Leaving the Shenandoah National Park in northern Virginia, the Appalachian Trail comes on hard times. North of State Route 55 at Linden, Virginia, the Trail becomes largely a matter of road walking until it leaves the Virginia-West Virginia line near Harpers Ferry, West Virginia, and crosses the Potomac River into Maryland. The last three miles of the Trail provide tremendous views of the Shenandoah and Potomac River Gorges and of the village of Harpers Ferry. It is safe to say that the 51-mile stretch of Trail between the Park and the Potomac is the one in the most critical danger and provides the lowest quality hiking experience of any comparable 51 miles throughout the 2000-mile Trail.

The Jefferson National Forest

The Jefferson National Forest comprises more than 1,500,000 acres. As of 1975, some 674,488 acres were actually owned by the United States. In 1972 the Jefferson purchased the 45,800 acre Garden Mountain tract, which was one of the largest single tract purchases made by the Forest Service in recent years and plans are being made to reroute the Appalachian Trail through this newly purchased land.

The Forest is divided into six ranger districts. Individual trails are described in succeeding pages in five of these districts and the sixth (Wytheville, Virginia, 24382, telephone 703/228-5551) is traversed by the Appalachian Trail. Forest holdings generally occupy the mountain ridge tops, and consequently the districts proceed in long narrow southwest-northeast strips from the Tennessee line in the south as far north as the James River, where the George Washington Forest begins.

Within the boundaries of the Jefferson are one National Recreation Area (Mt. Rogers, 150,000 acres, Marion Ranger District) and one Wilderness Area (James River Face, 8,800 acres, in the Glenwood Ranger District).

The Jefferson is administered by the Forest Supervisor Office in Roanoke. Maps and other information for the entire Forest or of the individual ranger districts may be obtained from that office. The address is: Jefferson National Forest, P.O. Box 241, Pott Federal Building, Roanoke, Virginia, telephone: 703/982-6276.

MARION RANGER DISTRICT
Mt. Rogers National Recreation Area
1102 North Main Street
Marion, Virginia 24354
Telephone: 703/783-5196

The Forest Service operates six National Recreation Areas (NRA's) in the United States. Two of them are in the mid-Atlantic region. One is Mt.

*Mount Rogers National Recreation Area looking north from
Wilburn Ridge. [Photo by U.S. Forest Service.]*

Rogers in southwest Virginia, an area that includes Virginia's two highest
mountains, White Top (elevation 5520 feet) and Mt. Rogers (elevation
5729 feet). Perhaps three-fourths of the Marion district lies within the
NRA and all of the trails we will describe are within the NRA.

In 1972 the Appalachian Trail was rerouted over Mt. Rogers. The former route, which followed the crest of Iron Mountain and contained
three trailside shelters, is still maintained as a hiking trail but is now
yellow-blazed. The combination of the new and old Trail routes along
with a number of connecting trails makes for a delightful network. In
addition, there are five new campgrounds in the NRA, all of them with a
generous number of campsites and one, Grindstone, has 100 camping
units and several bathhouses with hot water showers and electricity. At

least one camping loop is open all year round. Hiking groups often use the campgrounds as a base of operation for both day hiking or backpacking trips.

In short, the Mt. Rogers National Recreation Area is a beautiful piece of real estate with delightful trails and excellent campgrounds. There are no large centers of population nearby and it actually is underutilized.

Now for a description of its hiking trails. To avoid repetition we list the USGS Quad maps and other maps only once. Thereafter, for each trail, we will show the name, distance, and description. The following USGS 7½ minute quads cover all of the NRA: Damascus, Konnarock, White Top Mountain, Trout Dale, Glade Spring, Chilhowie, Marion, Atkins, Cedar Springs.

In addition one may obtain the following Forest Service maps: Appalachian Trail in the Jefferson National Forest, Appalachian Trail in the Mt. Rogers NRA (not always in print), Jefferson National Forest, Marion District.

Central Circuit Trail
Distance: 13.5 miles
Description: This trail can be used for an all day or an overnight hike. Begin hike at the Appalachian Trail (A.T.) parking lot, east of Grindstone Campground, on State Route 603, head south on the A.T. past Old Orchard Shelter to the top of Pine Mountain. Here the open scenery, at elevations above Northern hardwood forests, will remind many of that found out west — grasslands, rock outcrops, and a wild herd of ponies. Follow the A.T. west through Rhododendron Gap (so named because of the profusion of purple and pink rhododendron that grows here) to the summit of Mt. Rogers. The crest of Mt. Rogers is capped by a spruce-fir forest, similar to those found in Canada and the northern United States. At lower elevations, a northern hardwood forest again predominates. The thick undergrowth of ferns and mosses is attributed to the large amount of rainfall on this part of Southwest Virginia.

From the top of Mt. Rogers, descend to Deep Gap, turn right on the blue blazed Mt. Rogers Trail and descend to Route 603. At that point turn right (east) and return to the parking lot. This circuit can also be used in conjunction with the Iron Mountain circuit.

Hikers planning to travel through this country from the month of October through the month of April should take into consideration the highly variable climate. Nights can be extremely cold, despite warm days, and rain and snow are frequent.

Iron Mountain Ciruit Trail
Distance: 7.5 miles
Description: This trail will take part of one day to hike. Start on State Route 603, just west of Grindstone Campground, where the Flattop Trail (blue-blaze) has its southern terminus. Go north on this trail (a jeep route which leads to Forest Service Road 84) until you meet the

yellow-blazed Iron Mountain Trail. Turn right (east) on the yellow-blazed trail to the point where it crosses the A.T., then turn south on the A.T. and hike until reaching State Route 603. Follow the road west until you return to starting point. This circuit can easily be used in conjunction with the Central Circuit.

Hurricane Circuit Trail
Distance: 10 miles
Description: This all day circuit hike begins where the Barton Gap Trail crosses Forest Service Road 84. The trail (motorbikes allowed) goes south to meet the A.T. Follow the A.T. south for a short hike to the Iron Mountain Trail (yellow-blazed). Turn right (west) on Iron Mountain Trail until you meet Forest Service Road 828, which you will follow north past the beginning of the Roland Creek Trail at Hurricane Gap. Follow the scenic Roland Creek Trail north as it winds back and forth over the stream and passes Roland Creek Falls before it joins Forest Service Road 643. Stay on this road (hiking east) until it comes to the northern end of the Barton Gap Trail. Turn south on the latter trail and follow it back to the starting point on Forest Service Road 84.

This circuit can be enlarged by starting at the Hurricane Campground and going on the Dickey Gap Trail until it meets the A.T. Stay on the A.T. until it crosses the yellow-blazed Iron Mountain Trail. Get on the Iron Mountain Trail and follow it as before, but at the junction of the Barton Gap Trail and Forest Service Road 84, hike east on the road to get back to the campground. This adds about five miles to the overall hike.

Hurricane Campground is open from April to November. It has 30 developed camping sites, two bathhouses with hot water showers and electricity.

Hurricane—Skulls Gap
Distance: 10.5 miles
Description: From State Route 650 (near Hurricane Campground) proceed west on Forest Road 84 (a closed work road part of the way), a multi-purpose trail used frequently by motorcycles. You will cross several streams during the hike. Upon reaching State Route 600 at Skulls gap, the hiker will find one of the NRA's picnic grounds. The trail parallels the Iron Mountain Trail throughout its entire length.

Roland Creek Trail
Distance: 2 miles
Description: Begin this hike at the parking area at the western end of Forest Road 643. The trail crosses Roland Creek several times before reaching its end, at Hurricane Gap on Forest Road 84, west of Hurricane Campground.

Mount Rogers National Recreation Area—Comers Rock
as seen from the air. [Photo by U.S. Forest Service.]

Not far from the starting point, the hiker can view the beautiful little Roland Creek Falls. Dense rhododendron thickets and an oak forest characterize the other sights along the trail.

Mount Rogers Trail
Distance: 4.5 miles
Description: Trail leaves State Route 603, just east of Grindstone Campground, and ascends to the north slopes of Mt. Rogers, Virginia's highest

peak. Just before connecting with the A.T. at Deep Gap, this blue-blazed trail enters the edge of the spruce-fir forest type unique to this area of the state. During April, May and June, wildflowers grow in abundance along this trail.

Iron Mountain — West
Distance: 20 miles
Description: Horses can be used on this trail, which prior to 1972 was the official route of the A.T. One portion is open to motorbikes from May to November. Start this ridgetop hike at Damascus; follow the A.T. a short distance until you come to the yellow-blazes of the Iron Mountain Trail.

The Iron Mountain Trail will take you past three shelters — at Sandy Falts, Straight Branch and Cherry Tree. From many points along the trail, you can view the rural valleys below and the forested ridges that run parallel with Iron Mountain. Both Whitetop Mountain and Mt. Rogers can be sighted from the Iron Mountain Trail.

Several streams pass through the area, providing fishing as well as cooking water. Hunters use the trail during deer season.

The eastern end of this portion of the Iron Mountain Trail, is on State Route 16, at Iron Mountain Gap just north of Troutdale. The community of Sugar Grove is just over six miles north of the terminus.

Dickey Knob Trail
Distance: 2.5 miles
Description: Begin in Raccoon Branch Campground, climb to the summit of Dickey Knob to the site of an old fire tower, about 2.5 miles. Several vistas are encountered along the trail, and in late summer huckleberries are ripe in the opening of the Knob. At the foot of the trail is a nature walk (less than ½ mile long) used as an interpretive trail for campers. The walk features the trees and other plant life common to the area.

Raccoon Branch Campground has 20 developed sites and two bathhouses (no hot water). Two trout streams pass near the campground and one terminus of the Virginia Highlands Horse Trail is just outside the campground entrance.

Pine Mountain Trail
Distance: 4 miles
Description: This all-purpose trail is used by jeeps (just to the mountain summit) and horses. Begin from State Route 603, just east of the Fairwood Livery. The trail climbs four miles to the summit of Pine Mountain to "the Scales." From here, hikers and horseback riders can gain access to the high country, unique to this portion of Virginia.

The trail passes through a northern forest at its lower elevations, but comes out in open grasslands similar to areas in the western United States. In late summer and early fall, Pine Mountain is a favorite spot for huckleberry pickers. A herd of untamed horses, as well as cattle owned by private individuals, inhabit Pine Mountain. Hunters frequent the area during deer season.

Beartree Gap Trail
Distance: 3 miles
Description: This trail connects the A.T. to the Iron Mountain Trail in the Beartree Gap area. It crosses the road to Beartree Campground and U.S. Route 58.

Virginia Highlands Trail No. 1
Distance: 28 miles
Description: This is the route of the Virginia Highlands Horse and Wagon Trail between U.S. Route 21 and State Route 601 (east of Sugar Grove). It may be used by motorbikes from May through November. The trail crosses two roads, State Route 798 and Forest Road 16, where access may also be obtained. During the month of July, an organized "Wagon Train" passes through this area.

Virginia Highlands Trail No. 2
Distance: 6.5 miles
Description: A horse and hiker trail, it begins near Raccoon Branch Campground and goes 6.5 miles to a dead end. The trail follows the contour of the ridges in the area, passing over a couple trout fishing streams.

Raccoon Trail
Distance: 3 miles
Description: Begin in Raccoon Branch Campground; proceed to the Virginia Highlands Horse Trail (going southwest) for a short distance. Then follow the blue-blazed Raccoon Trail to the Appalachian Trail, passing the Raccoon Branch Trail shelter.

Iron Mountain — East
Distance: 2.5 miles
Description: This yellow-blazed hiking trail covers the 2.5 miles between Comers Rock Campground and Hale Lake. If traveling east to west, begin where Forest Service Road 57 joins the trail on the east side of Hale Lake. Once on the trail, you will cross a road before entering a stand of white pine, in which an old logging road is located. Forest Service Road 57 is at the right of the trail as the hiker climbs to the ridge crest of Iron Mountain. Once headed down, the trail passes through an area of large boulders before reaching the road to Comers Rock Campground, which is designed for picnickers and primitive camping. Comers Rock provides a good overlook for the surrounding countryside.

West End Circuit Trail
Distance: 18 miles
Description: This trail begins at the town of Damascus. Follow the A.T. north until its intersection with the yellow-blazed Iron Mountain Trail.

Turn left on latter trail proceeding east until reaching ridgetops which provide many views of scenic areas in southwest Virginia. At approximately six miles you will reach Sandy Flats trail shelter (water). Continue east on Iron Mountain Trail, cross Forest Service Road 90, and after another mile turn right (south) onto blue-blazed Beartree Gap Trail at Shaw Gap. Follow the blue-blaze trail until it joins the A.T. Turn right on A.T. and take it back to the starting point in Damascus.

The Beartree Campground is open from May until October each year. It has more than 100 camping units and several bath houses with water showers and electricity. When complete, this camping complex will also boast a small lake.

The cricuit can be enlarged if you bypass the turn at Shaw Gap and keep going on the Iron Mountain Trail until you arrive at a trail at Straight Branch shelter, 11.5 miles from Damascus. Turn right on this side trail which leads to Beartree Campground. Follow the campground road until it reaches the Beartree Gap Trail and turn left on that trail and complete the hike as before. This adds about 8.5 miles to the circuit.

BLACKSBURG RANGER DISTRICT
Blacksburg, Virginia 24060
Telephone: 703/552-4641

Cascades Trail
Distance: 4 miles
Maps: USGS Eggleston Quad.; Jefferson National Forest Map, Blacksburg District, which is applicable to all trails in Blacksburg District.
Description: This trail is in central Giles County, Virginia, four miles north of Pembroke on State Route 623. It is a loop trail that departs from the Forest Service parking lot, crosses over to the east side of Little Stony Creek, and follows the stream upstream for one mile. You will pass an old steam boiler used years ago in a saw mill operation and will gain a fine panoramic view of Barney's Wall from the bottom. The Wall is a sheer bluff rising from the creek bottom to 3640 feet.

At the one mile point the trail crosses over Little Stony Creek to the west side again before it proceeds on upstream. At this point there is also a return trail to the parking lot. From the one-mile point the trail continues upstream to the Cascades Falls, a magnificent waterfall of some 60 feet, tumbling into a large pool at the base. From the falls the return trail remains on the west side of the stream as it leads back to the parking lot. The terrain on the ascending trail is mostly steep and rocky and the return trail follows an old logging road that provides excellent hiking. Little Stony Creek is also a native trout stream with fishing limited to artificial lures with barbless hooks. The entire hike requires about three and one-half hours. Drinking water and restroom facilities are provided at the Picnic Area at the beginning of the trail. However, no camping is allowed within the area or along the trail, which ranges in elevation from 2140 to 2860 feet.

Ribble Trail [Southwestern Giles County, Virginia]
Distance: 1.9 miles
USGS Quad: White Gate 7½
Description: The southern terminus of the trail takes off from Forest Service Road 201 at the point where the road makes a 90° turn and starts up the mountain, approximately a quarter mile east of the Wapiti Trail Shelter. From this point the trail heads north up the slope of Flat Top Mountain, terminating just below the crest at the point where the Honey Springs Cabin is located. The terrain varies from flat ridgetops to steep side slopes, rising from an elevation of 2480 feet to 3760 feet. Allow two hours for a leisurely walk of this blue-blazed 1.9 mile trail, which intersects the A.T. at both ends. Water is available from the spring at Honey Springs Cabin.

Virginias Walk
Distance: 1.5 miles
Map: Waiteville, Virginia, USGS Quad.
Description: This trail is on the north slope of Potts Mountain above White Rock Branch, in northern Giles County. It is a loop trail with both termini in the White Rocks Recreation Area. The trail departs from the campground and meanders around the north slope of Potts Mountain, crosses the heads of several small drainages, goes into West Virginia, then returns to the campground. The trail crosses White Rock Branch, which is a native trout stream. Deer and squirrel are common sights. Allow one hour for a leisurely walk. Elevation ranges from 3020 to 3160 feet. Drinking water, restroom facilities and campsites are available within the campground area.

Pandapas Pond Ecology Trail
Distance: 1 mile
Map: Newport, Virginia, USGS Quad 7½
Description: This is a one mile loop trail around Pandapas Pond, an eight acre man-made impoundment of the headwaters of Poverty Creek. Both termini of the trail, which was developed and constructed by the Forest Service and the Wildlife Society of Virginia Technical University, are at the parking lot. The primary purpose of the trail is to lend an insight into the ecology of the area, while at the same time providing a leisurely hike. There is a series of numbered markers along the trail designating various points of ecological significance. A guide book is provided to interpret and explain each numbered stop. The trail is just off U.S. Route 460, four miles north of Blacksburg.

War Branch Trail and Chestnut Trail
Distance: 3 to 4½ miles
Maps: Waiteville and Interior, Virginia. USGS Quads 7½
Description: This is a series of short trails that allow a casual loop hike. They are located on Salt Pond Mountain in Giles County within the Mountain Lake Scenic Area on State Route 613, approximately two miles

north of Mountain Lake. Park at parking area on Route 613 where there is a large wooden sign showing in color the network of trails. One can follow the Chestnut Trail and walk 1.25 miles to the War Spur Overlook. This trail traverses a forest with remnants of the old American Chestnut forest still remaining. The overlook provides a magnificent view of the upper John's Creek valley, as well as the wilderness aspect of the Mountain Lake Scenic Area. From the overlook you can proceed through a virgin hemlock, fir and red spruce stand while enjoying the splendor of rhododendron and mountain laurel. This section of trail then connects with the War Branch Trail, at which point you can turn north and intersect the Appalachian Trail in approximately 1.25 miles, or turn south and return to the parking lot on Route 613. The terrain is gentle sloping and it ranges in elevation from 3800 feet to 3100 feet. No drinking water or restroom facilities are available and camping is prohibited within the Mountain Lake Scenic Area.

The Narrows Overlook Trail [Bushwhacking]
Distance: Approximately 5 miles; required hiking time 4-5 hours.
Map: Narrows, Virginia-West Virginia, USGS Quad
Description: This is for experienced hikers only, who know how to use a map and enjoy exploring trailless areas. Here it is best to use two cars. Proceed west from Pearisburg, Virginia, on U.S. Route 460. Cross the New River and at 1.3 miles, just past the Celanese plant, turn right on state secondary road 641 and drive 1.7 miles. Park one car on the road where the Appalachian Trail intersects. In the second car, return to U.S. 460, turn right and drive 2.6 miles west to the traffic light at state road 61. Turn right at the traffic light and immediately (in 10 feet) turn left onto "old U.S. 460". Pass in front of hamburger stand and under the highway bridge ahead. Proceed 0.7 miles to barricade and park.

Drop down the grassy embankment to new U.S. 460 and proceed straight ahead west 33 feet past an old shed by the road with a house and garden behind it. Where the wooded embankment meets the road again, begin scrambling up the steep embankment to the right. Ascend very steeply through undergrowth diagonally away from the road. Bear a little to the left and follow in a northeasterly direction along the top of the rock outcrop. The underbrush opens up somewhat after the first 300 feet or so. Continue along the top shelf of rocks, from which you will see several outstanding views of The Narrows of the New River in about the first mile. Enjoy these — views of the wide river and its parallel rapids, with the railroad tracks and State Secondary Road 649.

Once you are up onto the level ridgeline of Peters Mountain, in a broad, nearly flat area with only light undergrowth, pick up the newly relocated A.T. before entering Forest Service property. Cross over one buried gas line (70 feet wide seeded area) and a 200 kv power line. This is the corner with West Virginia, since Virginia's Giles County juts into West Virginia a few miles on either side of the New River. Eventually you will pass a cable TV tower and come out by a pastured field at the top of the mountain. Here there is a beautiful view of the valley, the mountains of West Virginia, and the town of Petersburg.

At the northeast end of the open field, re-enter the woods. Hike under a second 200 kv power line and at the second power line tower pick up an old grassed road continuing northeast. About 100 feet further, the A.T. turns sharp left as it proceeds north; continue straight ahead on an old road which drops off to the right and leads down the southeast side of Peters Mountain, crossing back and forth under the power line as it descends very steeply down the rocky, badly eroded service road under the 200 kv power line. This is the former A.T. route and blazes or evidence thereof may be seen. Follow this main service road to the state secondary road where car number one has been parked. There are several springs and streams on the trail back to the car.

This route goes through hardwood forests, except for some scrub pine in the last half-mile or so. The land at the top of the mountain belongs to the Forest Service at an elevation of up to 3339 feet; the elevation along U.S. 460 at the start of the trip is 1609 feet. The land through which the hike begins is privately owned woodlands with no buildings and is not posted. There are small springs on the northwest side of swags in the ridgeline, surprisingly close to the top of the mountain. Once a wet spot is found, just dig it out a bit till it fills with water and settles clean; there is not much poing in going further downhill to find a better flow of water.

Butt Mountain — White Rocks — Mountain Lake Circuit
Distance: 23 miles
Maps: Eggleston, Virginia; Interior, Virginia, West Virginia; Waiteville, Virginia-West Virginia; USGS Quads. 7½ minute
Description: The suggested best starting and ending point is at the end of the pavement on State Secondary Road 613, a half-mile beyond Mountain Lake Hotel, at the outlet end of Mountain Lake. Cars may be left there, May through September, which are the months the hotel is open. All land adjacent to the highway is owned by the hotel, and during the rest of the year this area is fenced off and parking is not recommended. Arrange to park with the hotel caretaker, who lives by the crest of the paved road next to the hotel, or continue on down road 613 (once called the Salt Sulphur Turnpike) to park at the War Spur Trail parking area, 3.2 miles beyond the hotel.

Beginning on State Secondary Road 613 at the end of the pavement, and at the outlet end of Mountain Lake, walk to the near end of the wooden pier leading to the frame boathouse in the lake, turn right, and follow the clearly worn but unblazed trail along the shore of Mountain Lake in the direction of the hotel. This trail goes all the way around the lake and is an enjoyable circuit in itself. There are other hiking opportunities on Mountain Lake Hotel property, a 3000-acre tract all around

Mount Rogers National Recreation Area—looking at
Mount Rogers from Pine Mountain. [photo by U.S. Forest Service.]

Mountain Lake. Inquire at the hotel desk.

At 1.9 miles turn sharp right uphill onto gravel State Secondary Road 714. Ascend steadily. At Pacers Gap (2.8 miles) there is a good view of Salt Pond Mountain behind to the southeast. On the right, at 3.4 miles, is a good spring, out of a pipe. Pass under signs referring to the Little Meadows Hunting Club. From here on, the road is a Forest Service access road, and according to the Forest Service, they have only the width of road access into and through this private land, instead of the 30 foot right-of-way customary in this part of the country. There are hunting camps and lodges in this area, nearly all posted. There has alledgedly been considerable vandalism of these camps. While the occupants of these camps would not hesitate to render aid to a passerby in genuine difficulty, it is otherwise best for strangers to avoid the camps and stay on the road.

Cross Little Stony Creek at about 4.8 miles, and a short way beyond enter the Little Meadows area, which is a beautiful sight from the road. Cross Meredith Branch and ascend gently up the ridge of Butt Mountain, taking care to follow the main road. At about 8.5 miles the road levels out and the land opens up into high meadow with beautiful views on both sides across flat to gently sloping ground. At 8.8 miles the road forks, the right fork continuing on around the mountain and the left going 650 feet to the Butt Mountain fire tower.

The best treat of the circuit is the view from the fire tower. The elevation here is 4202 feet. At 11 miles due west lies the Narrows of the New River, a gap in Peters Mountain. The land beyond Peters Mountain is West Virginia. The Angels Rest of Pearis Mountain, the flat-topped mountain 8.7 miles to the west-southwest, stands 1313 feet above the town of Pearisburg, at its foot. The cliffs of the New River may be seen 4.3 miles to the south, and between 6.2 and 9.3 miles due south are the gaps the New River has cut for itself through Brush, Gap and Spruce Run Mountains to north of the city of Radford. The top of the fire tower is kept locked, although the steps may be climbed. The tool shed behind the tower can give emergency shelter. Cistern water is questionable here.

When you return to the Forest Service road, continue west, descending very gently, and re-enter the woods. The A.T. comes up from the left at 12.8 miles. Baileys Gap shelter is 1650 feet down the hill to the left on the Trail. At 15.8 miles cross State Secondary Road 613, the Salt Sulphur Turnpike. The outlet end of Mountain Lake is 5 miles to the right; to the left, downhill through many switchbacks, is the White Rocks Recreation Area, a motor campground maintained by the Forest Service. A little way beyond the turnoff to the campground is state secondary road 635, which runs down the beautiful valley of Big Stoney Creek toward Ripplemead and Pearisburg.

Continue straight along the A.T., ascending steadily from the Salt Sulphur Turnpike. Travel 17.2 miles to the Wind Rocks, which lie to the left of the Trail. They give an excellent view of the Big Stoney Creek valley. Further along the A.T., at 16 miles, is the Stony Creek fire tower. You may climb and enter the room at the top, which has been severly vandalized. This gives an excellent view of the gentle ridges which make up this very high (3960 to 4290 feet) plateau north and west of Mountain Lake. Continue on A.T. At 17 miles come out into meadow. Just beyond end of meadow, the Trail turns sharp right for the descent toward War Spur. Continue straight along old wagon trail 1.3 miles past the turnoff, to the White Rocks, which are steeply pitched immense sheets of white sandstone. From here is a good view of the wooded Johns Creek valley in Craig county.

Returning to the junction with the A.T., turn left to continue on the Trail. Descend gently and then more steeply, and then at 18.6 miles turn sharp right uphill at a sign onto the War Spur Trail.

The War Spur Trail parking area on the Salt Sulphur Turnpike is 1.2 miles distant. About halfway to the road a sign points to the left to "Virgin Woods". This side trail makes a circuit through a stand of virgin hemlock, then there is a spur to the left leading down to a good overlook over Seven Mile Mountain and the War Spur valley. The trail next returns to the War Spur Trail parking area at the Salt Sulphur Turnpike, in 20.5 miles. Turn left toward Mountain Lake, following the road.

The Salt Sulphur Turnpike is probably so named because of the once considerable quantities of sodium sulfate hauled in the middle of the last century from mineral springs in Monroe County, West Virginia, to glass and dye manufacturers in the New River country.

This route also skirts the Mountain Lake Wilderness Study Area, an 8400-acre tract set aside under the Eastern Wilderness Act of 1974. Wildlife are extremely prolific here. On as few as a dozen trips in an automobile along the Salt Sulphur Turnpike, it is possible to see a black bear, a large covey of turkey, and several deer. Ferns in the woods alongside the road grow to unusual size in the boggy soil.

At 23 miles, you will pass the University of Virginia's Mountain Lake Biological Station on the left. A mile further is the outlet end of Mountain Lake, the end of the circuit. If the air temperature is at all warm, a dip in Mountain Lake, the largest natural lake in Virginia, is highly recommended.

The lake's elevation is almost exactly 3960 feet, and the water is pure enough to drink. The best place to swim is probably the rocks a couple hundred feet around on the shore to the left of the boathouse. Avoid contact with the bottom; there may be broken glass. This is easy because the lake is as much as 165 feet deep only a little ways out from the north shore, and then shoals steadily toward the hotel.

CLINCH RANGER DISTRICT
Wise, Virginia
Telephone: 703/328-2931

The Jefferson National Forest Map, Clinch Ranger District, scale one inch to the mile, will be found extremely helpful in locating all trails in the district. The Clinch Ranger District is in the extreme southwest corner of Virginia bordering on and in some places extending slightly over into Kentucky. Its trails are primarily hunter and fishermen access trails that are being used increasingly for hiking and backpacking. Since directional signing on these trails is not complete, caution is advised. Use the USGS quadrangle maps and check at the Ranger Office for information and advice.

Pine Mountain Trail #201
Distance: 23 miles
Map: USGS Quads: Jenkins East, Clintwood, Hellier, Elk Horn City 7½
Description: This trail begins on U.S. Route 23 in Pound Gap on the

boundary between Virginia and Kentucky. It is moderately difficult. From the starting point it proceeds northeast for its entire route, literally straddling the state line. The trail has many scenic vistas, and rock outcrops. Elevation is around 3000 feet for most of the distance. At milepoint 11.4, pass the lookout tower at Jesse Gap. The trail is poorly signed and ends on private land so be sure to carry map and compass. There are unimproved trails running from the main trail to county roads. At mile point 18 turn right at abandoned silica strip mine, down upper Skegg Branch Trail to State Route 612 and end of trail. Those wishing to extend the hike may stay on Trail #201 all the way to Breaks Interstate Park, a distance of 23 miles from the starting point at Pound Gap. There is a campground with 122 sites in the Park.

Big Stone Mountain #207
Distance: 11 miles
Maps: Appalachia, Big Stone Gap, Keokee, 7½ USGS Quads
Description: This trail begins on U.S. Route 23 at Roaring Branch approximately one mile south of the town of Appalachia. It provides moderate to difficult hiking and it is well maintained but poorly signed from U.S. Route 23 to the top of the mountain at the Wise-Lee County line. The same is true from Cave Springs Campground to about one mile east of Oligner Lookout Tower. The area between these two points has not been maintained on any regular schedule. On the east end of the trail, the route climbs steeply, with frequent rock steps, through some very large timber, mostly Hemlock, and past rocky waterfalls. The Cave Springs campground and a fire tower is at the western end. Many vistas from the higher elevations. The average elevation is 2600 feet, which drops to 2000 feet at the campground.

331 — Bear Rock Trail
Distance: 2.5 miles
Map: Toms Creek, Dunsanivon 7½ USGS Quads
Description: This trail is in the eastern end of Scott County near the intersection of Wise, Russell, and Scott County lines and the Clinch River. The trail begins on the north side of Little Stoney Creek on Road 701 about 0.7 miles South of the intersection of Forest Service Roads 700 and 701. It then proceeds for 0.2 mile east to the Falls of Little Stoney, a beautiful waterfall and undeveloped swimming hole. At the other end of the trail is the Hanging Rock Picnic Area, with some unusual rock formations. Trail is well maintained but is poorly signed. It follows a trout stream most of its length at an elevation of 2000 feet. There are undeveloped fishing trails up Little Stoney Creek from Bear Rock Road to Bark Camp Lake, and there is parking at both termini.

329 — Wallen Ridge Trail
Distance: 10 miles
Maps: Keokee, Big Stone Gap, 7½ USGS Quads
Description: This trail is in the eastern end of Lee County. Begin the hike

on State Route 619 and proceed generally northeast for the entire distance. The trail lies generally at 2500-2700 foot elevation and is easy to hike. The last maintenance work done in 1975; however, it is poorly signed. The trail is on top of Wallen Ridge for almost its entire distance and affords many scenic views. It ends at its intersection with State Route 641 approximately 3 miles south of Big Stone Gap. There are no Forest Service parking facilities at either end.

704 — Mountain Fork Trail
Distance: 2.8 miles
Map: Wise, 7½ USGS Quad
Description: This trail begins in the High Knob Recreation Area, which is in Wise County about 3 miles south of Norton. From High Knob Recreation Area, it follows a trout stream its entire length until reaching Forest Service Road 704. There are Forest Service parking areas at both termini.

GLENWOOD RANGER DISTRICT
Natural Bridge Station, Virginia 24579
Telephone: 703/291-2188

The Jefferson National Forest Map, Glenwood Ranger District, scale one inch to the mile, will be found extremely helpful in locating all trails in the ranger district. The District is located in the northeast corner of the Jefferson National Forest, being bounded on the north by the James River and the George Washington National Forest.

Apple Orchard Falls Trail
Distance: 10.5 miles
Maps: U.S.G.S. Quad: Arnold Valley, Virginia, 7½
Description: This trail begins at an elevation of 3500 feet on the Blue Ridge Parkway, at Sunset Field Overlook near Milepost 78. It leads in a northwesterly direction, crossing into the Jefferson National Forest at 0.1 mile and crosses the A.T. at 0.2 mile. At 1.1 mile the trail passes a huge overhanging rock on the right that would give shelter from rain. It begins a steep descent around the falls at 1.2 mile. At 1.3 mile, the hiker can look back for a beautiful view of the 200-foot high falls. The trail leads into the headwaters of North Creek. At approximately 3 miles, the northwest end of the trail (elevation 1500 feet) joins Forest Road 59 at the north end of the Cornelius Creek Trail (Note: At this point a circuit hike of 6.1 miles can be accomplished by returning to the Blue Ridge Parkway via the Cornelius Creek Trail).

From end of trail, follow Forest Road 59 west for 4.5 miles to junction with Virginia State Route 614, then 3 miles to Interstate 81, approximately 2 miles north of Buchanan, Virginia (Exit 48).

Cornelius Creek Trail
Distance: 10.6 miles
Maps: USGS Quad: Arnold Valley, Virginia
Description: This trail begins at elevation 3300 feet on the A.T., 1.2

miles south of Forest Service Road 812 (Parkers Gap Road). During its
3.1 mile northwesterly route to North Creek, the elevation drops to 1500
feet — at its junction with Forest Service Road 59 and Apple Orchard
Falls Trail (Note: At this point a circuit hike of 6.1 miles can be accomplished by returning to the Blue Ridge Parkway via the Apple Orchard
Falls Trail).

From end of trail, follow Forest Service Road 59 west for 4.5 miles to
its junction with State Route 614, then 3 miles to Interstate 81, approximately 2 miles north of Buchanan, Virginia (Exit 48).

Wildcat Mountain Trail
Distance: 4 miles
USGS Quad: Arnold Valley, Virginia
Description: This trail was developed primarily for use of campers at
Cave Mountain Lake. It is a loop trail from the camping area at an ele-
vation of 1200 feet, climbing to 2700 feet on Wildcat Mountain. The
total length is approximately 4 miles over rough terrain, requiring about
three hours hiking time.

JAMES RIVER FACE WILDERNESS AREA

In 1975 the Congress established the 8804-acre wilderness area within
the boundaries of the Glenwood Ranger District. The following trails are
within the boundaries of the newly established wilderness area.

Piney Ridge Trail
Distance: 3.5 miles
USGS Quad: Snowden, Virginia, 7½
Description: This trail begins at a point on the A.T. 2.8 miles north of
Petites Gap and 0.5 mile north of Marble Springs shelter near the Rock-
bridge-Bedford County line. Elevation there is 2450 feet. The trail leads
in an easterly direction down Piney Ridge between Snow Creek and
Peters Creek, losing altitude to an elevation of 900 feet at its junction
with Forest Service Road 54. Follow gravel surfaced Forest Service Road
54 to the northeast approximately 0.5 mile to its junction with U.S.
Route 501.

Balcony Falls Trail
Distance: 5.5 miles
USGS Quad: Snowden, Virginia
Description: Trail begins near the Rockbridge-Bedford County line on
the A.T. 0.5 mile northeast of Hickory Stand, which is 5.1 miles north of
Petites Gap. The trail follows an old fire road in a northerly direction for
1.35 miles to the end of the road where the trail continues northeasterly
out the ridge top for approximately 1 mile. Timber type changes often
from southern pine to mixed hardwoods. Scenic views from the top of
the ridge include to the left, the community of Glasgow and to the right
the James River Gorge. The trail drops off to the left in a northwesterly
direction, with switchbacks to a junction with State Route 782. Follow

Route 782 west 1.8 mile to junction of State Route 759, go north approximately 0.5 mile to junction with State Route 130 at Natural Bridge Station, Virginia (headquarters of Glenwood Ranger District).

Gunter Ridge Trail
Distance: 4.3 miles
USGS Quad: Snowden, Virginia, 7½
Description: Trail begins at 2500 feet elevation at a point on the Belfast Trail 0.4 mile west of the A.T. at Hickory Stand. It makes several switchbacks over steep ground before reaching State Route 759 at an elevation of 800 feet. Follow the road north 1.5 mile to junction with State Route 130 at Natural Bridge Station, Virginia.

Belfast Trail
Distance: 2.8 miles
USGS Quad: Snowden, Virginia 7½
Description: Trail begins at Hickory Stand on the A.T., 4.5 miles north of Petites Gap and 2.2 miles north of Marble Spring shelter. The elevation here is 2650 feet. The trail leads in a southwesterly direction passing junction with Gunter Ridge Trail at 0.4 mile, descending very steeply into Belfast Creek. At 1.5 mile, you pass Devil's Marble Yard, a scenic outcrop of loose boulders. At 2.8 miles, elevation of 1000 feet, the east end of trail crosses a footbridge over Elk Creek to State Route 781. From the trail's end, go northwest 1.5 mile to junction with State Route 759 and then north for 3.2 miles to junction with Virginia Route 130 at Natural Bridge Station, Virginia.

George Washington National Forest

The George Washington (frequently referred to as the "GW") has approximately 1,794,014 acres within its boundaries, of which some 1,038,447 acres are owned by the United States. The GW is bordered by the James River and the Jefferson National Forest on the South, by West Virginia and the Monongahela National Forest on the west and by the Shenandoah National Park on the north and east. The forest is divided into six ranger districts and in the ensuing pages, trails from four of these districts are described. The northernmost ranger district, the Lee, is only 100 miles from Washington, D.C. The first 100 miles of the Blue Ridge Parkway goes through the Pedlar District of the GW and through the Glenwood District of the Jefferson National Forest.

Administration of the GW is from the Forest Supervisor Officed in Harrisonburg. Maps and other information for the entire Forest or of the individual ranger districts may be obtained from that office. Complete address is: George Washington National Forest, Federal Building, Harrisonburg, Virginia 22801, telephone: 703/433-2491.

DRY RIVER RANGER DISTRICT
510 North Main Street
Bridgewater, Virginia 22812
Telephone: 703/828-2591

All trails described for the Dry River Ranger District can be located on the George Washington National Forest Map, Dry River Ranger District. Scale is one inch equals two miles. The map shows land status as of June, 1972. This district is in the center of the GW, it runs in a southwest-northeast direction and on its western side it straddles and extends two to four miles over into West Virginia.

Trails in Hone Quarry Recreation Area

There are five trails close to this quiet and somewhat remote recreation area, and one can hike all five without moving his car from his campsite. To reach the recreation area proceed from the headquarters of the Dry River Ranger District in Bridgewater, where you will already have checked (if you are prudent) with Forest Service personnel as to the condition of the trails you plan to explore. Proceed west on State Routes 727, 613, and 257. Inside the Forest Service boundary, the road turns south and is numbered 924. Proceed straight ahead into Hone Quarry Recreation Area on Forest Service Road 62. Park in the recreation area, which has 30 picnic spots and 10 campsites.

I will relate my own experience in this area which will give you some idea of the situations you may encounter occasionally in locating and hiking these trails.

I had stopped at the Bridgewater office and reviewed the maps with the officials and received instructions on how to reach the Hone Recreation Area, a spot I had visited some years before when it was still a primitive campsite. I parked near picnic area and tried to find starting point of Big Hollow Trail. Having no luck, I inquired of a Forest Service work crew. One member of the crew was familiar with the trail and gave me explicit directions as to where to begin, but was uncertain if trail was open all the way to the ridge. I started hiking on the trail; there were no signs, no blazes but it was wide, of good grade, and easily followed. I went on for approximately 1 mile, then the trail began to narrow and was less easy to follow. At 1.5 miles, it evaporated completely.

I retraced my steps slowly, looking for the spot where I might have lost the main trail, but found no other trail. I returned to recreation area conceding only temporary defeat. I again located the work crew and inquired how I could locate Hone Quarry Ridge Trail at its intersection with State Route 924. They gave me explicit directions, but with the warning that the sign might have been destroyed but the sign post would probably still mark the spot. I drove to the area and proceeded very slowly along the road and saw neither sign nor post. Stopped at several likely looking spots and hiked into the forest but could locate no trail of any sort, so I returned to the recreation area and this time obtained directions to Hone Quarry Dam and lake. I followed road in the hot sun and found the dam. One minor accomplishment — two major defeats. Such was my grade for the day as peerless pathfinder.

But in truth, no day is a failure if it permits me to get out into the forest for the better part of the day, eat my lunch near a quiet stream, and allows me to get in a few hours of hiking. And it must be remembered that all of the trails about to be described are in the Forest Service approved trail system and either have been, are now, or again will be brought up to Forest Service trail standards. So check your maps, check with Forest Service personnel, and even then be prepared for an occasional disappointment. Here are the five trails. Since they are all in the same area I will omit much of the road approach instructions. Three USGS Quads — Brandywine, Reddish Knob, and Briery Branch — all in Virginia — cover all five trails.

Big Hollow Trail
Distance: 2 miles
Description: Begins at point on Hone Quarry Run just above the campground at approximately 2000 feet elevation. Proceeds up the trail, which is wide during the first mile and is on a good grade. The trail becomes narrower at higher elevation and joins the Hone Quarry Ridge Trail at 3200 feet.

Mines Run Trail
Distance: 3 miles
Description: Caution — This trail follows Mines Run as its name indicates — it does not follow Hones Quarry Run, as shown on the Forest Service Map. The trail begins on State Route 924 at a point just above Briery Branch Dam and it follows Mines Run, a trout stocked stream for 3 miles dead-ending at that point.

Slate Springs Trail [A]
Distance: 4 miles
Description: Trail begins at point where Rocky Run joins State Route 257 near Forest Service Boundary. Proceed up Rocky Run crossing Oak Knob at 3500 feet, skirting to the north of Pond Knob and joining the Slate Springs Mountain Trail.

Slate Springs [AA]
Distance: 4 miles
Description: From the recreation area, proceed on a dirt road to the Hone Quarry Dam. Pick up Slate Springs (AA) Trail at that point. The trail follows Hone Run for approximately 2 miles, then veers to the north, climbing steadily until it reaches Slate Springs Mountain Trail, near Flagpole Knob on Forest Road 85. This is a strenuous hike. The elevation at campground is approximately 2000 feet; it is 3400 feet at the dam, and 4200 feet at the end of the trail.

Hone Quarry Ridge Trail

Distance: 8 miles

Description: Proceed from the recreation area on Forest Service Road
62; turn right on State Route 924 and go south for ½ mile. Pick up the
trail at that point, where the elevation is 1700 feet. For the next 8 miles
you will be proceeding west — and up, up, up, heading for end of the
trail near the West Virginia state line at 3900 feet elevation. At 3 miles
the trail to the left leads to Briery Branch dam, and at 4 miles the trail to
the right is Big Hollow Trail leading to Hone Quarry Recreation Area. At
5 miles the trail to the left leads to Mines Run and the Mines Run Trail.
At 6 miles it comes out on a dirt road, which it follows until its junction
with Forest Road 85 at the end of trail.

OTHER TRAILS IN THE DRY RIVER RANGER DISTRICT

Slate Springs Mountain Trail

Distance: 8 miles

USGS Quads: Brandywine, Virginia; Rawley Springs, Virginia

Description: This trail begins at Flagpole Knob on the dirt Forest Service
Road 85 at 4000 feet, almost at the West Virginia state line. It proceeds
east and north connecting up with the two Slate Springs Trails (A and
AA). From there it goes north through the tiny community of Maple
Springs before veering east and descending down Chestnut Ridge. The
trail leaves the GW forest just before reaching the village of Rawley
Springs at elevation 1800 feet. U.S. Route 33 is but a scant half-mile
beyond. Note: The two Slate Springs trails, in conjunction with the Slate
Spring Mountain Trail, make for some interesting circuit hikes. For an
even more strenuous circuit, one could proceed up either one of the
Slate Spring Trails, go south on the Slate Spring Mountain Trail, Forest
Road 85, east on Hone Quarry Ridge Trail, and back to the recreation
area via the Big Hollow Trail.

Timber Ridge Trail

Distance: 8 miles

USGS Quad: Reddish Knob, Virginia

Description: This is another "top of the mountain down to the valley"
type of trail. The trail heads can be reached at either end by car, but we
will begin this one from the fire tower at Reddish Knob, elevation 4397
feet. It has been some years since I was up on this knob, but I remember
that the drive up was somewhat of an adventure itself, and once at Reddish Knob I felt like I was on top of the world with the tremendous view
to both West Virginia and Virginia. To reach Reddish Knob, take State
Route 924 for approximately 10 miles (from the forest boundary near
Hone Quarry) until you reach Forest Service Road 85. Turn left (south)
on this road for an additional two miles to the Knob.

Proceed east on the trail from the fire tower. At 0.5 mile the trail
forks; the left fork goes down California Ridge trail and the right fork
continues on the Timber Ridge Trail. At 4 miles Sand Spring Mountain
Trail comes in on the left, while Timber Ridge again bears right. Beyond

this intersection the Trail begins descending Hearthstone Ridge until, at the end of the trail, it reaches Forest Service Road 101, 4 miles south of its intersection with State Route 924. The eastern trailhead is just north of Hearthstone Lake.

Sand Spring Mountain Trail

Distance: 3 miles

Description: This trail is in the same area (same USGS map) as Timber Ridge Trail. Its western terminus is at the midpoint of Timber Ridge Trail at 3700 feet, from which it descends in southeasterly direction until it terminates on Forest Service Road 101, two miles north of Hearthstone Lake. Both these trails can be used to make a 9 mile circuit hike, using Forest Road 101 as the third leg in the circuit.

Trails in the Todd Lake Recreation Area

The following three trails can be easily reached from the Todd Lake Recreation Area. From Bridgewater (Ranger District Office) proceed south on State Route 42. Just south of town, turn right on State Route 727 and stay on that road for approximately 6 miles until reaching State Route 730. Follow Route 730 for approximately 4 miles and then turn left on Forest Service Road 95 reaching the Todd Lake Recreation Area in about 3 miles. The following USGS Quads, all in Virginia, cover this three-trail area: Stokesville, Reddish Knob and Palo Alto.

Chestnut Ridge Trail

Distance: 7 miles

Description: Trail hike can be started in two places from its eastern end. The trail officially begins on Forest Service Road 95, approximately 0.3 mile west of its intersection with State Route 730. Or from the recreation area one can cut off some mileage by entering the trail from the Little Skidmore jeep road, which begins at the recreation area. Trailhead elevation on Road 95 is approximately 1600 feet. The trail proceeds generally east and somewhat north. After intersecting the aforementioned Little Skidmore jeep road, it climbs up Chestnut Ridge, turning north briefly to intersect the Grooms Ridge Trail at 3200 feet; then it turns back south briefly before going west in its steady climb to Little Bald Knob at 4300 feet.

From the Knob a trail leads southwest for approximately 3 miles, reaching Camp Todd on Forest Road 95. Another trail leads north from the Knob for approximately 5 miles joining Forest Service Road 85 near the West Virginia state line at a point approximately 1 mile north of the Shenandoah Recreation Area.

Note: Jeep and motorcycle travel is permitted on all of this trail except for one mile at its western end.

Grooms Ridge Trail

Distance: 4 miles

Description: This trail begins on Forest Service Road 101 approximately

1.5 miles south of Hearthstone Lake at elevation 1700. In its 4 mile traverse it makes almost a half-circle, at first climbing west from the road, then swinging south along Big Ridge until its intersection with the Chestnut Ridge Trail at elevation 3200.

North River Trail
Distance: 4 miles
Description: This trail begins on Forest Road 85 across from the Shenandoah Mountain Recreation Area at elevation 3600. It descends south along the North River until it terminates on Forest Road 95.

Shenandoah Mountain Trail [South]
Distance: 3.5 miles
USGS Quad: Palo Alto, Virginia
Description: There are two Shenandoah Mountain trails in the Dry River District. The one described here is really an extension of the trail by the same name that is described in the Deerfield Ranger District. This trail, which is not in the Forest Service inventory of trails, is actually Forest Road 85, which serves to connect the long Shenandoah Mountain Trail (described in the Deerfield Ranger District) with the Shenandoah North Trail in the Dry River District.

Shenandoah Mountain Trail [North]
Distance: 6 miles
USGS Quad: Brandywine, Virginia 7½'
Description: This trail is a disconnected piece of the long Shenandoah Mountain Trail that is described under the Deerfield Ranger District trails. A study of the map would seem to indicate the easiest approach to this trail would be from U.S. Route 33, the trail's northern terminus. Wrong. Forest Service officials advise that the best access from U.S. 33 is via a jeep road over private property. Note that Forest Service right-of-way privilege extends only to Forest Service vehicles. Therefore access must be made from the south off Forest Road 85 at Bother Knob, and involves a bit of cross country hiking. Check with the Forest Service office for exact point of entry. The trail proceeds north in the 3600-4000 feet elevation and literally straddles the Virginia-West Virginia state line. The northern-most point of the trail that is on Forest Service property is at High Knob.

LEE RANGER DISTRICT
Professional Building
Edinburg, Virginia 22824
Telephone: 703/984-4101

Visitor Center is on U.S. Route 211 between Luray and New Market open seven days a week from April to November. Telephone: 703/740-8310.

On the organization charts of the U.S. Forest Service, the Massanutten Mountain area is nothing more than a part — though a large part to be sure — of the Lee Ranger District of the George Washington National

Forest. But the Massanutten is much more than that. It is somewhat of a geologic oddity, in that it rises abruptly out of the floor of the Shenandoah Valley of Virginia, near Strasburg, extends southwest for 60 miles, then disappears just as abruptly, near Harrisonburg, Virginia. On the north, State Route 55 almost touches the Massanutten at Signal Knob. And on the south, U.S. Route 33, running from Harrisonburg, Virginia to Elkton, Virginia, skirts it near Massanutten Peak. U.S. Route 211, from Luray to New Market, bisects the Massanutten at New Market Gap, resulting in the logical designations of "South Half" and "North Half." The attractive Forest Service Visitor Center is situated on U.S. 211 near the top of the gap.

Owing to its proximity to the Washington and Baltimore metropolitan areas, the Lee Ranger District has received some allotments of both money and labor to construct hiking trails and other facilities, especially in the Northern Section. This Section has two other distinctions. It contains the rather well preserved ruins of the Elizabeth Furnace, an ironmaking furnace that operated throughout much of the nineteenth century. Secondly, at what is now Camp Roosevelt, the first Civilian Conservation Corps camp opened in 1933. A sign marking the site reads as follows:

CAMP ROOSEVELT

Site of the first Civilian Conservation Corps Camp in the United States. Operated April 4, 1933 through May, 1942. This recreation area is dedicated the 17th day of July, 1966 as a tribute to the men of the Civilian Conservation Corps and their accomplishments.   George Washington National Forest

Whereas the Shenandoah National Park and its famed Skyline Drive receive tremendous visitor use, the Massanutten, some 10 miles to the west, is, if anything, somewhat underused. During the course of two midweek visits in July, 1975, we found the campgrounds only partly full and the hiking trails sparsely used. But on some week ends, I am informed, the campgrounds and certain trails receive heavy use. Hopefully this book, plus two new hiking trail maps issued in 1975 by the Potomac Appalachian Trail Club (Map H for the Southern Section, Map G for the Northern), will help to funnel more hikers to the Massanutten.

Some 54 miles of the 250 mile Big Blue—Tuscarora Trail (described in detail under West Virginia trails) goes through the Lee Ranger District.

Massanutten North has trails for all types of visitors. A scant hundred yards from the visitor center is a macadam trail of gentle grade that can be negotiated by those confined in a wheelchair. And some six miles north of the visitor center on Forest Service Road 274, is a trail for the blind developed in cooperation with the Lions Club. It attempts to make the hiker use his senses of touch, hearing, and smell to better appreciate the mountains around him. There are a number of interpretive stations on the trail, all connected by rope so that the blind can guide themselves. At each station there is a conventional sign for those who see and a braille sign for those who cannot.

Elsewhere on Massanutten North there are day hike trails of short or long duration, circuit hikes and two long trails for the backpacker who wishes to stay overnight on the trail. Wild food enthusiasts will be interested to know that the area contains heavy concentrations of two easily identified and easily harvested wild foods, the milkweed and the poke salad plant.

Massanutten South (PATC Map H) is wilder and more rugged than the Northern Half and its trails are not so well defined. I have described only one of its trails, Bird Knob. The Boone Run Shelter was constructed in 1971. I stayed overnight there on the day of its dedication in October. It is four miles from the southern boundary of the District and can be reached via Cub Run, Route 636. There is a good trail leading south from the shelter (see map) but in 1975 it was unsigned and unblazed.

Bird Knob Trail — From Forest Service Picnic Ground one-half mile east of Visitor Center in New Market Gap (U.S. Route 211)

Distance: 9 miles

Maps: USGS Quads: Hamburg, Tenth Legion, Stanley, all in Virginia; PATC Map H

Description:

From the picnic area a sign directs hikers to summit of Bird Knob (4.6 miles). The trail is orange-blazed (freshly blazed and brushed out by Youth Conservation Corps in 1975). In mid-July, 1975, with photographer Kevin Johnson, I hiked part of the trail, but it is to Rita Cloutier of the Potomac Appalachian Trail Club that I am indebted for the trail description that follows. In August of 1975, Rita led a group of PATC hikers on a scheduled hiking trip to the top of Bird Knob and beyond. Here is her description:

From the picnic area off U.S. 211 in New Market Gap, take the orange-blazed Bird Knob Trail, approximately 50 feet in on right hand side of picnic road. The trail runs generally north for about ¼ mile. At 4-way intersection, turn left on center double orange-blazed trail leading westerly uphill. At the top of the lower ridge (don't follow the red-banded trees on the right), turn left at the orange-blazed rocks guarding a benchmark, proceed southwesterly along the ridge and follow the trail up past two outstanding viewpoints of the Shenandoah Valley to the west. Continue on the trail for about 3 miles to the foot of Bird Knob where there is a wildlife clearing with a scummy pond. At roughly the northeast corner of the clearing, find and follow the road north for about ¼ mile to the point where it runs into another road. Turn left (northeast) and follow the second road about one-tenth mile to a major wildlife pond deep enough for swimming. Return on same route.

This alternate return is for *experienced* hikers only: Retrace steps and then follow second woods road out to a gravel road and Forest Service gate. Turn left on the gravel road and walk approximately .40 mile along it uphill. At the point where the gravel road makes a sharp right-hand turn uphill, continue straight ahead (northeasterly) through the Forest Service gate to an old woods road (jeep trail on maps). Follow this road, taking the *right* branch of the fork approximately one mile in, until a wildlife clearing is reached. Go to not quite the northwest corner of this clearing and bushwhack to the right (northwesterly) about 200 feet to the Bird Knob Trail. (Contrary to the maps, we did not locate the spot at which the jeep trail intercepts the Bird Knob Trail — it may no longer exist.)

Note: There is a considerably more detailed description of this 9-mile hiking trail than other comparable trails in this book. This description illustrates quite well the type of decisions a hiker must make when following even a fairly recent map. It explains why good hike leaders like to check out a trail on the ground before leading a group of other hikers over it. Note particularly the reference to the jeep trail intersection which "may no longer exist," which is another good example of why it is desirable to check out maps and hiking trails with local offices or knowledgeable people. Jeep trails can become abandoned and overgrown, or conversely, they can be improved into all-weather roads traversable by automobiles.

Length of time required for this trail hike: 4 to 4½ hours.

Water: Some of the PATC-ers drank from the stream which feeds the swimming/wildlife pond. They lived! You may wish to carry enough water with you for the entire hike.

Massanutten Mountain Trail — From State Route 619 through Elizabeth Furnace and south to Camp Roosevelt.

Distance: 23 miles

USGS Quads: Strasburg, Bentonville, Rileyville, Luray, all in Virginia. PATC Map G.

Description: The trail follows the ridge line of Massanutten Mountain. There are two ways to reach it from the north. To hike the entire 23 miles one would locate the intersection of the trail (orange-blazed) at its junction with State Route 613 approximately one mile east of the intersections of State Route 613 and 678. The trailhead (not visible from the road) is across the road from the fish hatchery near the home of the Superintendent. The second, and easier, way to locate the trail is to start at the bridge over Passage Creek at the north end of the picnic grounds in Elizabeth Furnace Recreation Area. (Cars left in the picnic grounds over night should have note displayed that car owners are hiking). At the bridge, pick up the blue-blazes of the Big Blue trail and follow that trail east and southeast for 1.5 miles to its junction with the Massanutten Mountain Trail in Shawl Gap. The elevation at Elizabeth Furnace is about 700 feet, whereas on top of the ridge it is 1500 feet.

At Shawl Gap the Big Blue and the Massanutten Mountain trail follow the same route south for approximately 6 miles to Veach Gap. The hiker follows both blue-blazes and orange-blazes. Those who are backpacking

*Two of the four bunks at the Little Crease Shelter,
one of the more comfortable overnight shelters.*

are urged to stay overnight at the excellent Little Crease shelter in Veach
Gap.

I have a particular interest in this shelter. In 1970, shortly after the
conclusion of my 2,000 mile Appalachian Trail hike I was invited by
Forest Service employee Charlie Huppuch to spend a day at Harrison-
burg, Virginia, with employees of the George Washington National
Forest supervisor's office. From my notes and from memory, I told the
Forest Service people of some of the better shelter design features I
came across in my inspection of the 240 shelters that dot the A.T. from
Georgia to Maine. Many of these ideas, plus some improvements developed by the Forest Service people were incorporated in a new shelter,
Boone Run, in the southern section of the Massanutten (see PATC Map
H). Having built that one, the Service made a few more improvements
when it built the Little Crease shelter described in this chapter. It is big,
well lighted, and has plenty of sleeping space in its four bunks and
ample floor space. The traffic areas in front of many shelters become
muddy holes in even moderately wet weather. Not at Little Crease! The
area in front of the shelter is paved with heavy field stone. It has table

Masonry work in front of the Little Crease Shelter.
[Photo by Kevin H. Johnson.]

space, a toilet, and a good source of water in the little stream in front of the shelter.

From the shelter the trail goes generally east to regain the ridge elevation. One mile from the shelter the two trails split, the Big Blue going east toward the South Fork of the Shenandoah River, while the orange-blazed Massanutten Mountain trail goes south. In 4 miles the white-blazed Milford Gap trail goes east to the Hazard Mill Canoe Camp. The main trail continues southwest, crossing another side trail 4.5 miles farther on. About 4 miles beyond that junction, a side trail heads to Kennedy Peak and the observation tower, at elevation 2560. Continuing on south on the main trail for 2 more miles leads the hiker to State Route 675. Bear right on Route 675 for 1.7 miles to the Camp Roosevelt campground.

Duncan Hollow Trail — From Camp Roosevelt to U.S. Route 211
Distance: 8 miles
USGS Quad: Hamburg, Virginia; PATC Map G
Description: This trail is, for all practical purposes, a continuation of the

Massanutten Mountain trail. However, on the trail maps, and on sign posts it bears the name Duncan Hollow Trail, so to be consistent we call it that. The trail begins from State Route 675 about .1 mile east of Camp Roosevelt. The wooden sign at that point with arrows pointing south reads: Duncan Hollow Trail, Big Run — 6 mi, Waterfall Mtn. 7

The trail goes south from Route 675 along a dirt road through Duncan Hollow. After about a mile, the road becomes a foot trail and approximately 3 miles from Route 675, the blue-blazed Peach Orchard Trail leads to the right for 2 miles to the Crisman Hollow Road (Forest Service Route 274). Continuing on south for another 2 miles the Duncan Hollow Trail intersects the yellow-blazed Scothorn Gap Trail, which also leads off to the right and joins the Crisman Hollow Road. Going on south, the Duncan Hollow Trail ends on U.S. Route 211 about 1.7 miles east of the Forest Service Visitor Center. There is red flagging on the north side of the highway to identify the trail and ample hard surface parking.

Signal Knob Circuit Hike

Distance: 10 miles

USGS Quad: Strasburg, Virginia; PATC Map G (see in particular the enlarged inset map of the Elizabeth Furnace area on reverse of Map G).

Description: Signal Knob is a historic spot where both Confederate and Union troops maintained a signal station during the Civil War. The stone breastworks built to protect the site from attack are still evident. There are several ways that one may reach Signal Knob, but since circuit hikes are always more interesting than straight "up and back," hikes we will describe a circuit taken in mid-July, 1975, with my son Kevin and three other members of Explorer Post 681 of Falls Church, Virginia.

We had camped overnight at the family campground in the Elizabeth Furnace Recreation Area. Early next morning we walked to the campground entrance and across the hard surface Route 678. The trail sign at that point read:

Bear Wallow Trail	0.6 miles
Signal Knob	5.1 miles
Signal Knob Parking Lot	1.7 miles

A ten minute walk brought us to the Bear Wallow Trail, which we followed until it cut across with the Big Blue Trail. Turning left on the blue-blazed "Big Blue" (excuse the alliteration!), we followed both trails until their intersection with Little Passage Creek. The Bear Wallow Trail ends at that point.

To reach Signal Knob, turn right (northeast) on an unblazed but clearly defined trail. In 0.3 miles, pass Sand Spring on right, the sole source of water for Confederate troops stationed on the Knob. Follow the trail for approximately 2 miles to the top of Signal Knob at 2105-foot elevation. From the Knob one has an unobstructed 180° view of the Shenandoah Valley. The spot is still used for communications, but today the communications take the form of an educational television transmitting equipment tower.

For your return trip take the *unblazed* trail past the television tower. PATC Map G shows this as a red blazed trail but the map is incorrect. The trail goes generally south and east. Plan enough time for the return trip so that you can enjoy the outstanding views from the Shenandoah Valley Overlook at 1900 feet, the Fort Valley Overlook at 1800 feet, and the Buzzard Rock Overlook at 1500 feet. In July and August allow additional time for picking and eating blueberries at many spots along the trail. About .2 miles before reaching the Signal Knob parking area, the trail crosses a gushing stream which emanates from a walled-in enclosure some 50 feet off the trail. Upon reaching the parking area, one can return to the starting point via Route 678 or one can postpone the road walking a bit by taking the yellow-blazed trail from the parking lot which intersects the road near the picnic area.

Allow approximately 5 hours for the hike. Water is available at several points along the circuit.

Other Elizabeth Furnace Trails — (See enlarged inset map on the reverse side of PATC Map G).

Two extremely interesting interpretive trails begin and end near the picnic area. One such trail shows and explains the steps involved in making charcoal. This trail contains a reconstructed collier's hut and a huge pile of hardwood arranged in a manner that would be suitable for a slow burning charcoal-producing fire.

The other trail, called the "Pig Iron Trail," leads the viewer past the big stone Elizabeth Furnace that functioned well into the nineteenth century. Signs mounted on stone pedestals explain and illustrate the method by which the charcoal was used to heat the iron ore and to produce the pig iron.

Sugar Knob Cabin Trails and Wardensville, West Virginia

Distance: 15 miles

USGS Quad: Woodstock, Virginia, and Wardensville, WV; 7½ minute; PATC Map M, Strips 5 and 6

Description: The following trails are for anyone wishing to hike them, but especially for those who are staying at or camping in the vicinity of the cabin. To stay at the cabin, obtain key from and make reservations in advance with the Potomac Appalachian Trail Club, 1718 N Street N. W., Washington D.C. 20036. There are six trails in the vicinity of the cabin and some of these can be combined for circuit hikes:

Pond Run Trail	2.23 miles
Peer Trail·	3.18 miles
Half Moon Trail to Lookout Spur	0.57 miles
Half Moon Trail, Spur to Road	2.25 miles

| Half Moon Lookout Spur | 0.67 miles |
| Mill Mountain Trail | 6.17 miles |

PEDLAR RANGER DISTRICT
Federal Building
Buena Vista, Virginia 24416
Telephone: 703/261-6105

All trails described for the Pedlar Ranger District can be located on the map of the George Washington National Forest, Pedlar Ranger District, scale of one inch equals two miles. The map shows the land status as of September, 1973. The six trails included for the District are all in the northernmost part and they are either in or lead to the Big Levels Wildlife Management Unit. Green Pond, a sink hole on top of the plateau, is mentioned in several of the trail descriptions.

Cold Springs Trail
Distance: 4.5 miles
USGS Quad: Big Levels, Virginia
Description: To reach the beginning of the trail, proceed north on State Route 608, then turn right on Forest Road 41 for approximately 0.5 mile, then north on Forest Road 42 for 3 miles to Cold Springs Branch, where you will find the trail. Elevation at beginning of hike is approximately 2100 feet. At the top of Big Levels, elevation 3400 feet, the trail comes into a jeep road, which is now used only for foot and horse traffic at lower elevations.

Follow the jeep road past the intersection with Stony Run Trail, to Green Pond at elevation 3208, at which point the Kennedy Ridge Trail and St. Mary's River Trails intersect. Here the jeep road becomes Forest Road 162 and leads south past Bald Mountain to the Blue Ridge Parkway. (Note: Instead of continuing all the way to the Blue Ridge Parkway, you can take a circuit hike of some 14 miles by returning on the St. Mary's River Trail and then going north on Forest Service Road 42 back to the starting point.)

St. Mary's River Trail
Distance: 6 miles
USGS Quad: Vesuvous and Big Levels, Virginia
Description: To reach the beginning of hike, proceed north on State Route 608 to Forest Service Road 41. Follow Road 41 to the Forest Service Parking area at the gate. This trail is actually an old road (now blocked to vehicular traffic) that follows the river for 2 miles before Sugartree Branch comes in from the south. The trail (road) goes up Sugar Tree Branch and past the mines. For an interesting side trip, follow the river about a mile past the point where Sugar Tree Branch comes to a low waterfall and pool and to the beginning of the gorge. To go up the river beyond this waterfall is difficult, especially during high water in the winter and spring. The old road is difficult to follow at one point, where it passes through one of the upper mines, but it continues

through to Green Pond on top of Big Levels. The trail crosses the river three times at its lower end and is difficult to negotiate in winter.

Stony Run Trail
Distance: 3 miles
USGS Quad: Big Levels, Virginia
Description: To reach beginning of the Stony Run hike, proceed north on Forest Road 42 for about 7 miles north of its intersection with Forest Service Road 41. This trail is a jeep road used by hunter access to Big Levels. The trail starts at 1819 feet at the road, and climbs to 3219 feet at the junction with Cold Springs Branch Trail.

Kennedy Ridge Trail
Distance: 3.5 miles
USGS Quad: Big Levels, Virginia
Description: To reach beginning of hike proceed east on Forest Road 42 to a point approximately 2 miles east of its intersection with Forest Road 52. This trail at upper and lower ends is a former jeep road. It begins at 1800 feet on the road and climbs to over 3000. This trail is not blazed and may be difficult to find and follow.

The next two trails begin at the delightful Sherando Lake recreation area, with its two man made lakes, excellent swimming and camping facilities. It is readily accessible both from nearby Waynesboro, Virginia, and from the Blue Ridge Parkway, and both trails appear on the Big Levels USGS quad. I did not scout these two trails but Sherando brings back memories of our Boy Scout Troop 681 of Falls Church, Virginia, which camped here for week-long periods in the late 1950's. In 1970, during the course of my 2000 mile A.T. hike, I was intercepted at the nearby Parkway by Forest Service employees Joe Hudick and Charlie Huppuch, who took me over to Sherando for a steak supper and put me up overnight at the bunkhouse — courtesies greatly appreciated by a tired hiker.

Sherando Lake to White Rock Gap
Distance: 6 miles
Description: The trail begins from the upper lake and climbs to White Rock Gap on the Parkway. Fairly easy to follow, it is marked with red paint blazes where the route might be confusing. The trail stays in a hollow for its entire length and parts of it follow an old jeep road used only by a few hunters from adjacent private land. The hiker will encounter considerable brush growth during the summer months.

Sherando Lake to Bald Mountain
Distance: 4 miles
Description: The trail proceeds from the Recreation Area on Forest Road 91 to the Blue Ridge Parkway at the Bald Mountain Overlook. The trail that is blue-blazed from the recreation area to the top of Torrey Ridge heads northwest past the campground water tank and climbs up to Torry Ridge, gaining 800 feet elevation in the first mile. At 1.3 mile the

Torry Ridge trail intersects another blue-blaze trail that goes down a side ridge to Forest Service access Road 91 to Sherando Lake. The two blue-blazed trails, together with Road 91, can be used to form a loop trail.

In proceeding on the Torry Ridge trail past the blue-blaze trail intersection, the going becomes more difficult near the top of the ridge, for the trail is somewhat overgrown. It bears northwest on the ridge top and climbs up Bald Mountain and to the site of the former lookout tower. The elevation here is 3587 feet. A dirt road runs northeast from Bald Mountain to the Bald Mountain Overlook on the Blue Ridge Parkway.

DEERFIELD RANGER DISTRICT
2304 West Beverly Street
Staunton, Virginia 24401
Telephone: 703/885-1911

All trails described for the Deerfield District appear on the map of George Washington Forest, Deerfield Ranger District. Scale of one inch equals two miles. The map shows land status as of July, 1974. The Deerfield is one of four ranger districts in the GW that is within 150 miles of my home, and these, along with the Shenandoah National Park (60 miles from home) I have come to regard as being somewhat as my private hiking domain.

I have spent the night in Sexton, one of PATC's 15 locked cabins, which is located in the northern part of the District, some 3 miles north of U.S. Route 250, and have hiked the surrounding trails many times. Adolph T. (Sam) Samuelson, Assistant Supervisor of Trails for PATC, has personally maintained the 15-mile network of Sexton trails for many years.

Elliott Knob, in the midpoint of the District atop Great North Mountain, at 4463 feet, is the highest point in the forest. In the southern part of the District, the beautiful Maury River flows through the mountain at an even more beautiful spot called Goshen Pass. Nearby is the Goshen Camp, the Council Camp for the National Capital Council, BSA.

Elliott Knob Trail
Distance: 5 miles
USGS Quad: Elliott Knob, Virginia
Description: This trail leads to Elliott Knob, which is some 400 feet higher than its highest rival, Hawksbill, in the Blue Ridge Mountains in Shenandoah National Park. It has been 15 years since I climbed Elliott Knob on a warm July day, but I can still remember the tremendous view from the top of the fire tower and the cool breeze that refreshed me after the hot climb.

There are several ways to approach Elliott Knob, but I will first describe the north-to-south route that is listed on the Forest Service map as Elliott Knob Trail. To reach the beginning point of hike, proceed by car south from Churchville, Virginia on State Route 42 for 6 miles. Turn right on State Route 688 and follow for 4 miles to the mountain crest. Watch for a sign reading Elliott Knob and look for the trail's yellow blazes. The trail begins on the south side of the road at about the 2600 foot contour line and climbs slowly to the top of the ridge at an elevation of about 4000 feet, and proceeds south. As it nears Elliott Knob it comes out on a jeep road. Turn right on this road as it goes uphill past a communications facility and on to the firetower.

There are several possibilities for return trip. If you are backpacking you can continue south on the North Mountain Trail for another 10 miles and come out on State Route 687 near Craigsville. You can go east from the Knob on the jeep trail and come out in about 3 miles on State Route 42 near the village of North Mountain. Another possibility: proceed west from the Knob on the foot trail for about 3 miles until you reach a series of roads heading north to State Route 688. From here you return to the parking area.

There is a pond and cleared campsite a short distance east on the dirt road. The pond is easily spotted from the road but it may take a little searching to find the campsite.

Question: What is the actual elevation of Elliott Knob?? Here are some answers:

Source	Elevation Given
Map, George Washington National Forest	4462
Virginia Official Highway Map	4458
A Backpacking Guide to the	
Southern Mountains (Blankenship)	4450
American Automobile Association Road Map	4456

When tempted to become too precise I think of the words of John Ruskin, the English philosopher: "It is the mark of an educated intellect to seek only so much exactness as is required by the nature of the subject matter and the purpose to which it is to be put."

North Mountain Trail

Distance: 10 miles

USGS Quads: Elliott Knob, Deerfield, and Craigsville, all in Virginia

Description: This trail can be hiked either from Elliott Knob or from State Route 687 in the south. The map shows the trail continuing on south past State Route 687 almost to Goshen, but Forest Service Personnel advised against attempting to continue past State Route 687. Since in the preceding trail description we have already taken you to Elliott Knob we will describe the trail in a north-south traverse.

Leaving Elliott Knob at 4458 feet, follow ridge crest generally southwest, gradually descending. After about one mile, the trail to the right leads to Chestnut Flat Springs, 0.3 miles away. If you continue on the main trail for 3 miles you'll reach Hite Hollow Road or Forest Service Road 82, at 3300 feet. Proceed southeast for another 5 miles at the 3300 to 3000 foot elevation. For the remaining 2 miles of the trail, you des-

cend gradually, reaching State Route 687 at about 2100 feet. State Route
687 is identified as Ramsey Draft Road. Do not confuse it with Ramseys
Draft Road further north, which leads off U.S. Route 250.

Crawford Mountain Trail

Distance: 6 miles
USGS Quads: Elliott Knob, West Augusta, and Stokesville, all in Virginia
Description: Car approach and parking is same as for Elliott Knob Trail.
From the parking area on State Route 688, proceed north on the yellow-
blazed trail. This is a jeep trail which begins at about 2600 feet and climbs
to 3600 feet on Crawford Mountain. At 2 miles the trail intersects
Chimney Hollow Trail, which leads to the left; and 200 yards further on
it intersects Crawford Knob Trail, going off to the right. As it nears U.S.
Route 250, the Crawford Mountain Trail begins to descend rapidly, and
at its terminus on U.S. 250, its elevation is some 1800 feet.

Chimney Hollow Trail

Distance: 3 miles
USGS Quads: Elliott Knob and West Augusta, Virginia
Description: This trail begins at its intersection with the Crawford Mountain Trail and proceeds generally in a northwesterly direction until its
intersection with U.S. Route 250 one mile east of the village of West
Augusta and immediately east of Forest Service Road 96. It is a yellow-
blazed trail that is signed on U.S. Route 250. Elevation at its beginning
on Crawford Mountain is over 3600 feet and at its terminus on Route 250
it is 1933 feet.

Crawford Knob Trail

Distance: 4 miles
USGS Quads: Elliott Knob and Churchville, Virginia
Description: This trail proceeds east from its intersection with Crawford
Mountain Trail until it reaches Jerusalem Chapel in the valley on State
Route 720. From its point of origin the trail proceeds southeast over
Crawford Knob at 3728 feet and then drops down steeply until reaching
the 3000 foot level. As it nears the valley it joins the dirt Forest Service
Road 289, which it follows until it reaches State Route 720 and the end
of the trail.

   Note: The last three trails described — Crawford Mountain, Chimney
Hollow, and Crawford Knob — can be used in conjunction with some of
the secondary roads to make some interesting circuit hikes. They would
be especially convenient for those headquartering at Sexton Cabin.

Shenandoah Mountain Trail

Distance: 31 miles
USGS Quads: Williamsville, Deerfield, McDowell, and West Augusta, all
in Virginia.
Description: The distance of 31 miles is roughly the distance from State
Route 27 in the southern part of the Ranger District to the point where
the trail literally goes off the map in the north. Actually the Shenandoah
Mountain Trail continues north into the Dry River District, following the

state line past such impressive peaks as Reddish Knob, Bother Knob, and High Knob.

The 23.5 mile section from State Route 627 to U.S. Route 250 has received but limited maintenance, is not blazed and only partially signed. Forest Service personnel report that in spite of this, the trail receives enough hiker traffic to make it reasonably easy to follow. North of U.S. 250 the Shenandoah Mountain Trail and the network of trails surrounding the PATC Sexton Cabin have been well maintained for many years by one man — Adolph (Sam) Samuelson of the Potomac Appalachian Club. These latter trails are blue-blazed and signed. They are described in more detail under "Sexton Cabin Trails."

Begin the Shenandoah Mountain Trail from the Scotchtown Draft Road (State Route 627) at a point approximately 3 miles east of its intersection with State Route 678 (the village of Ft. Lewis is 4 miles south of this intersection). From the trailhead proceed north, climbing from the road elevation of 2000 feet and shortly crosses over top of South Sister Knob and skirts North Sister Knob at the 3000 foot elevation. At 5 miles, a side trail to the right leads to Wallace Peak. At 8 miles the Jerkemtight Trail bears off to the left. Continuing on at the 3000 foot level, the trail at 14 miles passes to the west of The Bump 14 miles further on, and at 17 miles it crosses Forest Service Road 173. The trail continues northeast, straddling the Highland County—Augusta County line until it reaches U.S. Route 250 at 23.5 miles, with a little drop in elevation.

North of U.S. 250, the trail goes along the ridge with occasional views west into the valley and at 26.5 miles it reaches the Jerrys Run Trail (the locked PATC Sexton Cabin is 0.4 mile to the right). From here it proceeds north past Hardscrabble Knob, skirts Tearjacket Knob, and runs on to Forest Road 95 in the Dry River District.

Jerkemtight Trail
Distance: 4.5 miles
USGS Quads: Deerfield and Williamsville, Virginia
Description: Trail begins at a point 4 miles south of Deerfield on State Route 629. It follows a dirt road at its beginning along a stocked trout stream, proceeds south and west until joining the Shenandoah Mountain Trail in the vicinity of Wallace Peak. The elevation at the beginning of the hike is 2000 feet and rises to 3600 feet at the intersection with Shenandoah Mountain Trail. The distance of hike can be extended by going north on Shenandoah Mountain Trail for 3 miles, then descending to the west on the western segment of the Jerkemtight, reaching State Route 614 in an additional 4 miles.

Sexton Cabin Trails
Distance: 15.5 miles
USGS Quads: 7½ minutes. West Augusta, McDowell, Virginia; PATC Map E, Sexton Shelter Area, Virginia
Description: The Potomac Appalachian Trail Club maintains 15.54 miles of trails in the Cabin area. These trails are:

Shenandoah Mountain Trail	7.53 miles
Jerry Run Trail	2.04 miles
Hardscrabble Knob Trail	0.40 mile
Ramsey Draft Trail	5.57 miles

The trails are blue-blazed and signed. PATC Map E is at a scale of one inch to the mile. The map covers an area 20 miles north and south of U.S. Route 250 and 10 miles east and west.

One of the more popular hikes is to go from the cabin southwest for 0.4 miles, turn north on blue-blazed Shenandoah Mountain Trail for approximately 5 miles, then south on the blue-blazed trail to Hardscrabble Knob. The return route would be via the Ramsey Draft Trail to Jerry Run Trail and then a right turn on Jerry Run Trail back to the cabin. The length of this circuit is about 12 miles.

Jerry Run Trail is a connector between the Shenandoah Mountain Trail (elevation 3200 feet) and the Ramsey Draft Trail (elevation 2544 feet).

The Ramsey Draft Trail runs from U.S. 250 north to the point where the stream divides into the Left Prong and the Right Prong. In earlier years this was a road passable by vehicles.

The short (4 mile) Hardscrabble Knob trail is a dead-end leading to the site of the former fire tower on top of the 4200 foot Knob. On one of my hikes out of Sexton Cabin some years ago, I met a lone logger sawing and hauling timber out from the forest. He related his experiences as a former tower man at the fire tower on top of Hardscrabble. He worked six days a week and on the seventh he would walk 7 miles to a spot where he could pick up a ride home and get resupplied with groceries. Then he would go back to the tower. The most vivid thing I recall of his experience was his practice of throwing table scraps out of the tower after his evening meal and listening to the wild cats fight and snarl over the food!

Shenandoah National Park

This 300 square mile park lies astride an 80-mile length of the Blue Ridge Mountains in northern Virginia. The 105-mile scenic Skyline Drive winds its way through the entire park, beginning near Front Royal in the north and extending to the southern end of the park on U.S. Route 250 (Interstate 64) near Waynesboro. On a road map the park looks like a thin ribbon, as thin as three miles in some places, widening out to seven or eight miles in others. The A.T. winds along the top of the mountain for 94 miles, sometimes on one side of Skyline Drive, sometimes on the other. The Trail and the Drive intersect in 25 places. Most long-distance hikers of the Trail consider that the 94 miles within the Shenandoah

National Park is the best designed and best maintained of any comparable area in the entire Trail.

There are three types of maps available for hikers who travel over this area. The first is the USGS 7½ minute quads to which we have been referring throughout this book. The second is a set of three maps also developed by the U.S. Geological Survey, covering the northern, central and southern sections of the park. Order these from the USGS address given in the introductory chapters of this book and specify Shenandoah National Park and which of the three maps you desire. The third set of maps, and probably the most convenient for your use, are the three Potomac Appalachian Trail Club (PATC) maps; Map 9 for the northern section, Map 10 for the central, and Map 11 for the southern. These maps are available from PATC, 1718 N Street N.W., Washington, D.C., 20036. Write for price list.

PATC has been in existence since 1927 and it seems that Dr. Egbert H. Walker has been chairman of the Maps Committee most of that time. His maps are of one quality only — excellent. They are multi-colored affairs, with contour lines and a wealth of useful information printed on the reverse side of the map. Map 10 was last reprinted in January, 1975, at which time 35,000 copies were produced. One can only conclude that the hiking trails in the central section of the park are getting a tremendous amount of use. A portion of Map 10 has been reproduced on these pages by permission of PATC (see page 75).

Overnight accommodations in Shenandoah National Park cater primarily to those seeking the more expensive hotel-type accommodations or to those using trailers or tents in the four large public campgrounds. The park concessionaire, ARA-Virginia Sky-Line Company, Inc., of Luray, Virginia 22835, provides lodge and cottage accomodations for over 900 guests.

The four public campgrounds in the park provide hot and cold water, trailer sewage disposal stations, showers, laundry, stores, and for tent campers, a cleared tent area with fireplace and picnic table. The four campgrounds are:

NAME OF CAMPGROUND	NUMBER OF CAMPSITES	COST OF CONSTRUCTION
Loft Mountain	231	$410,593
Lewis Mountain	32	Unknown
Big Meadows	255	$348,822
Mathews Arm	186	$616,348

Two of these campgrounds are relatively new, Loft Mountain having been built in 1966 and Mathews Arm built in 1968. The other two have been enlarged and modernized in recent years.

This is an impressive display of facilities for car campers, but the backpacker, in comparison, has little going for him. There were 21 trailside shelters, most of them built in the 1930's for overnight use by backpackers. But in 1974 the Superintendent of the Park declared these shelters out of bounds for overnight use and he had the solid oak and chestnut bunks torn out of the shelters and destroyed. And a special set of rules was established for the backpacker and published in the Federal Register to give them the force and effect of law. Most of them are common sense rules which most good backpackers would follow anyway. But some of them become very irksome to the backpacker when he compares the restrictions placed upon him to the freedom allowed the picnicker or the car camper. Here are the most improtant rules that apply to the backpacker in the Shenandoah National Park:

Permits are required for "backcountry" camping. Backcountry is defined as 250 yards from a paved road, .5 miles from park facilities other than trails, unpaved roads, and trail shelters. Permits are available without charge at park headquarters, entrance stations, visitor centers, or from any ranger. Requests for permits must be accompanied by the campers' name, address, number in party, and the location and date of each overnight camp. No party may include more than 10 persons. Send requests for permits to: Shenandoah National Park, Luray, Virginia, 22835.

No one may camp within 250 yards or in view of any paved road or the park boundary or within .5 miles in view of any park development or facility, except a trail, unpaved road or trail shelter. Nor may anyone camp in view from a trail or unpaved road or in sight of any sign posted as a no-camping area. No one may camp within 25 feet of a stream.

Also, no one may camp in view of another camping party or inside or in view of a trail shelter. However, in severe weather campers may seek shelter or sleep inside or near a trail shelter with other camping groups.

There is a two-night (consecutive) limit for backcampers in any location. Open wood and charcoal fires are prohibited, except in shelter fireplaces. Small gasoline, propane or solid fuel stoves are recommended.

Possession of food or beverages in discardable glass containers is prohibited and all other material must be packed out. Dogs are prohibited in certain posted trails and must be on a leash at all times.

These rules are enforced with a zeal that would be commendable had it been used to "regulate" rather than to "eliminate." Perhaps the frustrations of the backpackers in this park can best be illustrated by a postcard written in the summer of 1975 by a couple from Hawaii, both in their 60's, who were routed out of their tents on two successive nights by park rangers:

"The rangers didn't find us the first night. We were looking for them to get a permit. The second night they found us at 10 p.m. and issued a permit and warning—we were camped near a road and in sight of a trail. The third night they found us again . . . out of sight of the shelter but close to a stream and trail. So we had to move in the dark or pay $25.00. We hiked down

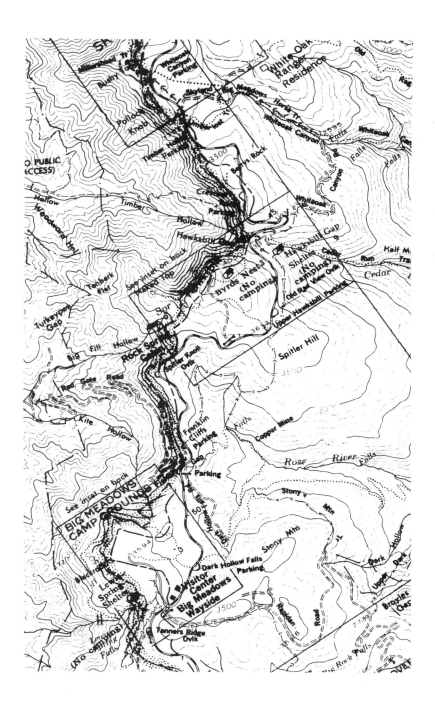

the road, slept behind a stone wall, and hitched out next day thoroughly disgusted. We are 62 and 64 and from Hawaii, doing the entire trail.

Aloha, Jane Kaopuiki

P.S. Shenandoah Park is geared to motorists."

One of the reasons given for closing the shelters in the park was the terrific overuse of the Appalachian Trail and of the shelters, but many of us maintain that except for certain times in June, July and August the hiking facilities are underused, if anything. Stan Horzempa, of Chester, Pennsylvania, hiking south to north through the Park in October and November 1975 encountered the following numbers of people:

Day and Date	No. of back-packers met on trail	No. Day Walkers on trail	Place Camped	No. of people camped with
Sat.—Oct. 25	0	0	near trail	0
Sun.—Oct. 26	0	20 (around Loft Mt. campground)	around Pine-field shelter	0
Mon—Oct 27	2 backpackers 13 Boy Scouts	0	High Top shelter	0
Tues—Oct 28	0	0	South River shelter	0
Wed—Oct 29	0	4 (on side trail)	Bear Fence Mt.	0
Thurs—Oct 30	0	0	Milam Gap	0
Fri—Oct 31	0	10 (on side trail)	Rock Spring cabin	2
Sat—Nov 1	6	80 (White Oak side trail)	Off White Oak Trail	0
Sun—Nov 2	5	50 (White Oak side trail)	Byrd Shelter No. 3	0
Mon—Nov 3	0	0	Elk Wallow Shelter	2
Tues—Nov 4	0	0	Indian Run Shelter	0
Wed—Nov 5	1	0	Mosby Shelter	0

Regarding his hike, Mr. Horzempa writes:

"I had a very nice time on my hike. For the most part, as my chart showed, the trail was almost totally deserted. I was surprized to find that, with the exception of side trails during week ends, the trails in the Shenandoah National Park were even more empty than trails in Pennsylvania and Maryland. Only in the park did I go entire days without seeing another person on the trails. I see no reason why the shelters in the park should not be used during the off-season."

Now to proceed to the trails. We have already discussed the A.T. briefly, and we will now discuss some of the many delightful side trails and circuit trails in the park and introduce you to one of the most valuable publications ever issued by PATC, *Circuit Hikes in the Shenandoah National Park.*

There are a variety of different kinds of trails, roads, fire-foot trails, etc., and the combination of these makes possible a wide choice of circuit hikes. *Circuit Hikes,* now in its ninth edition is a 4¼" x 7" book of 74 pages with a durable plastic cover, ideal for carrying in a large pocket of jacket or pack. It describes and provides a sketch map of 20 circuit trails (where the hiker need not retrace the same route on the return trip) and a number of non-circuit trails.

The 105-mile long Skyline Drive has mileage markers throughout its entire length. *Circuit Hike* uses these mileage markers as locator points for starting and finishing hikes. For example on Hike No. 11 — Hoover Camp (President Herbert Hoover's fishing camp) the book reads, "To start the hike, park at the Big Meadows Wayside just past milepost 51." That makes it quite precise and the full-length circuit hikes are described with the same precise and easy-to-follow directions.

One of the all-time favorites is the 8 mile circuit of Old Rag Mountain. This was the favorite mountain of the late Senator Harry F. Byrd, Sr., and in about 1960 he financed the construction of a large stone shelter with an indoor fireplace near the summit and it was named Byrd Nest No. 1. Later he financed construction of three more "Byrd Nest" shelters in the central and northern sections of the Park.

Old Rag is a somewhat isolated mountain east of the chain over which Skyline Drive is located. It is reached through the town of Sperryville, and those driving from the Washington and Baltimore areas need not go through the Park turnstiles or pay the entrance fee to make this hike, which involves much rock scrambling and brings the hiker out on a rocky summit where a fire tower was once located. It's a great place to loaf and enjoy fine views on a warm summer day.

The return trip brings you down the other side of the mountain, past another shelter, the original Old Rag shelter, and takes you back to parking area via a former road. The first week in May in this part of the mountains could be called "spring flower week" or even more specifically, "trillium week;" thus, those hiking Old Rag on the first Sunday of May will have much company on the trail.

Another of my personal favorites is the circuit hike into Hoover Camp. This is Circuit Hike No. 11 in PATC's *Circuit Hike* book but the 12 mile circuit described therein is not the circuit I prefer. The former involves too much road walking, much of it in the hot sun, for my tastes. "My" hike begins at Bootens Gap milepost 55, takes one down the beautiful little stream called Laurel Prong, through a stand of giant hemlocks, and into Hoover Camp. The return route is through Mill Prong, another stream that was the source of water for the Hoover Camp. The Mill Prong Trail connects with the A.T. in Milam Gap, at which point the hiker continues south on the A.T. back to his car at Bootens Gap. This

circuit is 8 miles long and even though it is near the popular Big
Meadows lodge and public campground, I rarely find people on this trail.

If my hiking time is short, I frequently park my car in Milam Gap and
hike the short 2 mile Mill Prong Trail into Hoover Camp, enjoy a few
minutes at this quiet and beautiful spot, visit the place where the Mill
Prong and Laurel Prong come together to become the Rapidan River, or
I just idle a few minutes on the wide veranda of the Hoover Lodge and
reminisce a bit. The Hoover Camp was donated by the former President
to the Boy Scout organization and maintained for years as a council
camp of the National Capitol Area Council of Washington, D.C. It was
later given to the National Park Service. Many of the buildings had fal-
len into disrepair and these were removed by the Park Service. Hoover
Lodge has been renovated and is now used occasionally, mostly on
weekends, by VIP's.

We have now described two of the circuit trails in the *Circuit Hikes*
book. Chuck Young, a veteran Scoutmaster from Fairfax, Virginia, states
that for years he was able to satisfy the hiking needs of his Boy Scout
troop by the use of four publications, the PATC Maps 9, 10 and 11 plus
Circuit Hikes. By the time he had exhausted all the hiking possibilities
offered by these publications, he had a new generation of Scouts in the
troop and he would start all over again.

We will now describe one more circuit hike which, while not included
in the *Circuit Hikes*, has become a favorite of mine in recent years. In
the beginning pages of this book, in discussing drinking water and water
purification, I mentioned the name of an elderly mountaineer, George
T. Corbin. The trail I am about to describe centers around this same
George Corbin, and the log cabin he built in 1910 near the headwaters
of the Hughes River, in Nicholson Hollow in the central section of the
park. The Corbin Cabin Circuit Hike, for want of a better name, is what we
shall call the shorter hike; and the Nicholson Hollow — Hannah Run
Circuit is what we shall call the longer one. Both hikes go past Corbin
Cabin.

To reach the Cabin, proceed south on Skyline Drive from Thornton
Gap (U.S. 211) for about 6 miles. At the 37.9 milepost there is macadam
parking area on the right. Directly across the Drive from the parking area
is a blue-blaze trail with a sign reading, "Corbin Cabin 1.4 miles." This is
the steeper of the two trails and is called the Corbin Cabin Cutoff Trail.
To reach the longer, less steep trail proceed further south to milepost
38.6 and park in the Stony Man Parking Area. Retrace your route, this
time by foot, on Skyline Drive until you reach a blue-blaze trail on the
right. The sign reads, "Nicholson Hollow Trail" and "Corbin Cabin 1.8
miles."

Proceed down this trail to the east, descending from elevation 3103
on Skyline Drive to about 2000 feet at Corbin Cabin. Cross the upper
reach of Hughes River as you approach the cabin. This is a locked cabin
maintained by the PATC and to stay overnight you should make a reser-

vation and obtain the key from the Club. The cabin is equipped with bunks, mattresses, pots, pans, dishes, kerosene lanterns, and kerosene. To complete the circuit, cross the Hughes River and begin the climb back up to Skyline Drive via the Cutoff trail. Enroute you will pass the ruins of two houses, formerly occupied by relatives of George Corbin. You will also pass the Corbin cemetery on the left shortly after leaving the river. All the graves except one are marked with field stones — the single exception has a concrete marker. It is the last resting place of George's second wife, who died in childbirth in 1924. Upon reaching Skyline Drive you may either (1) turn left and walk along the drive for about 1 mile to your car, or (2) return to your car via the A.T. which is just west of the drive at the point where the Cutoff Trail begins. The entire circuit covers about 4 miles.

For the longer circuit, park your car in the parking area near milepost 37 and proceed down the Corbin Cutoff Trail. After crossing Hughes River, turn left near the cabin and descend along the river for an additional 2 miles at which point the Hannah Run Trail comes in on the left. at an intersection marked with concrete signpost. Turn left and begin the long climb on a good grade back to Skyline Drive; you will pass the remains of a number of mountain houses enroute. The Hannah Run Trail is 3.7 miles long from its intersection with Nicholson Hollow Trail (elevation 1280 feet) to its intersection with Skyline Drive (elevation 3350 feet). At that point turn left and follow Skyline Drive for 1.6 miles until reaching Pinnacles Picnic Grounds. At the picnic area pick up the A.T. and follow it back to where the car is parked. Total length of circuit is about 10 miles.

Now a few words about George T. Corbin and the cabin he built in about 1910 near the Hughes River. George was about 21 or 22 years old at the time, and he and his second wife moved in. Three children were born in this cabin to the second Mrs. Corbin. But things must have been mighty grim when Mrs. Corbin died in the cabin shortly after the birth of their only daughter. It was the dead of winter, yet somehow the child survived. Later, George married again, to a 15-year-old girl, and a fourth Corbin child was born in this same cabin.

Years later, in 1936, the Shenandoah National Park was dedicated. The mountain people had been told they could remain in their homes and that many of them could work for the Park Service. So in 1938 George borrowed $500 to put a new metal roof on the cabin, but shortly thereafter word was received that all 433 families in the Park would be evicted. George received $500 for his cabin and the five acres that he owned.

The Corbin family, along with the other mountain families, were moved to a number of resettlement locations outside the park. The cabin remained vacant for many years but that new metal roof saved it from the rapid deterioration that beset the others. In 1953 the Potomac Appalachian Trail Club requested and received permission to renovate the cabin and include it in the system of locked cabins that are rented to both PATC members and to the general public. George was present at the dedication, which took place in 1954.

In October of that same year my son Dennis and I made our first visit to this latest PATC cabin. There was something very appealing about the little place and its surroundings. From that time right up to the present, my family and their friends have made many visits there.

In early January, 1962, I learned that George Corbin was living in my home town of Falls Church, Virginia, and that he worked as a janitor in the same school attended by my children. I promptly sought him out and within a week we took him down to his old cabin. There was much picture taking and George pointed out many points of interest in the area, the cemetery, the garden plot, the site of his father's home, and he told us what life was like when he lived there. We have had him down to his cabin many times since, twice in 1975.

A hand lettered *Story of Corbin Cabin* was prepared, inserted in a large glass protected picture frame and mounted on the cabin wall. A year or so later I recorded on tape an hour long interview with George, in which he described at length life as it was in the mountain hollows in the early 20th century. It's fascinating, almost unbelievable that life could have been so grim and primitive within our own lifetime, and not in some far away point on our planet but only 80 miles from the nation's capitol.

Today, George T. Corbin still lives in Falls Church. Widowed for the third time many years ago, he lives alone in an apartment. As in 1938 he lives with the threat of eviction hanging over his head, not from the National Park Service this time but from the developers who are converting an entire garden apartment complex into condominiums. At the age of 87, having worked hard all his life, we hope that he will be allowed to live out his remaining years without another eviction.

The presence of the George T. Corbins and of the other 432 families who were evicted from the Park in 1938 seems to permeate the Park atmosphere. Some who desire a complete wilderness experience without seeing any evidence of man may find the frequent evidence of man's existence in the Shenandoah Park to be objectionable. I find it fascinating.

I walk past the crumbling remains of an old cabin and note that the bottom part of the stone chimney (where the open fireplace used to be), has been completely filled in with stone and mortar. And in the chimney a little higher up there is a round hole in the chimney to accomodate the stove pipe for a new stove. I look around me and remember George remarking that "my father owned the first stove in Nicholson Hollow." I see a deep depression in the ground near the remains of a cabin. A root cellar, of course. And I remember George telling me of the difficulty of storing fruits and vegetables over the winter "before we had root cellars." I see what looks like a piece of metal grillwork half buried in the soil and as I unearth it with my boot I recognize the one word worked into the design . . . "*Singer.*" So somebody had a sewing machine. And so it goes. Uncared for family cemeteries, decaying old apple orchards, split rail fences, stone walls. Shenandoah has character as well as beauty and one should not hurry too quickly along its quiet trails.

I cannot leave Shenandoah without expressing the tremendous gratitude that so many of us feel to two groups of people, the one group that was successful in creating this narrow 100-mile long national park, and the second group, the National Park Service, that preserves it on behalf of all the people. It must be remembered that the Federal Government paid no part of the acquisition cost of the land. The land was acquired by the people of Virginia and then turned over to the United States. This was in the early 1930's in the depths of the Depression, when pennies, nickels, and dimes were hard to come by. Collections were made in schools throughout the state and the State Legislature appropriated a substantial amount of the money. But it was dedicated people who brought this about, people like the Governor Harry F. Byrd, Sr., George Freeman Pollock who, for a half-century operated the Stony Man Camp in what is now the central section of the Park, and Ferdinand Zerkel, a realtor from Luray, Virginia. It is to these people and many more to whom we are indebted for having the vision and the tenacity to make the proposed park a reality.

For 40 years the National Park Service has been the custodian of this 300 squire mile acres of Blue Ridge Mountain land. The A.T. has been my cup of tea for almost a quarter-century and I can become bitterly critical of the Park Service for its almost contemptuous indifference to the plight of the A.T. during these past seven years; and for what I consider its thoroughly unjustified action in closing all the shelters in the Park. And yet, overall, I have the utmost respect for this Service and the people in it, for the thoroughly professional job they do in protecting, preserving, and making available to the public the 30 million acres of the nation's choicest real estate that we have entrusted to their care.

BIG BLUE — TUSCARORA TRAIL

This 242 mile trail begins on the Appalachian Trail in the Northern Section of the Shenandoah National Park, swings west into the George National Forest, then north into West Virginia, Maryland, and Pennsylvania. It rejoins the Appalachian Trail near Harrisburg, Pennsylvania. Of its total 242 miles, some 105 miles lies in Pennsylvania-Maryland, and the remaining 137 miles is in Virginia and West Virginia.

The part of the trail south of the Potomac River is described under West Virginia.

Other Trails in Virginia

Douthat State Park
Distance: 100 miles
Map: Handout Map is available either at the park or from the Department of Conservation and Economic Development, Richmond, Virginia
23219. Scale: 2½ inches to the mile
Description: This 4493 acre park situated near Clifton Forge, Virginia,
contains an extensive system of foot trails. Elevation of the campground
lake is 1445 feet and some of the trails climb to 3500 feet. It has been
many years since I have hiked the trails at Douthat but I can vouch for
the fact that they are strenuous.

Seashore State Park
Distance: 40 miles
Map: A handout Map is available either at the park or from the Department of Conservation and Economic Development, as above. Scale: 2
inches equal one mile.
Description: This network of trails is in the Seashore National Area of
the Seashore State Park near Virigina Beach, Virginia. The Natural Area
covers 2800 acres and there is a Nature-Trail Center with a naturalist on
duty. It is open daily during the summer and on week-ends, except from
mid-November to April 1. The trails themselves are open every day of the
year from early morning until sunset.

1. APPALACHIAN TRAIL
2. MONONGAHELA NATIONAL FOREST
3. BIG BLUE-TUSCARORA TRAIL
4. HARPERS FERRY NATIONAL HISTORICAL PARK

West Virginia

WILD WONDERFUL WEST VIRGINIA
THE MOUNTAIN STATE . . . With 986 Miles of Hiking Trails

To obtain the Official Highway map, calendar of events, camping, state park brochures, write to:

> West Virginia Department of Commerce
> Travel Development Division
> State Capitol
> Charleston, West Virginia 25305

For Park and Forest information, reservations, hunting and fishing information, other data on outdoor recreation, write to:

> West Virginia Department of Natural Resources
> Division of Parks and Recreation
> State Capitol
> Charleston, West Virginia 25305

The Appalachian Trail in West Virginia

Throughout its almost 500-mile traverse of Virginia, the A.T. is never very far from the West Virginia state line. In two places it actually crosses over into West Virginia for short distances.

The first of these is near the town of Pearisburg. From the outskirts of Pearisburg, the Trail proceeds west and north and crosses into West Virginia on Peters Mountain. It proceeds along the West Virginia side for some miles before turning east into Virginia and on to the Blue Ridge Parkway area north of Roanoke.

In northern Virginia as the Trail approaches Harpers Ferry, West Virginia, it again swings over into West Virginia for several miles before descending onto U.S. Route 340 and crossing the Potomac into Maryland.

Monongahela National Forest

The Monongahela contains some 1,600,000 acres within its boundaries, of which 830,000 acres are owned by the United States. The forest stretches over the Allegheny Mountain range in eastern West Virginia and shares a common boundary with the George Washington National Forest for many miles. The Spruce Knob—Seneca Rocks National Recreation Area and two designated Wilderness Areas — Otter Creek and Dolly Sods — are located in the Monongahela. The same law that established these two Wilderness Areas (Public Law 93-622, of January 3, 1975) also designated a sizeable chunk of the Cranberry Back Country as a Study Area — to be treated as a Wilderness Area until Congress makes a final determination.

The map situation is different from that of the two other national forests in Virginia that we discussed on previous pages. Maps of the individual six ranger districts are not issued, but the Forest provides free a so-called Mini-Map of the entire Forest. This is in very small scale (1" equals 10 miles), about the same as a highway map, and no trail information is shown. Those desiring more detailed information may send a check for $1.00 to the Forest Service and receive two maps, North Half and South Half, scale ½" equals 1 mile; detailed hiking trail information is shown. However, each of these two maps is 44" x 32" in size, somewhat unwieldy for the hiker to be whipping out of his pack for handy reference.

But the Monongahela does have one thing going for it that few other national forests have — a guide book that describes each ranger district and every hiking trail in the entire forest in considerable detail. The hiking trails were researched and the book put together by many volun-

Backpackers enjoy a scenic hiking trail in Monongahela National Forest [Potomac Ranger District] near Spruce Knob, West Virginia. [Photo by U.S. Forest Service.]

teers from the West Virginia Highlands Conservancy, a relatively new (1967) but dynamic organization of some 700 members that concerns itself with a wide range of conservation issues. The full name of the guide is *Hiking Guide to Monongahela National Forest and Vicinity.* A third edition of the book became available in November, 1975. Cost: $3.00.

Administration of the Monongahela is from the Forest Supervisor Office in Elkins, West Virginia. Maps and other information for the entire forest or for the ranger districts may be obtained by writing to that office. The complete address is: Monongahela National Forest, Federal Building, Elkins, West Virginia 26241. Telephone: 304/636-1800.

MARLINTON RANGER DISTRICT
Marlinton, West Virginia 24954
Telephone: 304/799-4334

Much recent trail work has been done and written up in this district. In reviewing the detailed trail logs, I found that all measurements were noted in the old surveyor's tried and true method of chains. Eighty chains equalled one mile and it was necessary for me to make some quick conversions in preparing my trail descriptions. But the district recently purchased a new five foot circumference measuring wheel which measures distances down to the foot and to the inch. No more chains and chain conversions!

I found that Marlinton Ranger Gary Lytle came from the same part of Minnesota in which I was born and raised and that we had each played high school football (a slight quarter century apart!) against some of the same St. Paul-Minneapolis suburban teams.

The Youth Conservation Corps and the Operation Mainstream programs have provided the labor for recent trail construction work. These two programs, using people at opposite ends of the age span (young people and those over 55), have made significant contributions to the trail construction and maintenance operations of many national forests. In the Marlinton district one of the most productive Operation Mainstream workers is 78 years of age.

Tea Creek Trail
Distance: 10.4 miles
USGS Quad: Mingo
Description: This trail is really comprised of two trails connecting on top of Gauley Mountain to form a circuit. The circuit begins and ends at the Tea Creek Recreation Area. To reach the hike's starting point, proceed north from Marlinton on U.S. Route 219 for 3.5 miles, then turn left on State Route 17 and follow it for about 8.0 miles until it intersects Forest Service Road 86 inside the boundary of the Monongahela National Forest. Turn right on Road 86 and follow it for 3.0 miles until you come to the Tea Creek Recreation Area. Upon entering, proceed to the east end of the parking area and find the sign reading:

Tea Creek Trail   Tea Creek Mountain Trail

Follow the trail for 100 years at which point the two trails split; Tea Creek goes to the left and Tea Creek Mountain Trail runs straight ahead. You can make the circuit either way, but we will take it up here to Tea Creek and come back the other way. The Tea Creek Trail goes north for 2.7 miles along an old railroad grade, passes a beaver dam and crosses the right fork of the Tea Creek at two locations. Except during high water levels, the stream can be easily forded by rock hopping. The trail bears generally east for an additional 3.8 miles until it intersects Tea Creek Mountain Trail at a point 6.9 miles from the starting point.

At this point, begin the return hike to the Tea Creek Recreation Area. At 7 miles you reach the high point of the trail on Tea Creek Mountain, at elevation 4575 feet. At 10.4 miles begin your descent and at 12.0 miles cross the Williams River Trail. Almost immediately after that trail, go over Tea Creek bridge into the Tea Creek Campground, and this is the end of the circuit.

I visited this area in mid-September, 1975, ate my noon-day lunch at the Tea Creek Campground, located an old apple orchard (apples dead ripe) and then hiked up parts of both trails. Recent trail construction work was clearly evident, with fresh blue paint blazes identifying the trails. There are 12 camp sites at the recreation area, and State Route 150, the Highlands Scenic Highway, passes within a mile of the area. followed this delightful highway south to the Cranberry Mountain Visitor Center, maintained by the Forest Service at the intersection of State Route 39 and 150.

Laurel Creek Trail

Distance: 9 miles — Average elevation 2500 feet

USGS Quad: Minnehaha Springs

Description: This is a circuit hike trail constructed in September, 1975, by Operation Mainstream. In fact, the trail had been so recently constructed that Forest Technician Jack Bowen wrote up the description for me while I was in the office.

The trail leaves the Rimel Parking area on State Route 39 about 0.7 miles west of the Virginia state line and about 0.5 miles west of State Routes 39 and 92 intersection. From the trail parking area proceed east, crossing the Old Lockridge Mountain Jeep trail. Continue around slope and old road in Laurel Creek. Ascend Lockridge Run to near the top of Lockridge Mountain. Here the trail then goes south, passing a wildlife clearing, and at approximately the 5.5 mile point it reaches a trailside shelter and a wildlife water hole.

From the shelter the trail proceeds along the east side of Lockridge Mountain and at about 8 miles it passes near another wildlife water hole. From that point it proceeds for an additional mile down the west side of the mountain until it returns to the starting point at Rimel Parking area.

Beaver Creek Trail

Distance: 2.1 miles

USGS Quad: Marlinton

Description: This trail was constructed in 1975 by the Youth Conservation Corps. It starts at the Watoga State Park campground on the east side of the park and ends at the Beaver Lick Tower Road, or Forest Road #343. This is a very scenic trail along the head waters of Beaver Creek, it takes the hiker through a great variety of timber types. The entire trail has been marked with blue paint blazes.

487 — Williams River Trail

Distance: 2.5 miles

USGS Quad: Mingo

Description: This trail follows an old railroad grade along the north side of the Williams River. It starts at the Tea Creek Campground and ends on the west bank of Little Laurel Creek. By continuing across the creek and following an old road, it is possible to reach the lake on the Handley Public Hunting Area. The entire trail was freshly marked with blue paint blazes in 1975.

POTOMAC RANGER DISTRICT
Route 3, Box 16F
Petersburg, West Virginia 26847
Telephone: 304/257-7111

(Office is 3 miles west of Petersburg on State Route 28)

I made two trips to the Potomac District—the first in September 1975, at which time I visited trails in the Dolly Sods Wilderness Area and in the Spruce Knob-Seneca Rocks NRA. The second trip was in November 1975, when I spent 10 hours with Supervisory Forester Jim Bruce reviewing and preparing writeups of trails.

The Potomac Ranger District is unique among all Forest Service Ranger Districts in the United States. Why is this the case? Consider that the United States Forest Service administers but six National Recreation Areas (NRA) in the entire United States. One of these, the Spruce-Knob-Seneca Rocks NRA is located in the boundaries of the Potomac District. Consider that the Congress has, to date, designated only a handful of Wilderness Areas pursuant to the Wilderness Act of 1975, Public Law 93-622. One of these areas, Dolly Sods, is also included in the Potomac District. So here we have a ranger district of some 280,000 acres, and of that total about 100,000 acres is in an authorized NRA, and another 10,215 acres is within the Dolly Sods Wilderness Area.

The Potomac District is the most northeasterly of the six ranger ·districts in the Monongahela. Most of it lies in two counties, Pendleton and Randolph. In the ensuing pages we will first outline the trails in the Spruce Knob-Seneca Rocks NRA and second, those in the Dolly Sods Wilderness Area.

SPRUCE KNOB-SENECA ROCKS NATIONAL RECREATION AREA

National Recreation Areas have been described as places that are half-way between a national forest and a national park. They are areas the Congress has sought to preserve and protect because of their outstanding scenic beauty. Congress has sought also to encourage their use for recreation to permit the multiple use concepts of the Forest Service.

This NRA of 100,000 acres of lush backcountry is also unusual in that it is comprised of two distinct units. One, Spruce Knob, is on the western side of State Route 28 and therein rises the 4860 foot high Spruce Knob, highest point in West Virginia, with its big stone observation tower and interpretive trails. On the eastern side of State Route 28 is the Seneca Rocks unit, with its North Fork Mountain, its Eagle Rock, the Smoke Hole canyon and its two privately owned caves, Seneca Caverns and Smoke Hole Caverns. While the term "Seneca Rocks" is the name given to the entire unit, to many people the term applies more specifically to the 1000 foot quartzite formation that juts above the North Fork Valley at the Mouth of Seneca Creek. In addition to its scenic attractiveness, Seneca Rocks is considered one of the best climbing areas in the

East. It is a favorite of the Mountaineering Section of the Potomac Appalachian Trail Club, which is seeking to build a cabin in the area for use by climbers.

The two recreation units jointly share Seneca Creek which originates in the Spruce Mountain Area of Spruce Knob and drops into the valley, flowing through the settlements of Seneca, Onego, and Mouth of Seneca. The creek joins the North Fork at Seneca Rocks.

Now that we have noted some of the interesting features of the area we will describe the trails and the maps of those trails. The USGS quads covering the Spruce Knob Unit are Spruce Knob, Circleville, Whitmer, Onego, all 7½ minutes. Those covering the Seneca Rocks Unit are: Petersburg West, Upper Tract, Hopeville and Franklin, all 7½ minutes.

The one Forest Service map that is most helpful is a 1969 Spruce Knob-Seneca Rocks NRA map, scale ½" equals 1 mile, which shows, not only the NRA but also the complete Potomac District. The map is in process of revision; the revised edition to be available in 1976.

Seneca Creek Trail
Distance: 14.5 miles
Description: This trail, signed and blue-blazed, begins on Forest Service Road 103 (so shown on map; sign on road reads "112") about 6 miles west (by road) from the observation tower on Spruce Knob. The trail proceeds generally north until its junction with State Route 7 at the trail's end. From the beginning on Forest Road 103, it is 1.25 miles to the intersection with Tom Lick Run Trail, 2.25 miles to Swallow Rock Trail, and 4 miles to Judy Springs walk-in Campground (toilets, tent pads, drinking water from pump). At the campground the Bear Hunter Trail goes to the left and the Judy Springs Trail (1 mile) goes to the right acting as a connector between the campground and the Horton-Horserock Trail.

The Seneca Creek Trail proceeds north from the campground, and at 5.6 miles it intersects the Horton-Horserock Trail. At 6.3 miles, observe the Upper Seneca Falls just to the left of the trail, visible — and audible — as you approach. At 11 miles the Falls of Seneca are also visible from the trail. Continue north on the trail (now a jeep road through pasture lands), reaching Whites Run Road (State Route 7) at 14.5 miles.

Horton-Horserock
Distance: 8 miles
Description: This blue-blazed trail begins outside the NRA on State Route 29 approximately 1 mile south of the community of Whitmer (signed at trailhead). It proceeds east, ascending Allegheny Mountain and interesecting Allegheny Trail at 2 miles. The trail goes on east and descends, intersecting Seneca Creek Trail at 3.1 miles; then it proceeds south on the latter trail before turning left up Spruce Mountain. At 4.35 miles it intersects Judy Springs Trail and at 4.6 miles it intersects the Lumberjack Trail. Ascending Spruce Mountain for 0.75 miles the Trail

ends at intersection with the Huckleberry Trail. Beyond the intersection is a spring and camping area.

Huckleberry Trail

Distance: 3.5 miles

Description: Trail begins at Spruce Knob Observation Tower Parking Lot and goes north on Spruce Mountain (fantastic views east and west). There is a spring and camping area to the right at 2.2 miles marked by a sign. At 3.5 miles Huckleberry Trail dead ends temporarily. To continue, use this alternate route. Turn left (side trail to the right leads to spring and camping area) on Horton-Horserock Trail for 7 miles, then right on Lumberjack Trail until it ends on Strader Run Road for a total distance of 11.2 miles.

Huckleberry Trail, when finished, will parallel Lumberjack Trail but will be .5 mile to 1 mile further east on the crest of the mountain. It, too, will terminate on Strader Run Road, for a total distance of 11 miles. The last 2 miles of trail is a jeep road over private land and is neither signed nor blazed.

Allegheny Trail

Distance: 13.6 miles

Description: The trail is signed and blue-blazed and begins on Forest Service Road 103 (so shown on map; road sign 112) 1.5 miles east of Spruce Knob Lake. Two trails begin here -- the other -- Big Run proceeds west to Gandy Creek. For the first 6.3 miles the trail follows the Wildlife Access Road. Proceed north following the joint boundary of the NRA and the Pioneer Zone. Trail intersects the Tom Lick Run Trail at 2.1 miles, North Prong Trail at 2.3 miles, Leading Ridge Trail at 3.1 miles, and at 3.3 miles the Swallow Rock Run Trail comes in on the left.

At 4.7 miles Bear Hunter Trail leads right to Judy Springs Campground and at 6.3 miles the Wildlife Access Road turns left to Gandy Creek while the Allegheny Trail, now a foot path, continues north reaching Horton-Horserock Trail at 6.5 miles. At 8.3 miles leave the Allegheny Trail, which turns left and dead ends in .7 miles. Continue north on Little Allegheny Trail and stay on it for an additional 5.3 miles to the end of the Trail at Whites Run Road (State Route 7).

North Mountain Trail

Distance: 23 miles

Description: Trail begins at U.S. Route 33 approximately 4 miles east of Judy Gap (intersection of U.S. 33 and State Route 28) and about 1 mile east of the picnic ground and the observation point overlooking Germany Valley. The trailhead is at a large turnout on the north side of U.S. 33. Its beginning point is further identified by a cable across the old road which the trail follows at the start of its route. Although this trail is generally signed and blue-blazed, the trailhead is on private property and landowner does not permit use of signs. Look for the blue blazes that identify the trail, which proceeds north from U.S. 33 to an unusual rock outcropping 23 miles north known as Chimney Rocks.

After leaving the trailhead on U.S. 33 and proceeding north on the ridge, the hiker will enjoy tremendous views of Germany Valley, a designated national landmark and an area containing many limestone caves. At 5 miles, a side trail (identified by sign and blue blazes) leads 2 miles to a spring. Approximately at the midpoint of trail (11 miles) is the North Mountain lookout tower (still in use). From the fire tower, the trail follows Forest Service Road 79 for 1.5 miles, then leaves Road 79 and becomes a footpath, again with views to the west of the Allegheny Front and the Roaring Plains. There are two springs (both identified by signs) at the point where the Trail leaves Forest Service Road 79. These may fail in extremely dry weather.

At 21.5 miles Landis Trail (signed) leads to the right for 2 miles, where it joins Forest Service Road 74. Hikers may wish to leave the Trail at this point or they may elect to hike the North Mountain Trail to its terminus at Chimney Rocks. If the latter course of action is taken, the hiker will need to backtrack for 1.5 miles and turn left on Landis Trail to reach Forest Road 79.

Redman Run Trail
This 2-mile trail is a connector that intersects the North Mountain Trail at mile point 16 and proceeds east to its junction with Forest Service Road 74.

Landis Trail
This is another 2-mile connector trail intersecting North Mountain Trail at milepoint 21.5 and proceeding east to Forest Service Road 74.

TRAILS OUTSIDE THE NATIONAL RECREATION AREA

Gandy Creek Trail Network
Distance: 17.7 miles
Description: This network, all in Randolph County, can be reached from Forest Service Road 103 (112), from a number of points on the Allegheny Trail, or from State Route 29, which parallels Gandy Creek. The trails by name and distance are:

Big Run Trail	3.5 miles
Two Springs Road Trail	4.0 miles
Elza Trail	2.0 miles
Bee Trail	1.5 miles
Swallow Rock Trail	2.2 miles
Spring Ridge Road Trail	2.0 miles
North Prong Trail	2.5 miles
TOTAL MILEAGE	17.7 miles

Although individual trails add up to 17.7 miles, the hiker can, by use of Forest Road 103, the Allegheny Trail, and State Route 29, plan circuit hikes that would involve many more miles of hiking.

DOLLY SODS WILDERNESS AREA

Public Law 93-622 approved January 3, 1975, established the 10,215-acre Dolly Sods Wilderness Area in Tucker and Randolph counties. This is a rugged mountainous area, much of it at the 4000 foot level. It is a land of contrasts, much open pastureland ("sods"), second growth hardwoods, beaver ponds, thick stands of rhododendron, and a harsh climate. It has a network of more than 25 miles of hiking trails, a number of which are described in this book. Most of them are blue-blazed and signed. Note: *Permits are required by anyone entering the wilderness area.* There is no charge for them, and they may be obtained from the Potomac Ranger District Office on State Route 28, about 3 miles south of Petersburg, or from any of the other ranger district office or the Forest Supervisor's Office in Elkins. They may be obtained also by phone or by mail. One signed permit is required for each entry of an individual or group. The information needed for issuance of the permit is: Applicant's name and address; expected date and duration of visit; location of entry and exit; number of people in party.

The following USGS Quads pertain to all trails described in the Wilderness Area: Blackwater Falls, Blackbird Knob, Laneville and Hopeville, West Virginia. Actually the hiker will not need to acquire the quads, because the Forest Service has developed a 1975 handout map, scale 1" equals 1 mile, that is given free to anyone to whom a permit is issued.

As this book goes to press we learn that a new book *Dolly Sods Trailguide and Management Plan*, cost $3.00, will be available in mid-April, 1976. It may be obtained from: West Virginia Highlands Conservancy, Box 711, Webster Springs, West Virginia 26288.

TRAILS IN THE DOLLY SODS WILDERNESS AREA

Blackbird Knob
Distance: 2 miles
Description: The start of the hike is on Forest Service Road 75, at Red Creek Campground. The trail proceeds west through some red spruce areas and past beaver ponds, and crosses Red Creek. It terminates on the southern side of Blackbird Knob where it joins the Red Creek Trail.

Red Creek Trail
Distance: 6.5 miles
Description: This is the main north-south trail running through the wilderness area. It follows Red Creek for its entire length and takes its name from the creek. I visited this area in September, 1975, and would not go so far as to say the water was red, but it is at least decidedly dark in color. The trail can be hiked in either direction. I hiked from the southern end, entering the trail at the Laneville Wildlife Cabin (parking available near the cabin). I went north past the intersection with the Stonecoal Run Trail and then with the Fisher Spring Run Trail. At 6 miles, the

trail leaves the Wilderness Area and at 6.5 miles it terminates at its intersection with the Blackbird Knob Trail. Camping facilities are 2 miles east on the latter trail.

Breathed Mountain Trail
Distance: 3.5 miles
Description: This trail and Big Stonecoal Run Trail both begin on Forest Service Road 80 at a point just inside the Wilderness Area boundary where Road 80 becomes impassible for vehicles. Trail goes past beaver dams and ponds, through forested areas and open spaces. It terminates at its intersection with the Red Creek Trail in an area that has good camping spots.

Big Stonecoal Trail
Distance: 4.5 miles
Description: As stated in the preceding description, this trail also begins at a point where Forest Service Road 80 ceases to become a road and becomes suitable for foot traffic only. The trail goes generally south following the stream and for some distance a former railroad bed. It intersects Dunkenbarger Run Trail at 2.5 miles. The hiker will see numerous waterfalls and rapids and will pass four designated camp spots. At 3.25 miles the Rocky Point Trail leads off to the left and at 4.5 miles the trail terminates at its intersection with the Red Creek Trail.

South Prong Trail
Distance: 5.5 miles
Description: Trail begins at Forest Road 19, .5 miles south of Dolly Sods Picnic Ground. It follows along the Allegheny Front for 2 miles, then swings down into South Prong Gorge. It intersects Forest Road 70 (a hiking trail only) at 3 miles and terminates on Boars Nest Trail at 5.5 miles.

Forest Road 70
Distance: 3.5 miles
Description: Trail begins on Forest Road 19, .75 miles south of Dolly Sods Picnic Area. It runs due south and terminates at a gas pipeline (cleared area) where the Roaring Plains Trail begins.

Boars Nest Trail
Distance: 3 miles
Description: Trail begins on Forest Road 19, 1 mile east of Laneville Wildlife Cabin, proceeds south for .5 miles, crosses South Prong, goes uphill to Flat Rock Plains and terminates on Forest Road 70.

Roaring Plains Trail
Distance: 3.0 miles
Description: Trail begins at intersection of pipeline and the end of Forest Road 70 and then proceeds south and west. It dead-ends at a point 1 mile east of Mt. Porte Canyon.

GREENBRIER RANGER DISTRICT
Bartow, West Virginia 24920
Telephone: 304/456-4635

The Greenbrier District lies almost in the exact center of the Mononga-hela. It is roughly bisected by U.S. Route 250, which goes by the front door of the Ranger Station in Bartow. And once you reach Bartow you will have no trouble finding the Forest Service Office. A 1966 publica-tion lists the population of Bartow as an even 100 people, making it the smallest ranger district headquarters town that I've ever visited.

The Greenbrier has no Wilderness Area within its boundaries, no Na-tional Recreation Area, no huge backcountry area like the Cranberry (Gauley District). But the Greenbrier need make no apologies. Through it runs two of the more prominent and beautiful rivers in the State, the Greenbrier and the Cheat. It has some 35 hiking trails concentrated in its two mountains, the Shavers Mountain and the Middle Mountain. And of the 10 highest mountain peaks in West Virginia, five are located in the Greenbrier District. It's a big rugged district with high mountains and beautiful streams, and if you like solitude in your hiking this is the place to go.

The District has two manmade attractions which are certainly worth a visit; the National Radio Astronomy Observatory (NRAO) just south of Bartow at Greenbank and the Cass Scenic Railway.

The NRAO is a government-owned facility built under the general auspices of the National Science Foundation. My duties as Finance Of-ficer for the Foundation brought me to Greenbank as early as 1958 when construction of the 140 foot movable "big dish" antenna was in its in-fancy. It was in connection with these trips that I became acquainted with the Greenbrier District, hiked a few of its trails, and came back on a long weekend to camp on its Middle Mountain.

One of the NRAO employees, Ted Riffe, was living in nearby Cass in 1960 when the lumber company there decided to call it quits after 58 years of operation, during which time two billion board feet of timber had been harvested. Riffe immediately began beating the drums to have the State of West Virginia acquire the big Shay locomotives, the other equip-ment, and the 11-mile stretch of track for a scenic railway. His efforts were successful and now the big steam locomotives take passengers to the top of Bald Knob, the state's second highest mountain, with an eleva-tion of 4842 feet. I must confess that my only ascent of Bald Knob has been, not by foot, but over the 11 miles of track in a motor car operated by Ted Riffe. Now let's get back to the hiking trails.

"Uniformity is the hob goblin of little minds."

Author unknown

Throughout this book we have shown hiking trails in a fairly uniform manner — name of trail, length, names of maps that pertain to the trail, and then, a description of the trail. To demonstrate that we are at least a little bit flexible, we will show the trails in the Greenbrier in a slightly different manner.

I had visited the Bartow office in mid-September, had examined some of the trail logs and discussed the trail system with Marv Schuman, the assistant ranger, and with Sam Jennings, the clerk. Later I received from Ranger Roger Bucklew a detailed listing of the 24 hiking trails currently maintained, plus an unusual map on which someone had painstakingly delineated each trail in a prominent fashion and had further identified each trail with a numbered tab glued to the map. Both the list and the map are reproduced in this book (see pages 97 and 99).

The list that has been reproduced is especially significant because it reflects the most important information that is contained in the Forest Service computer bank of all trails (hiking and otherwise) that are included in the Forest Service approved system of trails. Periodically the computer prints up the information in the form of listings that are sent to each ranger district for review and correction. These computer print-outs are very helpful, up to a point. For example, look at the information shown for the Lynn Knob Trail, Trail 317. It shows the mileage: 4.2. And it shows that the trail begins on Forest Road 17 and ends on Forest Road 14. But *where* on Road 17 does it begin? *Where* on Road 14 does it end? Each of these roads are many miles long. Elevation, water supply, campsites, or streams to be forded are not cited, but such information must be obtained elsewhere. In many cases I have visited Forest Service offices and written down the information as I obtained it from knowledgeable people or from the detailed hiking trail logs maintained in many ranger offices. In other cases I have gleaned information from more general books, guide books, and handouts describing the trails in some detail. In the Monongahela I relied heavily on the *Hiking Guide to the Monongahela National Forest and Vicinity*. The 1975 (third revision) cost $3 and may be obtained from outdoor stores or by ordering from: West Virginia Highlands Conservancy, Box 711, Webster Springs, West Virginia 26288.

The amount of detail devoted to describing some of the trails in that hiking guide are impressive. The Laurel River Trail, 18.6 miles long, is described in four full pages of fine type. The hiking guide has achieved a reputation as being extremely accurate. The volunteers who developed the information and the editor, Bruce Sundquist, are to be commended.

In transmitting the hiking list and map to me, Ranger Bucklew also supplied the following information:

> "All trails are classed as hiker trails. They are signed, desig-
> nated with blue paint, and receive maintenance annually. All
> trails can be located with the aid of the Momongahela Forest
> Map, available at a minimal charge. The free Forest Map does
> not show the trail system.

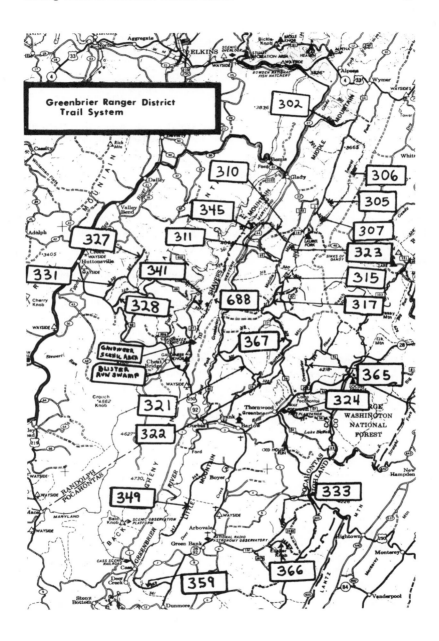

The attached map shows the existing trail system in black and probably the most used trails in yellow. All other trails shown are not existing and/or not maintained as system trails."

The map that was sent shows the two longest trails (Laurel River and North-South) marked in yellow, plus four short trails; the remaining 18 trails are marked in black. We will describe both of the long trails plus a representative number of the others. The USGS Quad maps that pertain to the Greenbrier District are: (all West Virginia) Greenbank, Hightown, Paddy Knob, Beverly East, Glady, Whitmer, Thornwood—all 7½ minutes; plus 15 minutes Cass and Durbin quads.

306 — Laurel River Trail

Distance: 18.6 miles

Description: This is a north-south trail that runs roughly parallel to and from 1 to 4 miles east of Forest Service Road 14. The Laurel Fork Recreation Area (camp sites for 6) is situated about 10 miles from the northern end of the trail. Starting point of trail on the north is 5.1 miles south from Wymer on Forest Road 14. Trail begins on the east side of the road at a point 100 yards south of Beaver Dam Run, marked by Forest Service sign. To reach the starting point at the southern end, proceed south from Wymer on Forest Road 14 for 19.9 miles to the first intersection with Forest Road 97. Or, from the south, one can leave State Route 28 at Camp Pocahontas and drive north for 10.5 miles to the second intersection of Forest Road 97. The trailhead is marked with Forest Service sign. Here, we will follow the trail from its southern end.

The trail follows Forest Road 97 east for 1.5 miles, then turns north off the road. At 4 miles it intersects Trail 315 and from that point on it follows Laurel Fork on old railroad grades. At 6.6 miles the Beulah Trail (310) comes in from the left and at 8 miles you reach the Laurel Fork Recreation Area.

North of the Recreation Area the trail continues to follow Laurel Fork, with much evidence of wildlife including beaver and deer. At 9.5 miles (1.5 miles north of the Recreation Area) Trail 307 comes in on the left (and connects to Middle Mountain Road — Forest Service Road 14). At 12.3 miles another connecting trail, the Stone Camp Trail, also comes in on the left. At 16 miles the trail crosses Laurel Fork and within .3 of a mile it leaves Laurel Fork, turns left (west) and follows a tributary that leads to Forest Road 14 and end of the trail.

688—North-South [Shavers Mountain]

Distance: 16 miles

Description: Having described the one long trail on Middle Mountain, we now move west across the narrow valley to describe the one long trail on Shavers. This trail appears on some maps under its former number — 332 (Shavers Mountain Trail).

It can easily be reached by car from either end. The northern trailhead begins in the village of Glady, where a jeep road intersects State Route

22 immediately west of the intersection of Routes 22 and 27. Parking is a problem at the northern end. To reach the southern end, proceed west from Bartow on U.S. Route 250 and 92. About 6 miles west of Durbin, turn right on Forest Road 27, drive past Gaudineer Knob and on to Gaudineer Scenic Area. The trail begins at northern end of the Scenic Area; it is a ridge top trail for its entire length and much of the elevation is at 4000 feet and above.

Proceeding north from Gaudineer, the trail intersects the Johns Camp Trail and the Johns Camp Shelter at 3.1 miles. At about 10 miles from the starting point, you reach a second shelter — the Wildell Shelter. There is no water there. Just beyond the shelter, The Beulah Siding Trail, No. 345, comes in from the east. As it nears its northern terminus, the North-South trail comes out on a jeep road which it follows to the trail's end, on State Route 22.

Chart for Greenbrier Ranger District Trail system

MONONGAHELA NATIONAL FOREST
GREENBRIER RANGER DISTRICT
TRAIL SYSTEM

TRAIL NAME	NO.	MILES	FROM	TO
McCray Run Trail	302	4.7	State Route 27	FR#14
Stone Cam Run Trail	305	1.4	FR #14	Trail #306
Laurel River Trail	306	18.6	FR #14	FR #14
Middle Mountain Trail	307	1.7	FR #14	Trail #306
Beulah Trail	310	4.7	FR #44	Trail #306
County Line Trail	311	4.9	FR #35	Trail #310
Camp Five Run Trail	315	1.6	FR #14	Trail #306
Lynn Knob Trail	317	4.2	FR #17	FR #14
Span Oak Trail	321	3.7	FR #44	FR #15
Burner Mountain Trail	322	3.6	FR #15	FR #14
Forks Trail	323	1.2	FR #14 & 183	Trail #306
Smoke Camp Trail	324	1.8	FR #4 (State Route 28)	FR #58
Chestnut Ridge Trail	327	5.5	FR #92	State Route 39/1
McGee Run Trail	328	2.9	FR #56 (State Route 250/92)	Trail #327
Laurel Run Trail	331	2.9	FR #56 (State Route 250/92)	Trail #327
North Fork Trail	333	2.9	FR #197	FR #1681
Johns Camp Trail	341	.8	FR #27	Trail #688
Beulah Siding Trail	345	1.2	FR #44	Trail #688
Little Mountain Trail	349	7.5	State Route 28	Greenbrier River
Peters Mountain Trail	359	6.5	State Route 28/92	State Route 7
East Fork Trail	365	7.9	FR#270 (Island Campground) FR#51	FR #254
Rattle Snake Trail	366	3.2	FR#197	Elleber Knob
Hinkle Run Trail	367	3.1	FR#17	State Route 14
North-South (Shavers Mt.)	688	16.0	FR#27	State Route 22
TOTAL:	24	112.5		

The *Hiking Guide to the Monongahela* points out that this trail goes through one of the heaviest black bear populations in the state, and that the North-South Trail constitutes one of the best cross-country ski trails in the entire Monongahela. Although there are no developed campgrounds in the Shaver Mountain Area, there are many good camp sites and water sources. See the Hiking Guide for details.

327 — Chestnut Ridge Trail . . . . .5.5 miles
328 — McGee Run Trail . . . . .2.9 miles
331 — Laurel Run Trail . . . . .2.9 miles

Description: These three trails, all on the Durbin, West Virginia, 7½ minute USGS Quad, are concentrated in a tight cluster. Two of them, 331 and 328 have U.S. Route 250 as their southern terminus at points about 8 and 10 miles west of Cheat Bridge. The northern terminus for both of these 2.9 mile trails is Trail 327, which connects both trails and has as its northern terminus the Shavers Run Road and has Forest Road 92 as its eastern terminus. Trail 328 has several handsome waterfalls on McGee Run. The three trails used in conjunction with the two Forest Service Roads make possible a number of short circuit hikes.

345 — Beaulah Siding Trail . . . . .1.2 miles
310 — Beulah Trail . . . . .4.7 miles
323 — Forks Trail . . . . .1.2 miles

Description: These three trails are important because they form an important east-west connection between the two long north-south trails, the one on Shavers Mountain and the other on Middle Mountain. Proceeding from the west to east, the hiker would leave Trail 688 just north of the Wildell Shelter and turn east on Trail 345 until its termination on Forest Road 44. At that point he would proceed north on Road 44 for .5 mile, pick up Trail 310 and go east on that trail to its termination on Forest Road 14. Then he would merely cross the road to pick up Trail 323 and continue on east until Trail 323 terminated at its intersection on Trail 306, the Laurel River Trail at a point just south of the Laurel Fork Recreation Area.

To reach the two Beulah trails, drive south from Glady on Forest Road 44. At 3.4 miles you reach Beulah Trail and at 3.9, the Beulah Siding Trail. Both trails are signed at the road intersection. To reach Trail 323, drive south from Wymer on Forest Road 14 for 14.7 miles. The trail is signed at the road intersection.

349 — Little Mountain Trail
Distance: 6.5 miles
Description: This trail is the longest of the four that are in the southern part of the district, south of Bartow. To reach the starting point, drive north of the village of Boyer on State Route 28 for 1 mile and turn left on Brush Run Road (marked by road sign). Turn left again on Little Mountain Road (Forest Road 470 is a poor road). The trail follows the

old road and climbs Little Mountain, where it turns south and follows along the ridge. The average ridge elevation is 3000 feet. At 6.5 miles, trail 349 descends and terminates at Slavin Hollow Road, State Route 2.

GAULEY RANGER DISTRICT
Richwood, West Virginia 26261
Telephone: 304/846-6558

(The Ranger office is located 2 miles east of Richwood on State Route 39) The Gauley Ranger District has 156,000 acres within its borders, and for years it has maintained a special area of 53,000 acres known as the Cranberry Back Country. Public use of motor vehicles of all kinds was prohibited in the Cranberry area and it became kind of a special preserve for hunters, fishermen, and hikers. In recent years, a number of organizations and citizens have sought permanent protection for the area and petitioned the Congress to designate it as a Wilderness Area under the provisions of the Wilderness Act. The efforts were not quite successful, but almost. The Congress, under Public Law 93-622, approved by President Gerald Ford on January 3, 1975, set aside 36,300 acres of the Cranberry as a "Wilderness Study Area," which means that it will be treated as a wilderness area for a certain number of years until the Congress decides whether it should be designated as a Wilderness Area.

All of the trails we are about to describe are in the "Cranberry Area," a term I coined especially for this book to include the new Wilderness Study Area, plus places outside the Study Area but within the confines of the former Back Country Area. We might even sneak in a trail that lies partly outside of both areas. But from the hikers standpoint it matters little. The important things to remember are that the entire 53,000 acres receives 60 inches of rainfall a year, of which some 90 inches is in the form of snow (about 10 inches of snow equals approximately one inch of rainfall). Winter hiking can be exhilarating but temperatures on the ridges get down to zero.

My only serious hiking in this area was in July, 1960, with my son Dan. Fifteen years time can dim the best of memories but I do recall distinctly three things about our hike to the Mikes Knob area: (1) the tremendous view from atop the lookout tower on the Knob; (2) the big black flies that settled on our heads and necks as we hiked the trails; and (3) the general dampness of the trails and surrounding terrain.

All told there are 22 trails in the Cranberry Area, totaling 75 miles. Trails are well-maintained and are blue-blazed. There are eight shelters, plus two more in the Gauley district outside the Cranberry Area. A handout map entitled "Cranberry Back Country" may be obtained free from the Forest Service. The USGS Quad maps that cover the area (all West Virginia) are Webster Springs SE and SW, Bergoo, Lobelia (15 minutes), Richwood (15 minutes), Marlington (15 minutes), all 7½ minutes unless otherwise shown.

I visited the Gauley Ranger office for part of one day, spending time with Ranger Ron Scott but mostly with Lee Schaar who possessed a remarkable knowledge of the details of each trail.

Below are descriptions of 12 of the 22 trails — those that exceed 4 miles in length. The trail number, its name, and the length of all 22 trails are listed in alphabetical order in the handout map available from the Forest Service.

256 — Barrenshe Trail
Distance: 4.5 miles
Description: This trail begins on Forest Road 76, proceeds east along the ridge top north of Barranshe Run, skirts Briery Knob and terminates at Forest Road 99.

207 — Big Beechy
Distance: 4.5 miles
Description: Trail begins at Forest Road 108 at the point where Beechy Run joins the Middle Fork of Williams River. It proceeds east up Beechy Run for a short distance, then veers south, crossing the headwaters of Slick Rock Run and Steep Rock Run. The trail terminates at the junction of the North-South Trail and District Line Trail.

206 — County Line Trail
Distance: 11.5 miles
Description: Trail begins at Forest Road 108 across the road from where the Little Fork Trail begins. It proceeds generally northeast and at 6 miles crosses the top of the ridge that divides the Middle Fork and the Main Fork of the Williams River. The trail then follows the ridge line to intersection of District Line Trail (248), then drops down to cross Forest Road 86 and the main fork of Williams River. Normally the river can be easily forded, but in times of high water the crossing can be difficult. After crossing the river and the road, the trail proceeds east along the Pocahontas County line and terminates at its intersection with the Turkey Mountain Trail (209) at a point near where three county lines intersect — Pocahontas, Webster, and Randolph.

253 — Cow Pasture Trail
Distance: 7 miles
Description: This is a loop trail that goes, in part, along the southern boundary of the Cranberry Area at a point two miles northwest of the Cranberry Mountain Visitor Center on State Route 39. Start of hike is the gate across Forest Road 102 near the southern boundary of the Area. The 7-mile trail is well marked and signed and affords good views.

After periods of rain the trail crossing of the South Fork of Cranberry (north end of Glades) can be very wet. There are several hundred feet of muskeg to be traversed and with increased hiking use the muskeg has broken through. Heavy rains will raise the stream above the planking on the bridge crossing of the South Fork of Cranberry.

223 — Cranberry Ridge
Distance: 6 miles

Description: Trail begins on Forest Road 81 about 2 miles north of the Big Rock Recreation Area. From its starting point, the trail proceeds east crossing Glade Run and at 2 miles it arrives at Glade Run pond. From the pond it veers northeast, climbs to the top of and proceeds along the crest of Cranberry Ridge. It terminates on Forest Road 82 just west of Bishop Knob and just east of intersection of Forest Roads 81 and 82.

236 — Fork Mountain Trail
Distance: 9 miles
Description: The trail begins on State Route 39 at a point about 2 miles southwest of Mikes Knob. It climbs Fork Mountain and then proceeds generally west and north, crossing Bearwallow Knob and Rockcamp Knob. The termination near Richwood in the vicinity of Spencer Run at boundary of private land.

245 — Forks of Cranberry
Distance: 6 miles
Description: This trail begins on State Route 150, the Highland Scenic Highway at a point 6.5 miles north of the Visitor Center and proceeds generally northwest until terminating on Forest Road 102 about .3 mile south of its intersection with Forest Road 76. The trail stays in the 3500 to 4000 foot elevation for most of its length and provides excellent views from a number of points. The first 2.5 miles goes through an area that was badly burned in the 1937 Black Mountain Fire.

235 — Frosty Gap Trail
Distance: 6 miles
Description: Eastern terminus of this trail is at a point on the Kennison Mountain Trail about 1 mile north of State Route 39. Proceeding west it intersects Forest Road 232 at .6 mile and at 2.2 miles the trail crosses an old railroad grade. Continuing west the trail climbs Frosty Gap at elevation 4250 feet, then proceeds west and then north. Approximately 2 miles past Frosty Gap, a crossover trail leads to the left providing access to the Pocahontas Trail, which is .1 mile below Frosty Gap Trail at this point. The Frosty Gap Trail reaches its terminus on Forest Road 77, just before reaching the fire tower on Mikes Knob.

244 — Kennison Mountain
Distance: 10 miles
Description: The *West Virginia Highlands Conservancy Hiking Guide* rates this trail as "probably the nicest trail in the Cranberry Back Country." Had I known it rated this highly I would have hiked more of it than I did when I drove through the area on State Route 39 in September, 1975, on my way to the Gauley Ranger District Office. Seeing the sign "Kennison Mountain — 3988 feet," I stopped and reconnoitered a bit. There was also a trail sign and I hiked in a short distance in either direction from the road. The trail was well-maintained and blue- blazed. South from Route 39 it reaches its southern terminus in 1.5 miles as it approaches Blue Knob (elevation 4426 feet) and ends at its junction with the Pocahontas Trail.

North of Route 39, within a half-mile, the Frosty Gap Trail has its beginning and veers off to the west. It passes through spruce forest much of the way, staying at around the 4000 foot elevation during the first part of the hike and then dropping to 3500 near its northern terminus. Just before reaching its actual terminus on Forest Road 76, at the mouth of Houselog Run, the trail crosses the Cranberry River. There is no bridge at this crossing, which can present problems during periods of high water.

688 — North-South Trail
Distance: 19.5 miles
Description: A look at the map shows that this trail is more of an east-west trail, but the Forest Service has plans to make this one a part of a much longer trail that will run north-south. On some maps it appears as the Red and Black Trail. The northern (eastern?) terminus is at a point that could properly be named "Trail Termination Point" because three trails — Big Beechy, District Line, and the North-South — terminate here at a point about 2 miles west of the Highland Scenic Highway. From here the trail actually goes south, first for 2 miles along the ridgetop and then continuing south on Forest Road 76 (the gated crossing of Forest Road 86 and the Highland Scenic Highway makes a good place to get on the North-South Trail). The North-South Trail follows Forest Road 76 until it leaves the road to begin its long crosscountry trek westward, where it again joins Forest Road 76 at the trails termination point in the Cranberry Recreation Area (30 camp sites). On this westward route, it intersects Tumbling Rock Trail, and 2½ miles further on, the Birchlog Trail. Both of these trails lead to Forest Road 76 and to the Tumbling Rock shelter, a pleasant circuit off the North-South, especially if one wishes to stay overnight at the shelter. Just north of the North-South Trail, on the Laurelly Branch Trail, coal prospecting and core drilling activities began in 1975. Core drill roads cross the North-South Trail. Hikers should remember to follow the blue-blazed trail and ignore the core drill roads.

Continuing westward, the North-South intersects the Big Rough Run Trail, the Little Fork Trail, and then the Lick Branch Trail at which point the North-South begins to veer north crossing the headwaters of several small streams and intersection Forest Road 272. At this point it veers sharply to the left and terminates at Forest Road 76.

263 — Pocahontas Trail
Distance: 15 miles
Description: This trail begins at the Cranberry Visitor Center on State Route 39, which has a big parking area and is a good rendezvous point for beginning a hike, proceeds west intersecting the Kennison Mountain Trail near Blue Knob (Note: Some trail descriptions refer to that part of the Kennison Mountain Trail south of Route 39 as the Blue Knob Trail; the Forest Service now considers the Kennison Trail to extend all the way to its intersection with the Pocahontas), and then it swings north-

ward to cross Route 39 about 3 miles beyond Blue Knob and a mile east of the Falls of Hills Creek Scenic Area.

From Route 39, the trail proceeds northwest — intersecting Eagle Camp Trail, which provides access to State Route 39, then continues — to Mikes Knob (a popular spot; two trails and a Forest Service road either begin at or pass by the Knob), then continues on to the Summit Lake country to the Summit Shelter some 5 miles from the Knob, and skirts the Summit Lake Recreation Area (17 camp sites). Leaving the Summit Lake area, the trail goes west to terminate on Forest Road 99.

A study of the Pocahontas Trail route on the map shows that it never really enters the Cranberry Area. As it approaches Mikes Knob from the south, it begins to skirt the Cranberry boundary line and continues to skirt or straddle the boundary all the way to the Summit Lake country, from which it leaves the Cranberry Area and heads west. The West Virginia *Highlands Conservancey* book gives further information, stating that the Pocahontas follows in part a Seneca Indian Trail (now U.S. Route 219) and was also used by pioneers before the Civil War.

209 — Turkey Mountain Trail

Distance: 16.5 miles

Description: This long east-west trail is beyond the northern boundary of the Cranberry Area. The trail is about 2 to 4 miles north of and roughly parallel to Forest Road 86. Its western terminus is on a logging road leading northeast from State Route 46 (an extension of Forest Road 86) between the communities of Dyer and Donaldson. From the terminus (2500 feet elevation), it climbs to the top of Turkey Mountain and proceeds east along the ridge top (average elevation 3500 feet), overlooking the Gauley River to the north and the Williams to the south. At approximately the midpoint of the hike, the trail intersects Forest Road 133 near a marker indicating 3570 foot elevation. The eastern terminus of the trail is at Forest Road 135, about 4 miles north of that roads' intersection with Forest Road 86.

This trail was marked with blue paint in 1975 but as of November, 1975, had not yet been brushed east of Forest Road 133. During the summer months it may be difficult to follow.

Turkey Mountain Trail intersects with Twin Branch Trail #205 and County Line Trail #206, which provide access to the Williams River and Forest Road 86.

CHEAT RANGER DISTRICT
Parsons, West Virginia 26287
Telephone: 304/478-3251

The Cheat District is the northernmost district in the Forest, and within its boundaries lies the 20,000-acre Otter Creek Wilderness, designated by Congress on January 3, 1975. The trails about to be described occur within the District's two most delightful areas, Canaan Mountain and Otter Creek Wilderness areas. The Canaan Area is so attractive that it is

bordered by two state parks, Blackwater Falls State Park on the north
and the Canaan Valley State Park on the south. I visited here in mid-
September, 1975, hiked some of the trails in the Canaan Area, and
camped overnight at Blackwater Park. Here are the Canaan trails. All of
them appear on the following USGS Quads: Mozark Mountain and
Blackwater Falls, West Virginia.

Plantation Trail

Distance: 3.4 miles

Description: This trail bounds the northern side of the Canaan Spruce
Plantation until it reaches Fire Trail #6, the western end of the Plantation. The trail is level for the most part, although there are a few dips
near stream crossings. The general elevation is 3200-3500 feet. Several
small water dams are located along this trail, and water is available at
several small brooks. The average length of time it takes to walk the trail
is four hours.

Begin the hike about 2 miles southeast of Davis, West Virginia on
State Route 32, at a point .3 mile north of the Forest Entrance sign. The
trail proceeds in southwesterly direction. At 1.2 miles it crosses Fire Trail
3; at 1.8 miles a pipeline, and at 2.7 it crosses the Davis Trail #107.
Further on it crosses the Lindy Run Trail, at 5.1 miles, and the Railroad
Grade Trail at 6.3 miles. At 8.4, it reaches Forest Service Road 13, which
is the end of the trail and is 10.7 miles from the intersection of Forest
Service Road 13 with State Route 32.

Davis Trail

Distance: 2.8 miles

Description: This trail begins on the Canaan Loop Road, Forest Service
Road 13, 2.8 miles southwest of State Route 32 at Canaan Heights. It
crosses the Canaan Spruce Plantation, the Plantation Trail (Trail 101)
and parallels Engine Run to State Route 19/1 in Blackwater Falls State
Park. Access for fire-fighters is the primary purpose of the first 1.2 miles
of this trail, but from there on it is a hiking trail, and the tread is quite
rocky in many places. The trail is 2.8 miles long and takes the average
hiker about one hour and twenty minutes.

Mountainside Trail

Distance: 6.7 miles

Description: This trail makes a large loop along the southwest point of
Canaan Mountain, beginning 4.6 miles southwest of the Blackwater Falls
State Park sled area on the Canaan Loop Road and ending 3.25 miles
farther south on the same road in the Red Run drainage area. It follows
an old railroad grade for 6.56 of the 6.7 miles. After leaving the Canaan
Loop Road to the west, the trail crosses Laurel Run several times before
passing through the Red Run drainage area. At 6.5 miles the trail leaves
the railroad grade, climbs a short way up the adjacent slope, then turns
right and follows an old skid road and trail to the trail's end, on Canaan
Loop Road.

There are attractive camping possibilities at the head of Laurel Run where the trail crosses the Run at five different places. Water is available at several points. The end of the trail on Canaan Loop Road is 7.18 miles south of Blackwater Falls State Park sled area and .6 mile north of the Mozark Jeep Road.   Average hiking time; 3.5 hours.

109 — Lindy Run Trail

Distance: 3 miles

Description: The trail begins 4.7 miles southwest of Canaan Heights on the Canaan Loop Road (Forest Road 13). It bears in a northwest direction across Canaan Mountain, crosses Plantation Trail 101 at 1.3 miles, and ends on the Canaan loop Road near Lindy Run. The only water available for drinking is that in Lindy Run. Potability of such water is uncertain. Average walking time: 1.5 hours.

110 — Railroad Grade Trail

Distance: 3.3 miles

Description: This trail begins 6.7 miles southwest of Canaan Heights on the Canaan Loop Road (Forest Service Road 13). It heads in a northwest direction across Canaan Mountain and ends on the Canaan Loop Road, running parallel to the Lindy Run Trail.

The trail is nearly level all the way, although the tread is uneven due to the rotting away of the old railroad ties. This trail crosses the Plantation Trail (Trail 101) at 1.8 miles from its beginning. The first half of the trail lies in a northern hardwood stand and the second half is favored by spruce. There is a trailside shelter (shelter not shown on Forest Service map), 1.3 miles from the beginning at a stream crossing. The trail is 3.3 miles long and takes about 1.25 hours to hike.

TRAILS IN THE OTTER CREEK WILDERNESS

Public Law 93-622 approved January 3, 1975, established the 20,000-acre Otter Creek Wilderness located in Tucker and Randolph Counties. It includes almost the entire drainage area of Otter Creek and Shavers Lick Run and provides excellent opportunities for hiking and camping. Much of the area is in 60- to 80-year-old hardwood forest. The rainfall is 55 inches per year, and there are extensive areas of thick rhododendron, which makes for difficult off-trail hiking. Some 45 miles of hiking trails are located in and near the Wilderness, most of which we will describe. As in the Canaan Mountain Trails, these are laid out to permit a variety of circuit hike combinations. Most of the Trails are blue-blazed.

N.B.: Permits are required for anyone entering the Wilderness Area. There is no charge for them. They may be obtained from the Cheat Ranger District Office in Parsons, West Virginia, from any of the other ranger district offices, or from the Forest Supervisor's Office in Elkins. They may be obtained also by phone or mail. One signed permit is required for each entry of an individual or a group. The following is information needed for issuance of the permit: Applicant's name and address, expected date and duration of visit, location of entry and exit, and number of people in party.

The USGS Quad maps that cover the Otter Creek area are Parsons, Mozark Mountain, Bowden and Harman, West Virginia. Actually you will not need to obtain the quads, because with your approved permit you will received a 9" x 16" map free from the Forest Service, scale 1 inch equals 1 mile. All of the trails and the location of the two shelters are clearly shown. Some outdoor stores have small supplies of the maps and the postcard type application forms.

Otter Creek Trail

Distance: 11 miles

Description: This is the main north-south trail going through the Wilderness. It is to Otter Creek Area what Red Creek is to the Dolly Sods — a trunk trail off which many other trails branch. The entire trail follows an old railroad bed which offers fairly easy walking. You will encounter several springs during the course of the 11.4 mile hike. The trail crosses the creek three times and in wet weather requires some knee deep wading, occasionally waist deep (very invigorating in April and May!).

To reach the starting point, proceed east from Elkins on U.S. Route 33 for 12 miles. At Alpena Gap turn north on Forest Service Road 91. Proceed north for 2.5 miles to the end of the road and park. Just before reaching parking space you will have passed by Stuart Memorial Drive to your left. Bear Heaven Recreation Area (7 campsites) is about 2 miles west on that road.

Here are the principal points of interest on the Otter Creek Trail:

Trail head to Yellow Creek Trail	1.2 miles
Yellow Creek Trail to Mylius Trail	1.8 miles
Mylius Trail to Shelter (Moore Run Trail)	1.2 miles
Shelter to Green Mountain Trail	3.1 miles
Green Mountain Trail to Big Springs Gap Trail	1.3 miles
Big Springs Gap Trail to Mouth of Otter Creek	2.8 miles
TOTAL MILES	11.4 miles

The shelter has space for 6 people, and is located in a level area that is suitable for erecting tents. This is the most heavily used campsite in the Wilderness. Those looking for solitude should plan on setting up camp somewhere else. Although the Otter Creek Trail receives the heaviest use in the area, the branch trails all offer excellent opportunities for hiking and camping with less congestion. The branch trails in the area are described herein in a south to north fashion.

Yellow Creek Trail

Distance: 3 miles

Description: Proceeds west from Otter Creek Trail; passes through the Yellow Creek bogs and crosses Yellow Creek. Beyond the boundary of Wilderness Area the trail meets the end of the McGowan Mountain Road (Forest Service Road 324) which leads to Parsons. The Little Black Fork Trail connects to the Yellow Creek Trail about .3 mile from the terminus. Near the stream crossing there is a good campsite.

Mylius Trail
Distance: 2.4 miles
Description: This trail first crosses Otter Creek, then proceeds east, passing through a forest clearing enroute to its junction with the Shavers Mountain Trail at .7 mile. It then leaves the boundary of the Wilderness and descends steeply down the mountain until it is Forest Service Road 162 at 2.4 miles. The last .3 of a mile the trail follows an old road.

Moore Run Trail
Distance: 4 miles
Description: You'll find a shelter just north of Devils Gulch near the intersection of Moore Run Trail and Otter Creek Trail. To hike the Moore Run Trail, cross the creek just south of the shelter and begin the slow climb up the sides of McGowan Mountain. Trail passes through fine stands of hardwood with little underbrush. In 2.8 miles you will reach the intersection of Turkey Run Trail in an interesting bog area. The trail leaves the bog area about .5 mile beyond the Turkey Run Trail intersection and continues west until it terminates at its junction with the McGowan Mountain Trail .3 mile from the McGowan Mountain Road.

Turkey Run Trail
Distance: 4 miles
Description: This is a south-north trail that begins at its intersection with the Moore Run Trail. From there it first climbs over a spur of McGowan Mountain, then descends into Turkey Run. This is a pleasant trail with gentle climbs through spruce and hemlock stands. At 2 miles the trail joins and follows the Turkey Run Road (gated — no vehicles) for 1.8 mile to its connection with the Fernow Experimental Forest road system.

Green Mountain Trail
Distance: 4.2 miles
Description: This trail proceeds east and south from Otter Creek. During its first mile it involves a strenuous climb from 2250 feet to 3400 feet. After reaching the top of Green Mountain, it veers south and skirts the edge of a Canadian-zone bog at the headwaters of Shavers Lick Run. The trail terminates at its junction with the Shavers Mountain Trail 0.5 miles north of the Shavers Mountain Shelter.

Big Spring Gap Trail
Distance: 1 mile
Description: This trail, although only one mile long, is important because it provides access to Forest Road 701 in the Fernow Experimental Forest. It is actually an old jeep road. There is about a 500-foot drop in elevation from the trailhead to junction with the Otter Creek Trail.

Shavers Mountain Trail
Distance: 10.5 miles
Description: This is a ridgetop trail that follows close to the eastern boundary of the Otter Creek Wilderness. Its principal junction points are:

Alpena Gap Picnic Area to Hedrick Camp Cutoff   3.0 miles

Hedrick Camp Cutoff to Mylius Trail	4.3 miles
Mylius Trail to Shavers Mountain Shelter	2.2 miles
Shavers Mt. Shelter to Green Mountain Trail	0.5 mile
TOTAL MILES	10.0 miles

From the picnic area the trail ascends steeply through a series of switchbacks until it gains the crest of Shavers Mountain. From there the trail stays largely in the 3400-3800 foot elevation. A half-mile before reaching the Shavers Mountain Shelter, it passes by a virgin stand of giant hemlocks. The trail terminates at its junction with Green Mountain Trail close to the head of the Shavers Lick Run near the Tucker-Randolph county line.

Big Blue — Tuscarora Trail

In the early 1960's, the Appalachian Trail Conference, alarmed by the deteriorating condition of the A.T. in northern Virginia, authorized an alternate long distance trail that would depart from the A.T. in northern Virginia and rejoin the main trail in southern Pennsylvania. The alternate route would begin in the north section of the Shenandoah National Park, swing west into the George Washington National Forest, then north through Hancock, Maryland (crossing the Potomac River at that point) and into Pennsylvania. In Pennsylvania, the trail would follow the Tuscarora mountain ridge, then gradually swing north and east until rejoining the A.T. near the Darlington lean-to, approximately 12 miles south of the A.T. crossing of the Susquehanna River at Duncannon, Pennsylvania. Various names were suggested for this new trail, but it was finally agreed that in Virginia and West Virginia, it would be called the Big Blue Trail and be identified with blue blazes, whereas in Maryland and Pennsylvania it would be called the Tuscarora Trail and be marked with orange blazes.

The new trail would provide hikers with another side trail of some 250 miles off the A.T. As an alternate route, it would also provide insurance that if the situation in northern Virginia became intolerable, the main trail could be rerouted over the Big Blue-Tuscarora. The new loop presented the opportunity for hikers to take an almost 400 mile circuit hike using the Big Blue-Tuscarora for the major part of the circuit, and the A.T. for the remainder. A shorter loop or "Figure 8" would also be possible by using the Chesapeake and Ohio Canal Towpath along the Potomac River.

In the following pages we will describe that part of the new trail that exists in West Virginia and Virginia — approximately 137 miles. The remaining 105 miles is described in the Pennsylvania portion of this book.

Although the entire trail is generally referred to as the Big Blue-Tuscarora, we will, in describing the West Virginia and Virginia parts of the trail, refer to it hereafter as the Big Blue Trail or sometimes just the Big Blue.

The Potomac Appalachian Trail Club (PATC) is responsible for the creation and maintenance of the Big Blue.

The guiding force behind this activity from the time the first mile of trail was marked in 1967 up to 1972, was Fred Blackburn of Washington, D.C. (with very able assistance from his wife Ruth). He has been a member of PATC for all but one year of its half century of existence. In 1972, a mild heart attack plus advancing years convinced him to relinquish such strenuous activities to younger people. The Big Blue activities are now directed by Tom Floyd.

The big problem with the Big Blue is getting landowner permission for the trail to cross private property. Tom has crews working on this problem at both ends of the trail as well as the middle, and it is his goal to have a continuous trail in existence all the way to Hancock, Maryland by June, 1976. Some of the trail may initially run on narrow country roads but later, as landowner problems are worked out, the trails will be rerouted from roads into the more desirable wooded areas. Hikers planning to hike the entire trail should obtain the latest information and maps from PATC, 1718 North Street, NW, Washington, D.C. 20036.

The Big Blue is marked with 2 inch by 6 inch blue paint blazes, as is almost every other trail leading off the A.T. But many of the paint blazes on the Big Blue are in the shape of a big blue letter "T." The frequency of the "T" seems to vary with the particular overseer doing the painting. Some use it almost exclusively, some use it frequently, and some use it only at trail and road intersections.

The following Big Blue Trail descriptions are written on a north to south basis. Since the first half of the southbound route is incomplete, the description is more general and portrays the route that should be completed by mid-1976, indicating also those sections that are already complete.

The PATC maintains some 600 miles of foot trails. It accomplishes this by assigning to each of over 100 workers, or "overseers", responsibility for maintaining a particular trail. Each overseer maintains a trail of approximately 3 to 6 miles. For simplicity, our description of the south half, which is now complete, will use the same trail divisions and mileages that have been used by PATC in its trail overseer assignments.

One more word of explanation. Trail descriptions for the Big Blue are considerably more detailed than those for many other trails described in this book. We did this because these descriptions were developed expressly for this book. There are no other existing write-ups or guidebooks available. This is it — and we felt the detail was necessary.

Potomac River [U.S. Route 522] to Sleepy Creek Public Hunting and Fishing Area

Distance: 9 miles (completion expected early 1976)
USGS Quad: Hancock and Cherry Run, Maryland; Big Pool, West Virginia; PATC map to be published.
Description: The Big Blue Trail begins its southbound course where the Tuscarora Trail ends, on the Potomac River Bridge (U.S. Route 522) at Hancock, Maryland. The first 36 miles cross the eastern panhandle of West Virginia.

South of the bridge the Trail turns east and follows River Road. Here, along the Potomac, the Big Blue is at its lowest elevation, 400 feet. After about 3 miles, the Trail heads inland across several miles of private forest land, crosses Sleepy Creek, and comes to State Route 9 just below Sleepy Creek Mountain. The Trail follows Route 9 east for .5 miles then enters the General Adam Stephens Roadside Park, follows private roads uphill, and ascends Sleepy Creek Mountain on a well graded switchback trail constructed in 1975 by PATC work crews. About one mile from the roadside park, the Trail reaches state-owned land on the summit of the mountain, elevation 1540 feet (end of section). The one-mile mountain trail follows a perpetual easement donated by landowner Duane B. Dillard and the Tuscarora Land Company.

Groceries are available at Hancock and at a small store on State Route 9. Water is available at handpump in the roadside park. There are no camping areas on this part of the Trail.

Sleep Creek Public Hunting and Fishing Area
USGS Quads: Big Pond, Statlers Crossroads, and Glengary, West Virginia; PATC Map: To be published
Distance: 26 miles (approval of this route pending)
Description: The Potomac Appalachian Trail Club (PATC) presently is negotiating with the West Virginia Department of Natural Resources for permission to route the Big Blue Trail through this State owned property. If approved, the Trail will probably follow Sleepy Creek Mountain for 4 miles, then follow valley areas for most of the remaining route. Camping will be permitted only at Sleepy Creek Lake (11 miles from northern end of property).

Sleepy Creek Hunting Area to Gore, Virginia [U.S. Route 50]
Distance: 18 miles (not completed)
USGS Quads: Glengary, West Virginia; White Hall and Gore, Virginia; PATC Map: To be published.
Description: Here the Big Blue will cross wooded hills and rolling farmland in the area between Sleepy Creek and Great North Mountains. Almost all of the route is in Virginia. Much of it will follow private country roads and a few short sections of highway. Arrangements have been completed for a few miles of forest trail on private land in the central and southern sections. A campsite to be known as Caskey Highlands, with a nearby spring, has been approved on private land on the summit of Sleepy Creek Mountain, just beyond the southern boundary of the hunting area, 14 miles south of the Sleepy Creek campground. A parking

area and rest stop known as Ritter Wayside will be located on PATC owned land, donated by Clinton L. Ritter, just one mile south of Caskey Highlands. Ritter, with the help of landowner Theodore Pratt, Jr., donated several miles of perpetual easement for the trail on remote private roads and woodland footpaths south of Caskey Highlands. This section of the trail will be known as the Ritter section. Here, the trail passes by a 900-foot-deep artesian well available to hikers. The water flows from a pipe near a barn at the intersection of State Route 600 and 690. Another campground, known as Dresel Wayside, with a nearby spring, several secluded camping areas, and a deep pond stocked with bluegill, will be located just off the forested trail 7 miles south of Caskey Highlands. PATC will manage the campsite and spring under cooperative agreements with donors Robert F. Dresel and Paul H. Parker.

At the end of this section of the trail, at Gore, there is a grocery store, post office, and a motel.

Gore, Virginia [U.S. Route 50] to Loman Branch [Virginia Route 704]
Distance: 9 miles (not completed)
USGS Quads: Gore and Hayfield, Virginia; Capon Springs, West Virginia; PATC Map: To be published.
Description: The Trail here will pass through remote wilderness for 8 of its 9 miles. Most of the route will be along the side of Great North Mountain, a massive ridge formation that lifts 1400 feet above the valley. The Trail will ascend to the top of Pinnacle Ridge, where the view is on a grand scale. More than half of the Trail will cross Captain McDowell's Cove, a mountain retreat with several springs and extensive stands of timber. A side trail will lead to a campground, about 15 miles south of the last one described in the previous section. Another campground will be about 4 miles further south. Two miles of the trail will follow a right-of-way donated by landowner R.M. Larrick.

Loman Branch [West Virginia Route 704] to Yellow Spring Road
Distance: 4.2 miles
USGS Quad: Capon Springs, West Virginia; PATC Map: To be published
Description: Southbound the Trail is completed from this section all the way to the A.T. in Shenandoah National Park, a distance of 75 miles. From Route 704 the Trail follows the Lehew and Shilow Church paved road to the right for .4 miles, then turns left on the Loman Branch Road. It follows this seldom used secondary route for 3 miles past open fields and scenic forest including a grove of hemlock. The Trail turns left onto the Mt. Airy School road and soon bears right to ascend a wooded hillside on a switchback course. Beyond is the Mt. Airy school house, a one-room school that was closed in 1935. The route then crosses a road, ascends to a high meadow with views of the surrounding hills, then descends through woods to the Yellow Spring Road (end of section).

The Yellow Spring, West Virginia post office and a grocery store are 1 mile west.

There is no appreciable change in elevation in this section. The entire route is through private land. Hikers looking for a place to camp should continue at least another 3 miles to the national forest land.

Yellow Spring Road to Capon Springs Road

Distance: 3 miles

USGS Quads: Capon Springs and Wardensville, West Virginia; PATC Map M, Strip 4.

Description: This is a pleasant, scenic route over extensive meadows and rolling woodlands. Most of the Trail is at the 1300 foot elevation and varies no more than about 200 feet. The Trail crosses two creeks. The route begins at a farm gate on the Yellow Springs Road approximately one mile east of Yellow Spring, West Virginia.

From the gate, the Trail ascends on a private farm road to open pastures with views of rolling farmland, then winds its way through forested hills. Just inside the woods, the Trail is undefined, but paint blazes mark the route. For the next 2 miles, the hiker will meander along old forest trails atop level mountain ridges, then descend through scrub growth to an old railroad grade at Dry Run. Further on, the Trail follows a private road beside Capon Springs Run. It then crosses a bridge to Capon Springs Road (end of section) at a point about 1½ miles west of Capon Springs, a popular resort area that President Franklin Pierce visited.

Both Yellow Spring and Capon Springs have a post office and a grocery store. The next grocery store on the trail is 36 miles south, at Mauertown, Virginia.

Capon Springs Road to Hawk Campground

Distance: 3.81 miles

USGS Quads: Mountain Falls, Virginia, and Wardensville, West Virginia; PATC Map M, Strip 5

Description: Here the Big Blue makes its first entry into the George Washington National Forest, which it traverses for most of the next 54 miles. The section begins at the Capon Springs Road, 1.5 miles west of Capon Springs, West Virginia, and 1.5 miles east of State Route 259. After a short ascent, the going is easy all the way to Hawk Campground. The total climb is only 250 feet. Nearly all of the section is in the national forest.

Water is available from a handpump at the campground. Camping is permitted in the national forest, but the campground itself is sometimes filled to capacity.

Hawk Campground to State Route 55

Distance: 3.4 miles

USGS Quads: Wardensville, West Virginia and Mountain Falls, Virginia; PATC Map M, Strip 5

Description: From Hawk Campground the Trail ascends 1,000 feet to the Virginia-West Virginia state line on the crest of Great North Mountain, then follows a hogback ridge south 2 miles to Route 55. The blue-blazed route through the forest was marked but had not been cleared in October, 1975. The blazes follow an easy switchback route up the mountain, but on the ridge the going is somewhat rough where the Trail encounters outcrops and numerous rock slabs.

Hawk Campground, a national forest facility, is designed for car camping, but hikers may stay there if space is available. Hikers may camp elsewhere along the route, since almost all of the Trail is in the George Washington National Forest. Water is available at a handpump at the campground, but this is the last source of water on the south-bound route for 12 miles.

County Line Trail — State Route 55 to Waite's Run
Distance: 8.4 miles
USGS Quad: Wardensville, West Virginia; PATC Map M, Strip 5
Description: The Trail begins on Route 55 in the gap marking the boundary between Virginia and West Virginia. Most of the Trail is at the 2000-2200 foot elevation except for the last mile descending into Waites Run (1300 feet). The first 2 miles of the Trail follow an old narrow road which becomes a foot trail and at approximately 2.1 miles goes under-neath a powerline. At 4.2 miles there is a wooden trailside shelter main-tained by the Terrapin Trail Club of the University of Maryland (wood floor, sleeps 6-8). In places the Trail traverses a very narrow ridge with views of the valley both east and west. At 7.5 miles the Trail separates, one blue-blaze trail going straight ahead, the Big Blue with the "T" blazes bearing off to the left. Follow the latter until its junction with gravel road at 8.4 miles. This is the end of section. To continue, turn right, following blazes along the road.

Pond Run Trail and Half Moon Trail
Combined Distance: 3.5 miles
USGS Quad: Woodstock, Virginia; PATC Map M, Strips 5 and 6
Description: This is a strenuous hike involving a climb of 1700 feet from the gravel road paralleling Waites Run to the end of the section at the locked Sugar Knob cabin. The cabin is the smallest (10' x 10'), the most isolated, and least used of PATC's 15 locked cabins. At the beginning of the Trail, leave the gravel road following blue blazes and, within 100 yards, ford Waites Run. During most of the year this will be a simple rock hopping ford but at certain times (such as the miserably wet Labor Day weekend of 1975) it will be necessary to wade through a rushing torrent well above your knees. There will be 5 or 6 lesser fords as you proceed upward through much hemlock growth on the Pond Run Trail. At 2.2 miles you will reach the intersection with Half Moon Trail. Turn left and continue on Half Moon Trail, passing by signed trail to the right leading to Wolf Gap cabin 6.7 miles south. Shortly after passing Wolf Gap Trail there is an excellent but inconspicuous walled-in spring on the left, directly beside the Trail between two trees. Between the Pond Trail and Sugar Knob cabin, the Trail reaches maximum height of 3200 feet, its highest elevation except for the elevation at its terminus with the A.T.

After hiking on Half Moon Trail for 1.3 miles turn right on narrow trail with a sign pointing to Sugar Knob cabin. You will reach the cabin in 50 yards. Those desiring to stay overnight in the cabin should make reservation and obtain key from the PATC. There are a number of pleasant hiking trails in the Sugar Knob cabin area. These are described elsewhere with trails in the Lee Ranger district. There is a spring 150 yards south of the cabin on the Little Stony Creek trail.

Sugar Knob Cabin to Cedar Run

Distance: 5 2 miles

USGS Quad: Woodstock, Virginia; PATC Map M, Strip 6

Description: From the Sugar Knob cabin, the Big Blue descends for 1 mile to a trail intersection in a pass below Little Sluice Mountain. Here it bears left, ascends slightly, and skirts the slope of Little Sluice in a northerly direction. For some distance the cleared trailway cuts through tangled thickets of scrub oak, then follows the Virginia-West Virginia state line for about 2 miles along the broad crest of Little Sluice. A blue blazed side trail to the right leads to an overlook with views of distant mountains to the southeast. The Big Blue descends gradually to the east and terminates this section at Cedar Run.

The total descent is 1550 feet. The entire section is wooded and contains extensive stands of mountain laurel. The route is totally within the boundaries of the George Washington National Forest. The final descent crosses a part of the Scheffers Gap State Game Refuge, a cooperative state project administered on national forest land.

Water is available only at the beginning and end of the route. Hikers who wish to stay at the locked Sugar Knob cabin must obtain advance reservations from the Potomac Appalachian Trail Club, 1718 N Street, N.W., Washington, D.C. 20036. Camping is permitted on the national forest land. The Cedar Run area is accessible by car from Virginia State Route 604 at Van Buren Furnace.

Cedar Run to Fetzer Gap [Virginia Route 600]

Distance: 5.7 miles

USGS Quads: Woodstock and Toms Brook, Virginia; PATC Map M, Strip 6.

Description: After following Cedar Run upstream for some distance, the Trail ascends on a forest road to Scheffer Gap, then climbs to the crest of Little North Mountain, which the Trail then follows northeasterly about 4 miles to Fetzer Gap. The Trail climbs from 1450 feet at the beginning to 2200 feet on Little North Mountain, then descends to 1800 feet.

On Little North Mountain, the hiker will experience some of the roughest walking on the Big Blue. The Trail is merely a series of blue paint blazes through forest and underbrush, where no trail has been cleared. The route often seems to head directly into the rockiest areas, over huge outcrops, rough backbone ridges, and slabs along the mountainside over jumbles of broken stone and boulders. Not all of the Trail is rough. There are several stretches of level trail, particularly toward the end.

Almost all of the route is in the George Washington National Forest. The first third is also a part of the Scheffers Gap State Game Refuge. Water is available at Cedar Run and Gum Spring, the latter being only a half mile from Cedar Run near the beginning of the section. Gum Spring is the last potable water source on the Big Blue Trail for 16 miles. Camping is permitted along most of the Trail, since it is within the national forest boundaries.

Fetzer Gap [Virginia Route 600] to Maurertown [U.S. Route 11]

Distance: 6.0 miles

USGS Quad: Toms Brook, Virginia; PATC Map M, Strips 6 and 7

Description: The Trail in this section descends 1200 feet from Little North Mountain to Virginia's Shenandoah Valley. Most of the route is on country roads. The section ends at Maurertown on U.S. Route 11, location of a grocery store (beverages available) and a post office. The only water is a stream in the valley that is subjected to agricultural pollution. Camping is permitted only in the George Washington National Forest on Little North Mountain, and level sites are hard to find after the descent begins.

Details of the trail route: From Virginia Route 600 at Fetzer Gap, the Big Blue descends gradually on a graded trailway. The route is forested. Near the bottom the Trail goes onto a long, straight forest road that eventually leads out of the woods onto State Route 656. Proceed directly ahead on 656, then turn right at Route 623. From here to Maurertown, the route follows a network of roads, generally for less than a mile on each of the following routes: left onto Route 655, right at 652, left at 642, and then bear right on Route 657. Near Maurertown, the Trail crosses a fence stile and proceeds through woodland a short distance to U.S. Route 11. The main part of the village is to the right.

Maurertown [U.S. Route 11] To Powells Fort Camp

Distance: 5.07 miles

USGS Quad: Toms Brook, Virginia; PATC Map M, Strip 7

Description: On this section of the Big Blue, hikers will continue across the rolling farmlands of the Shenandoah Valley, cross the north fork of the Shenandoah River on a low water bridge, ascend the Doll Ridge escarpment of the Massanutten Mountain, and come finally into a narrow forested valley in the western range of the Massanutten. The ascent up the Doll Ridge route involves a climb of 1200 feet on a graded trailway. At the end of this section you will come to a pipe spring, the first potable water for a 16 mile stretch. Thirsty hikers may purchase beverages and milk at a grocery store in Maurertown near the beginning of the section. The Shenandoah River and a tributary stream may be polluted by agricultural runoff. Camping is permitted in the George Washington National Forest near the end of the route but not at Powells Fort Camp, which is reserved for large groups.

Detailed route information: From the north edge of the village of Maurertown, the Trail heads to the north and east following a service

road immediately to the left (west) of U.S. Route 11, turning right after
.7 mile crossing U.S. Route 11 onto Virginia Route 650. Where Route
650 turns to the left after another .7 mile, the Big Blue bears right and
connects soon with Route 648. Follow Route 648 downhill to the left,
cross a stream and turn right at Route 653. Continue straight ahead
toward the mountain for .4 mile avoiding a turn to the right, then enter
a farm road and descend to the north fork of the Shenandoah River.
After crossing the bridge, follow the road to the left leading up a slight
hill to farm buildings. The Big Blue bears right at the farm house, then
follows fence rows up through pastureland, coming finally to forest land
at the base of the mountain. From here the Trail ascends to Doll Ridge,
where blackjack and post oak thrive on shale barren, then continues to
the crest of Three Top Mountain, the westernmost ridge of the Massanutten. From Three Top, the Trail descends rather steeply through oak-
hickory woods to a graveled road at Powells Fort Camp. This section of
the Trail ends at the pipe spring just past the camp compound.

Powells Fort Camp to Elizabeth Furnace [Virginia Route 678]

Distance: 5.4 miles

USGS Quad: Strasburg, Virginia; PATC Map M, Strip 7

Description: Here the Big Blue Trail progresses through an isolated
mountain valley, ascends to a rocky ridge top, then drops down to the
popular Elizabeth Furnace Recreation Area in the George Washington
National Forest. This section of the Trail is located within the Massanutten Mountain range on national forest land. The entire route is covered
by an oak-hickory canopy with extensive growths of mountain laurel.
After a gradual climb of 900 feet, spread over nearly 4 miles, the Trail
descends about 1250 feet. The Trail is in good condition and includes
several graded switchbacks. Water is available at a pipe spring where the
section begins, at various points along a creek for the first 2 miles, and
at the end of the section. In the opposite direction (northbound on the
Big Blue), the pipe spring is the last potable water source for 16 miles.
Overnight camping is permitted on the national forest land but not at
Powells Fort Camp, which is reserved for groups. There is a car campground at Elizabeth Furnace.

Details of the trail route: From a graveled road at the pipe spring just
north of Powells Fort Camp, the Trail heads in a northerly direction up
Little Fort Valley, paralleling Little Passage Creek for 3 miles, and passing the Strasburg Reservoir about midway. The Big Blue turns sharply
right, where another trail continues ahead to Signal Knob, and ascends
on switchbacks to the rocky crest of Green Mountain, elevation 2100
feet. From here the Trail descends on switchbacks and long grades passing eventually over exposed shale barren where the woodland resembles
the scrub forests of the Southwestern plateaus. The Trail reaches the
Elizabeth Furnace picnic area at Virginia Route 678. The elevation here
is 840 feet.

Elizabeth Furnace to Massanutten Ridge

Distance: 7.2 miles

USGS Quads: Strasburg and Bentonville, Virginia; PATC Map G; PATC Map M, Strips 7 and 8

Description: Detailed description of this trail and the excellent Little Crease shelter will be found under "Massanutten Mountain Trail," Lee Ranger District, George Washington National Forest.

Massanutten Ridge to U.S. Route 340

Distance: 6.4 miles

USGS Quad: Bentonville, Virginia; PATC Map G; PATC Map M, Strip 8

Description: This section of the Trail begins on the east crest of Massanutten Mountain approximately 1 mile east of the Little Crease shelter. At this point the orange-blazed Massanutten Mountain trail proceeds southwest and the Big Blue proceeds generally southeast toward the South Fork of the Shenandoah River. Begin gradual descent on east bound Big Blue and, after 1 mile leave national forest property, go through gate and through succession of dirt roads and farm fields (private property). Be prepared for encounters with pigs, chickens, dogs. Trail blazes were infrequent when we hiked this area in July, 1975 and the Trail was somewhat difficult to follow. About .3 mile before reaching the river, the Trail leaves farm land and follows a narrow road. The road leads to the Bentonville Landing and the low water bridge. The trail crosses South Fork of the Shenandoah River at this point, continues on dirt road for some 200 yards and then turns right into the woods. Follow Trail through woods for 1 mile, then turn right on paved State Route 629. Follow Route 629 until its junction with Route 628. Turn left on State Route 628 and follow it until it reaches U.S. Route 340 at the end of section.

U.S. Route 340 to Overall Run

Distance: 3 miles

USGS Quad: Bentonville, Virginia; PATC Map M, Strip 8

Description: This section of the Trail begins where Virginia Route 628 reaches U.S. Route 340. It continues southeast for 3 miles, achieving a final gain in elevation of about 300 feet after crossing or skirting several small hills 400 to 500 feet above the starting point. The trail is marked with blue blazes that are quite visible except for where the Trail traverses an open pasture.

Details of route: Follow the blue blazes .16 mile southwest on U.S. Route 340. Turn left on gravel road and continue under a railroad embankment. After passing through a gate, begin a gradual ascent of .3 mile through a pasture before entering woods. The blazes in the pasture are on rocks and fence posts. Entering wooded terrain, follow the trail generally on old roads until entering Shenandoah National Park at .99 mile and reaching the stream bed of Sandbank Hollow at 1.03 mile. While this stream emerges above ground intermittently, it appears to be the sole natural source of potable water between the streams above the pasture on the east slope of Massanutten Mountain and Overall Run.

Ascending the hill, follow the well-marked Trail for 2 miles through wooded hills, reaching the end of the section at the Overall Run Trail after a total of 3 miles.

Overall Run to the Appalachian Trail

Distance: 4.5 miles

USGS Quad: Bentonville; PATC Map M, Strip 8

Description: This section begins where the previous section joins the Overall Run Trail. From there it is coterminous with Overall Run Trail, continuing southeast for 4.45 miles, where it meets the A.T. in the Shenandoah National Park. This section begins at an elevation of less than 1000 feet and ends at an elevation of over 3400 feet. At one point the trail goes up 1000 feet in one-half mile. This section goes through an area that has the Park's highest concentration of black bears.

Details of route: Turn left at the junction with the Overall Run Trail and continue upstream, crossing Overall Run twice. The steep ascent mentioned above begins about 1.3 miles from the starting point. The Overall Run Falls can be seen from two points reached by blue-blazed side trails at 1.6 and 1.8 miles. These falls have the longest drop of any in the Shenandoah National Park. At 2 miles the Trail passes a rock outcrop providing an overlook to the west. The Mathews Arm Fire Road is reached at 2.1 miles. Bear right and cross Gimlet Ridge Fire Road at 2.2 miles. The Trail continues, crossing a stream at 3.3 miles and reaching a trail intersection at 3.8 miles (the side trail at this intersection leads almost immediately to the Mathews Arm Campground Nature Trail). Turn sharp left and ascend to the A.T. at 4.5 miles. Here, at its highest elevation, the Big Blue Trail ends.

Harpers Ferry, West Virginia

Harpers Ferry! The words alone conjure up historic names and events — the Federal arsenal and armory built in 1796; John Brown's raid of October 16, 1859; the Potomac River; the Shenandoah River; the C&O Canal; and the Appalachian Trail. All of these places and events are related to the village of Harpers Ferry, nestled on a relatively tiny piece of rock between the Potomac and Shenandoah Rivers. The village is just the width of the Potomac away from the C. & O. Canal and its 184-mile hikeable, bikeable towpath. One day those using the Canal will have direct access to Harpers Ferry via a foot bridge to be built on the still useable stone piers which once supported the bridge crossed by John Brown and his men on his famous Sunday night raid. The headquarters of the Appalachian Trail Conference is also located here and, since the Trail comes with a scant two miles of the village, the Conference building has become a mecca for A.T. hikers, especially those making the long distance trek from end to end.

Harpers Ferry and its immediate environs became a National Historical Park in 1954, and since that time the National Park Service has steadily rebuilt and restored many of the more prominent buildings.

The last six weeks (October-November, 1975) of my writing activities for this book were spent in a 100-year-old house rented for the occasion from Grant and Ione Conway, fellow members of the Potomac Appalachian Trail Club. The house, situated high on a hill in Harpers Ferry, provided a wonderful setting for a book on hiking trails. Each day my morning constitutional took me down to the village, where within minutes I would catch sight of the Potomac and the Sandy Hook bridge over which U.S. Highway 340 passes. Sometimes I would stop at the A.T. Conference Office, sometimes at the National Park Service office, and now and then at the Fine Book shop, which sells books and pictures relating to this area. On some days I'd stop to watch with small-boy fascination the B&O train come charging out of the tunnel across the river and race across the bridge over the Potomac and proceed up river on the West Virginia side. Sometimes my walks would take me to High-acre, the century-old home situated in a prominent place in the village from whose attic window one can get a direct bead on the railroad tunnel entrance across the river. Highacre was donated to the Potomac Appalachian Trail Club by Kathryn Fulkerson, now deceased. From there my walks would take me down the steep steps past the Catholic Church which was used as a hospital during the Civil War, then down more stone steps carved out of solid rock, right down to the main street of the village.

And always my path led down Washington Street past a white house with a sign on the front reading: *Crowder Memorial World Nature Study Center*. This never failed to bring back memories of Orville Crowder, the fabulous little man who died in his 70's, in 1974, while getting ready to take off on another globe girdling plane trip. Crowder lived in the white house on Washington street and his memorabilia are still there. The study center is open to the public. He was an ardent hiker who had hiked the entire A.T. Hermann Postelthwaite (known more familiarly as "PW"), the genial curator of the Nature Center (it's a scant block from the Harpers Ferry Post Office where A.T. hikers pick up their mail) has stated that hikers are most welcome at the Nature Study Center — to eat their lunches on the wide front porch, to use the toilet facilities, or to camp out overnight in the spacious back yard. Every house in Harpers Ferry has character. So take a tip from me: Whether you're hiking on the A.T. or hiking or biking on the C. & O. towpath or just driving in the general area, don't miss Harpers Ferry!

Loudoun Heights Trail

Distance: 1.13 miles

USGS Quad: Harpers Ferry, West Virginia; PATC Map No. 6

Description: This is an important connecting trail from Harpers Ferry to the A.T. If and when the A.T. is rerouted through Harpers Ferry, it would quite probably go over this 1.13 mile link.

Start of the trail is at the western end of the bridge (on U.S. Route

340) that crosses the Shenandoah River. As it climbs the Loudoun Heights it provides excellent views of the Shenandoah River and the town of Harpers Ferry, and it intersects the A.T. at a point 1.13 miles from the bridge. From here it is 3.85 miles on the A.T. to the right to State Route 9. To the left it is 2.19 miles to the Sandy Hook Bridge over the Potomac.

A very pleasant circuit hike can be made by taking the Loudoun Heights Trail to the A.T. intersection; then go left on the A.T. to U.S. Route 340 and left again on 340 to the Shenandoah bridge. If you take this return route on the A.T., allow time to leave the A.T. briefly at several well marked spots and visit the overlooks that provide beautiful views of both rivers and of the village.

Maryland Heights Trail

Distance: 4 miles

Maps: PATC Maps 5 and 6

Description: This four-mile circuit involves some rather strenuous hiking, provides excellent views of the Potomac River Gorge and constitutes a lesson in Civil War history. The hike is described in much detail in both the *Guide To the Appalachian Trail* (From the Susquehanna River to the Shenandoah National Park) issued by the PATC, and in an 8½ x 11 inch handout sheet furnished by the visitor center at the Harpers Ferry National Historical Park. The Park Service handout sheet provides much historical detail and a map that is quite adequate. The entire hike goes across land that is part of the National Historical Park.

From the Visitor Center at Harpers Ferry, it is 4.1 miles to the starting point of the hike via U.S. Route 340 and the Sandy Hook bridge. Note that it is only 0.7 miles from the center via the railroad bridge across the Potomac River, but this is somewhat dangerous and the bridge bristles with "No Trespassing" signs. If you approach via the Sandy Hook bridge turn right at the Maryland end. The road passes a small picnic area, then circles down toward the river. At the stop sign, turn right. This takes you back under Sandy Hook bridge. Check your speedometer at this point as it is 0.6 miles from the bridge to parking space on the right side of the road, where the Maryland Heights Trail begins. From the parking area there are steps, marked with blue paint blazes, leading steeply up the bank. At 0.48 miles turn sharp right uphill. To the left are outstanding views of the confluence of the Potomac and Shenandoah Rivers and of Harpers Ferry. From this point begin a steady climb to the top of Maryland Heights.

The Park Service handout explains the various military defense ruins that you will see throughout the circuit. I hiked the circuit twice in 1975 and found that only about half of the significant points were identified by signs. The highest point on the trail (1475 foot elevation; 1200 feet above the river valley) is a sign reading *Survey Markers*. A very short distance beyond that sign, is an obscure orange-blazed trail leading off to the right. There is no trail sign at the intersection. The orange-blazed trail proceeds for 380 yards before the orange blazes are succeeded by the blue blazes. This is the Maryland Heights Elk Ridge Trail, by which one can hike all the way to the A.T. in Crampton Gap. Distance from Maryland Heights to Crampton Gap is 7.7 miles. An 18 mile circuit hike can be made using the Maryland Heights-Elk Ridge Trail to Crampton Gap, the A.T. south to the C & O Canal, and by turning right on the Canal back to the starting point.

To complete the Maryland Heights circuit, continue on the blue-blaze trail past the orange-blaze side trail and begin your return part of the circuit. Turn left on Military Road (marked by a sign) at 2.33 miles. At 3.3 miles at trail junction, turn sharp left and continue on to the starting point. The Park Service handout lists the hiking time as 3.5 hours, but it can be hiked in much less time than that by those in good condition.

Caution: This trail was somewhat overgrown in eary summer, 1975, and poison ivy was lush.

Other Hiking Trails in West Virginia

Cacapon State Park
Distance: 21 miles of hiking trails plus 10 miles of horsetrails.
Map: 8½ x 11 inch handout map from Cacapon State Park, Berkeley Springs, West Virginia 25411. Scale: 4 inches equals 1 mile
Description: This 6115-acre park is situated on and near Cacapon Mountain in the eastern panhandle of West Virginia. It has five maintained hiking trails, each marked with a distinctive color. On the reverse side of the handout map is a description of each trail, location of it's starting point, the length of the trail and time required to hike it. Some of the trails involve elevation changes of as much as 1000 feet.

Cedar Creek State Park [Gilmer County]
Distance: 10 miles of hiking trails
Map: 8½ x 11 inch handout map with trail descriptions on reverse side. Scale of map: 5 inches equals 1 mile
Description: This 2034-acre park is situated in the central part of the state, Route 1, Box 9, Glenville, West Virginia 26351. Primarily a day use park, it has six hiking trails laid out in the foothills of the Allegheny Mountains. The trails range in distance from .5 miles to 2.5 miles.

ALLEGHENY TRAIL

This is a proposed trail of roughly 200 miles that will begin with the intersection of the A.T. near Pearisburg, Virginia. It will proceed in a northeasterly direction following Peters Mountain for about 30 miles in the Jefferson National Forest. Near Hermatite, Virginia, the trail turns north into the George Washington National Forest and then enters the Monongahela National Forest on Little Allegheny Mountain. The trail will pass near Watoga State Park, the Huntersville anticline, through Seneca State Forest and up Back Allegheny Mountain.

At Cass, West Virginia, the hiker will have an opportunity to ride the Scenic Railroad. The trail will then parallel Shaver's Fork to Gaudineer Knob and then traverse to Shaver's Mountain past Alpena Gap, Otter Creek Wilderness and Fernow Experimental Forest, and on to Blackwater Falls State Park, the northern terminus.

For approximately 120 miles the Allegheny will be superimposed on existing marked trails. Of the other 80 miles, some 18 miles were constructed as of September, 1975. Estimated completion date is late 1977.

Hikers desiring to hike that part of the Allegheny Trail should write to: West Virginia Scenic Trails Association, Inc., P.O. Box 4042, Charleston, West Virginia 25304.

The Association welcomes volunteer help and new members. It has a big job to do!

1. APPALACHIAN TRAIL
2. CHESAPEAKE AND OHIO CANAL
3. ASSATEAGUE ISLAND NATIONAL SEASHORE
4. BALTIMORE METROPOLITAN AREA TRAILS

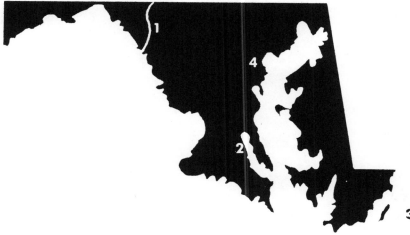

Maryland

To obtain the Maryland Highway and Natural Resources Map and other information on attractions and events, visit, write or call the:

Maryland Division of Tourist Development
1748 Forest Drive
Annapolis, Maryland 21401
Telephone: 301/267-1686

For information on State Parks write to:

Maryland Park Service
Tawes State Office Building
Annapolis, Maryland 21401
Telephone: 301/267-5771

For information on State Forests, write to:

Maryland Forest Service
Tawes State Office Building
Annapolis, Maryland 21401
Telephone: 301/267-5776

The Appalachian Trail in Maryland

The Trail enters Maryland on the east end of the Sandy Hook bridge (U.S. Route 340). It then drops down to the Chesapeake and Ohio Canal towpath, which it follows for 1.5 miles. Leaving the Canal, it crosses underneath U.S. Route 340 and then climbs Weverton Heights to the top of the ridge. There are excellent views of the Potomac River Gorge and of Harpers Ferry from lookout spots along the Trail.

From atop Weverton Heights, the Trail proceeds north along South Mountain for the remainder of its traverse through the state. It leaves Maryland at Pen-Mar on the state line after first skirting Camp David, the brief vacation spot for U.S. Presidents. In all, some 37 miles of the Trail goes through Maryland, and there are five shelters on this stretch. The State of Maryland has been making steady progress in acquiring land throughout the length of the South Mountain area.

Chesapeake and Ohio Canal

This 184-mile canal and towpath begins in the District of Columbia and follows the east side of the Potomac River for 184 miles, all to the way to Cumberland, Maryland. It has been owned by the U.S. Government since 1938 and is now a National Historical Park. It provides a hiking and biking path along it's entire length with hiker-biker campgrounds located about every five miles. Some 22 miles of the canal and locks have been restored. This part of the trail extends from Washington, D.C., to Seneca, Maryland, and is the most widely used area of the canal. In this span the canal offers not just hiking and biking, but boating, canoeing, and occasionally in winter, ice skating.

Construction on the canal began on July 4, 1828, with President John Quincy Adams turning over the first spadeful of dirt. A director of the canal company predicted that the canal vould be completed all the way to the Ohio River in three years. It actually took 22 years to reach Cumberland, Maryland, and it never did reach the Ohio River at Pittsburgh as had been originally planned. Still, the canal is an engineering marvel. It has 74 lift locks, all built of stone, each having the capacity to lift or lower a boat about 8 feet. Elevation of the canal at Cumberland is 615 feet; at Washington it reaches tidewater. In addition to the locks, the canal has 11 aqueducts that permit the flow of water and canal barges across the tributaries of the Potomac. Of these the Monocacy aqueduct, at milepoint 42, is the most impressive and is the most greatly admired structure on the canal. It is built of white granite, is 438 feet long and has seven arches, each with a span of 54 feet. Unfortunately, the aque-

Hills Creek Lower Falls. [*Photo by Roger L. Hughes.*]

duct was badly damaged by Hurricane Agnes in 1972. The Paw Paw Tunnel, at milepoint 155, goes through 3118 feet of rock and saved 6 miles of canal construction.

There are a number of books, guides, and maps that assist the hiker and biker in the traverse of the 184 mile path. The 11 x 26 inch folder issued by the C. & O. National Historical Park is quite useful; it has a good map on one side and much explanatory information on the other.

I had largely ignored the canal for almost 20 years, even though I lived within six miles of it, but, in 1968 I began making a number of Sunday hikes on the canal, going a bit further north each time until, by the end of the year, I reached Monocacy Aqueduct at milepoint 42. There are many access points by car throughout the entire length of the canal. When one is hiking by oneself from a car as I was, it requires hiking each mile twice. Two or more people, even with one car permits one-way hiking (each party begins hiking from opposite ends of the trail and they exchange the car key at midpoint). In my usual methodical fashion, I recorded on each map the day I had hiked, the total mileage, and the hours required. There are mile markers on the canal making it possible to compute hiking speed. In reviewing my map notes I find that I averaged about four miles per hour, my best effort being a 4.2 mile rate for one 6-mile stretch.

The canal is a great place for observing bird and animal life, trees, flowers, and other plants. Bird students make use of the place on a year-round basis. I have observed both raccoon and opossum on the canal and was surprised on one occasion to scare up a small white-tailed deer at milepoint 32.

The walkway-bikeway is an elevated trail varying in width to 12 feet. Bikeway detours have been provided at a few points where the going is unusually rough, but hikers can traverse the entire route on the towpath. The overnight accomodation — "biker-hiker overnighters" — provide water (generally from a pump), cleared areas for tents, picnic tables, and fireplaces. There are American Youth Hostels at Seneca, Sandyhook, and Cumberland (milepoints 23, 59, and 184 respectively with a fourth, at Williamsport, milepoint 100, due to open in the spring of 1976.

The current edition of the *American Youth Hostel C & O Canal Guide-book* can be purchased from bookstores or from the American Youth Hostel, 1520 16th Street, N.W., Washington, D.C. 20036; cost: $1.75.

Another excellent guidebook, which comes in a more convenient carrying size, is the *184 Miles of Adventure — Hiker's Guide to the C & O Canal,* issued jointly by five Council offices of the Boy Scouts of America. This 50 page 5.5 x 8.5 inch book has a separate page and map and an opposite page narrative for each 10-mile segment of the canal. It has a listing showing the exact location of every hiker-biker campsite and for each it shows exactly what conveniences the camper will find there. This book also contains the requirements for obtaining the BSA medals and patches for hiking all or parts of the 184 mile trail. The book costs $1 and may be purchased from book stores, outdoor stores, and from BSA Trading Posts.

Before leaving the C & O Canal I think it appropriate to mention the contribution of one man (one of many who worked so hard to preserve the Canal and to publicize its charms), Orville Crowder. The American Youth Hostel book, described above, contains the following acknowledgement:

> *"Special credit is due to Orville Crowder who made his exten-sive notes available to us. Mr. Crowder has walked the entire Canal on several occasions, and has measured the distances by means of a measuring wheel, comparing his figures with those of the official records of the old Chesapeake and Ohio Canal Company. This material has been an invaluable aid to William Clague who drew the maps. Mr. Crowder will expand these notes into a book to be called "Towpath Guide," which is eagerly awaited by outdoorsmen and historians."*
>
> [reprinted by permission]

Crowder never did write the book. In his later years he lived in a white house in Harpers Ferry (see West Virginia — Harpers Ferry National Historical Park), a five minute walk from the place where I put the finishing touches on this book. His detailed records on the C & O Canal were turned over to Thomas F. Hahn in 1970. Another Canal Enthusiast, Grant Conway, had accumulated voluminous records on the Canal over a 35 year period and these also were turned over to Hahn.

Hahn's four-volume *Towpath Guide* was published in four sections, from 1971 through 1973. Those desiring more information on the Canal may wish to buy this latest guide. The four volumes, published by the American Canal and Transportation Center, are available at book stores at a cost of $2.50 each or from the AC&TC, 809 Rathton Road, York, Pennsylvania, 17403 at the same price plus 35-cents shipping charge for each volume.

Assateague Island

Assateague Island National Seashore Trail
Distance: 29 miles
Map: National Park Service map "Assateague Island"
Description: A delightful variation from mountain hiking is the 29-mile beach trail hike along the east coast of the Assateague Island National Seashore; administered by the National Park Service. The island also includes the Chincoteague National Wildlife Refuge, administered by the Bureau of Sport Fisheries and Wildlife of the U.S. Department of the Interior. The island is the home of the famous Chincoteague ponies and each year during the last week in July all the ponies are rounded up and

herded into Assateague channel where they swim to Chincoteague Island for the annual auction. Those not sold are returned to Assateague for release.

There are but three walk-in campgrounds on Assateague Island, plus one youth group campground near the National Park Service ranger station in Virginia. There are a number of motels, cottages, and campgrounds in nearby Chincoteague. There is also a campground in the Maryland Assateague State Park, which is an enclave within the National Seashore at its northern end. The Park Service also maintains a campground adjacent to the state park on the north end of the island.

There is no marked trail, as such, but the hiker walks along the beach being forced to walk on higher ground near the sand dunes at high tide, but most of the time one is able to walk on the hard-packed sand. Mileage markers (the National Park Service ranger station at Chincoteague is the zero point) are posted just above high tide line.

There are two recommended ways of negotiating the 29-mile beach trail. One is to headquarter either in the town of Chincoteague or at one of the campgrounds at the north end of the island and hike a different section of the island each day — alternating the hiking with other activities such as swimming, fishing, crabbing, or whatever.

For those who wish to backpack straight through, a camping permit is required for overnight stops at any of the three walk-in campsites. Permits, maps, the Assateague Island National Seashore leaflet, and other information may be obtained by writing to either the: Superintendent, Assateague Island National Seashore, Route #2, Box 294, Berlin, Marylsnf 21811; or to: Virginia District Ranger, Assateague Island National Seashore, P.O. Box 38, Chincoteague, Virginia 23336.

The three walk-in camp sites are just that, no buildings except toilets and no water. From May 15 until the first frost in the fall, there is an insect problem. Hikers should bring insect repellant. For overnight camping, a tent with mosquito netting is advised.

The prevailing winds are from the sea and the insect problem is minimal when walking directly beside the ocean. Walking even in the hard-packed sand is somewhat tiring. The wind blows almost constantly and conversation is difficult. Nevertheless, hiking along the National Seashore can be very pleasant. The sight, sound, and smell of the wind and water combine to make one feel invigorated and relaxed. The hiker will suffer no ill effects from high altitude on this hike, for the highest elevation on the island is only 47 feet above sea level. But watch out for severe sun and windburn. Hikers should wear hats and be especially careful not to invite sunburn by over exposure. It is easy to forget about the sun when one is cooled by a constant breeze.

The island is actually 35 miles long but hiking is generally confined to the lower 29 miles. The upper six miles is partly on private property and the northern tip is reachable only by boat. With a long-time hiking friend, Maurice A. (Gus) Crews, I spent four days in mid-April, 1975, hiking in the Assateague-Chincoteague area. On a sunny Sunday morning we began hiking in the northern half of the island, but only after having been informed by a State Park attendant of the private land situation and having been warned not to tresspass.

Public use of the northernmost 6.5 miles of Assateague Island is limited because of the present ownership of the land. A 3-mile long zone immediately north of the Maryland State Park is closed to all public entry whether on foot or by vehicle. The National Park Service has closed the area because the former property owner still has an exclusive right of use and ownership of the premises as allowed by law.

Beyond this tract lies a 2.9-mile private enclave known as the Atlantic Ocean Estates. The National Park Service is currently negotiating to buy this area, for which only water access is presently available. At the north tip of the island lies a small tract of public land which is available by boat-in access from Ocean City. Trespass laws apply to areas not owned or controlled by the National Park Service, and visitors are asked to respect the rights of landowners in these areas.

Baltimore Metropolitan Area Trails

The three trails described in the next few pages are metropolitan type trails in the Baltimore region. A complete description of them (plus 37 other hiking trails and 8 canoe trips) appears in *The Baltimore Trail Book*, a paperback by Suzanne Meyer Mittenhal, published by the Greater Baltimore Group, Southeast Chapter, Sierra Club. Distribution rights to the book have been assigned to Appalachian Books, Box 249, Oakton, Virginia 22124. First published in 1970, the book has gone through three printings and as of October, 1975, was out of print. But it is soon to be reprinted with some revisions.

My hike on these three trails on October 7, 1975 was sheer joy. It was a crisp sunshiny day. And since my previous scouting trip had ended in four consecutive days of steady rain in Pennsylvania, the chance to hike in clear weather was doubly appreciated. Second, the areas through which these three trails took us were extremely beautiful. Finally, my "guide" for the trip was Carleton Gooden, from Maryland's Eastern Shore. Gooden, age 55, has become a hiking institution all by himself. Like his father before him, he operates a general store in Henderson, Maryland. And Gooden's firmly fixed hiking pattern is so unusual as to be worthy of description.

He works at the store five days a week, Wednesday through Sunday, 49 weeks of the year. On Mondays, he takes care of personal business matters away from the store. Each Tuesday morning finds him in his closed pickup truck headed for any one of hundreds of hiking trails within a 150-mile radius of his home. When he can arrange it he hikes

Mount Rogers National Recreation Area—typical Alpine scene on Pine Mountain. [Photo by U.S. Forest Service.]

with others. But each Tuesday he goes out and hikes. He writes up each hiking adventure in a friendly, informative manner and at two-month intervals mails his writeups to about 25 selected individuals. Also, each year he contributes some of his most interesting hike writeups for publication in the annual magazine issue of the *Potomac Appalachian Trail Club.* The trails we hiked on October 7, 1975 in the Gunpowder River area are among his favorites, and I share them with you as being typical of many that are described in *The Baltimore Trail Book.*

One final observation on Carleton Gooden. On Labor Day weekend each year he closes his store lock, stock and barrel and it remains closed for three solid weeks during which Carleton participates in a long back-

Backpacking provides fine opportunities for family recreation. These hikers enjoy the Shavers Mountain Trail, near Gaudineer Knob in Monongahela National Forest. [Photo by John Ballantyne, National Forest Service.]

packing trip, generally over some part of the A.T. (In case you haven't guessed it. Mr. Gooden is a bachelor. No married man could get away with such a life style!)

The Hereford Area of the Gunpowder State Park

To reach it from Baltimore (or even from Washington) get on the I-695 Baltimore beltway. Take the I-83 exit north. In 12 miles take the Hereford exit and drive east into the village of Hereford. Where the road dead ends, turn left on York Road and Proceed north from .8 mile. Watch for a small county road sign, "Bunker Hill Road", and turn left on that road, which takes you underneath I-83. Proceed for an additional mile and park in the picnic ground area of the 11,000-acre Gunpowder Park.

The Sierra Club maintains the trails in this area and the three we hiked received their tender loving care from Martin Larrabee and helpers. Trails are marked mostly with colored metal disks (painted tin can covers) with wooden arrow signs (painted the same color as the disks) and a few informational signs on which an embossing machine has been used to provide plastic strips giving names of trails and distances to significant points.

USGS Quad: The Hereford Area of Gunpowder Park appears on the 7½ minute Hereford quad.

Prettyboy Dam Circuit Hike

Distance: 4.2 miles

Description: This pleasant circuit provides two kinds of hiking, along the banks of the Gunpowder River below the dam, and a return along a higher elevation trail away from the river. The dam creates the Prettyboy Reservoir to supply water for the city of Baltimore. The controlled amount of water discharged from the dam means that the river almost always has a lively amount of water flowing through it — neither a raging torrent during periods of heavy rains nor a mere trickle in dry periods. The Gunpowder in this area has considerable distances of high rocky gorges. It's a place for leisurely walking, with frequent stops to enjoy the beauty of the river and surrounding area.

To begin the hike, park your car on Falls Road just south of the bridge over Gunpowder Falls (see map). Hike upstream on the Gunpowder South Trail to the foot of the dam. There are many lunch spots along the way; I recommend one in particular — a large flat rock projecting well out into the stream just below the dam. At the dam, which is 1.6 miles

*Mount Rogers National Recreation Area—Whitetop-Laurel Creek
near the Appalachian Trail. [Photo by U.S. Forest Service.]*

from the start, by all means take the time to walk to the top and enjoy
the view both of the big reservoir and of the river itself. On the return
trip, pick up the Highland Trail (pink markers) which leaves the Gunpowder South Trail about .25 mile below the dam. Ascend the Highland
Trail from west to east until it rejoins the Gunpowder South Trail beside
the river. At that point retrace your steps to where your car is parked.

Mingo Forks Circuit Trail
Distance: 3.8 miles
Description: I reprint (by permission) from *The Baltimore Trail Book*© to
give readers the flavor of this delightful little (7" x 4½") guide book.

> *"Easy 3.9 mile circuit, along woodland paths, beside attractive
> brooks, over open fields with extended views, and through an
> interesting pine grove. This hike combines a part of the Gun-*

Carleton Gooden, the dedicated backpacker from Henderson, Maryland, who literally locks up shop and hits the trail once a week.

powder South Trail with the Mingo Forks and Bunker Hill Trails. Park at the picnic area S of Gunpowder Falls on Bunker Hill Road [see map]. Start up the Gunpowder South Trail, between the pump house and the rest rooms. Almost immediately after entering the woods, turn right downhill, following the Gunpowder South Trail [blue markers] and avoiding the Bunker Hill Trail [pink markers]; here the latter trail, on which you will be returning; goes straight ahead. Cross Mingo Branch, ascend to the top of a ridge, and continue to the junction with the Mingo Forks Trail. This junction is high on the ridge, 0.6 mile from the start. Turn left up the Mingo Forks Trail [pink markers; and follow it east to west, according to the detailed description given above, to its end at Bunker Hill Road. Go *directly across the road and enter Bunker Hill Trail [pink markers; in the woods behind a power pole. Descend this trail, going directly across Bunker Hill Road again after another 0.9 mile. On reaching the Gunpowder South Trail, continue straight ahead to the starting place at the picnic area."*

Panther Branch Circuit Trail

Distance: 5.4 miles or 4.2 or 2.2 — depending upon which of the circuits is chosen.

Description: 5.4 mile circuit — this is a walk of moderate difficulty proceeding mostly along stream banks — Gunpowder Falls and Panther Branch. To start the hike, park at York road on either side of Gunpowder Falls. Proceed to the north side of the river and begin hiking generally east along the stream bank. There is an attractive lunch stop at Raven Rock Falls .9 miles from start of hike. At 2.6 miles, upon reaching Big Falls Road, cross the highway bridge and return in an upstream direction on Gunpowder South Trail. Reach Panther Branch at .5 mile, and 30 yards beyond turn left on Panther Branch Trail and follow it until it rejoins the Gunpowder South Trail near York Road. Here, turn left to your starting poing.

4.2 mile circuit — (the one taken by Gooden and myself) take the Gunpowder South Trail (instead of the Gunpowder North Trail) to the east end of the Panther Branch Trail. The still shorter circuit of 2.2 miles can be made by following the Gunpowder South Trail only as far as the Sandy Lane Trail and then returning along it and the Panther Branch Trail.

PENNSYLVANIA

11

1. APPALACHIAN TRAIL
2. ALLEGHENY NATIONAL FOREST
3. WESTERN PENNSYLVANIA
4. CENTRAL PENNSYLVANIA
5. EASTERN PENNSYLVANIA
6. OTHER TRAILS

Pennsylvania

To obtain copies of the Official Map of Pennsylvania and to obtain information on attractions, points of interest, resort areas, etc., write to:

Travel Development Bureau,
Pennsylvania Department of Commerce
Harrisburg, Pennsylvania 17120

For information on Pennsylvania's Game Lands and maps for same, write to:

Pennsylvania Game Commission
P.O. Box 1567
Harrisburg, Pennsylvania 17120

For information on State Parks, write to:

Bureau of State Parks
3rd and Reily Streets
Harrisburg, Pennsylvania 17120

For information on State Forests, write to:

Office of Public Information
Harrisburg, Pennsylvania 17120

Pennsylvania

With some 4700 miles of developed hiking trails, Pennsylvania very likely has the "mostest" of any of the six mid-Atlantic states described in this book. Also, the state and federal agencies and the hiking organizations have done a particularly good job of getting their trails signed and paint blazed and they have developed maps, handout sheets, pocket-size guide books and other materials which make it easy for the hiker to ascertain what hiking trails are available and precisely where he should go to get on them.

The Keystone Trails Association (KTA), a federation of some 33 organizations that maintain hiking trails within the state has become an effective agency for promoting trails, developing guidebooks and trail books, and for working to obtain legislation to protect the A.T. and to develop a state-wide system of trails. The KTA, under the leadership of the indefatiguable Madeline Fleming, developed some 20 years ago a publication entitled *Pennsylvania Hiking Trails,* which describes the major hiking trails in the state. Now in its 7th edition (1974), this publication has 91 pages of 8½ x 11 inch trail descriptions, arranged by geographical area. It gives the name and address of the 33 member organizations, lists names and addresses of hotels, motels, campgrounds, and eating places near the various hiking trails and provides indices and sources of purchase for state game land maps, public use maps, and U.S. Geological Survey quadrangle maps. The book and many of the KTA members and clubs have been most helpful to me in developing information for this book.

Club membership is $5 per year; individual membership is $2. Write to the Secretary, Maurice J. Forrester, Jr., R.D. #1, Box 91, Ramich Road, Temple, Pennsylvania 19560. I have been a member for years and highly recommend the organization.

A copy of *Pennsylvania Hiking Trails* may be obtained from: Appalachian Trail Conference, P.O. Box 236, Harpers Ferry, West Virginia 25425. Retail price of the book in 1975 was $2.50.

The Appalachian Trail in Pennsylvania

From Pen-Mar on the Maryland-Pennsylvania line, the A.T. extends for 215 miles across the state until reaching the spectacular Delaware Water Gap which separates Pennsylvania and New Jersey. After leaving Maryland, the Trail continues on South Mountain almost to Harrisburg. It leaves the Blue Ridge at that point, crosses the Susquehanna River at Duncannon, ascends steeply to the crest of Peters Mountain and proceeds northeast on Blue Mountain.

The area east of the Susquehanna seldom involves elevations exceeding 1500 feet, but the footway is so extremely rocky that long distance hikers, remembering their sore feet and worn out hiking boots, speak of the Trail in Pennsylvania with considerable respect. Midway in the state is the 15-mile St. Anthony's Wilderness, one of the more interesting stretches in the entire Trail. The mountain ridge east of the Susquehanna is very narrow and the hiker can frequently see vistas on either side of the ridge.

Hikers approaching the Delaware River should reserve sufficient time to enjoy the views from the numerous vantage points provided. This river gorge, and the Potomac gorge separating Maryland and Virginia, are two of the most spectacular river gorges in the East.

Allegheny National Forest

The Allegheny, a forest of some half million acres, is one of but four national forests in the six mid-Atlantic state covered by this book. It is located in the northwestern part of Pennsylvania and touches New York State and New York's Allegany State Park on its northern boundary. The northern part of the forest surrounds Allegheny Reservoir, with its 12,000 acres of water surface and 91 miles of shoreline. A number of the recreation sites are accessible only by boat.

The Allegheny River which bounds the forest on the west is a beautiful river with a lively history of river trade in furs and commodities and of logging rafts and log cabins. One of the trails we hiked, the Tanbark Trail, has its western terminus directly on the river.

There is an excellent map available which shows all of the hiking trails and campgrounds. Write to Allegheny National Forest, P. O. Box 847, Warren, Pennsylvania, 16365, and ask for the map of the Forest, plus the narrative description of each of the marked trails and the names and descriptions of the campgrounds. The reverse side of the map has a listing of the 32 recreation sites, with an indicator showing which of these also has camping facilities. Don't make the mistake we did by assuming that each of those red tee-pee pictures on the map indicates a campsite. Furthermore, even when you have ascertained which of the recreation sites has a campground you can't be sure when the campgrounds are open. All of them are open in the summer months, but only a few stay open year round. Therefore, when you first arrive in the forest it is wise to visit the nearest of the four district offices (located at Sheffield, Marshburg, Marienville, and Ridgway) and obtain up-to-date information as to campsites, trails, and roads.

All of the trails described are marked with either white or blue blazes, but there is little uniformity in the shape or the size of the blaze. The smaller, neater ones were about 2.5 inches by 7 inches with a smaller blaze above the vertical one (the two blazes together look like the letter "i"). But we saw blazes of almost all sizes, the biggest ones having a bottom blaze 20 inches high and four inches wide and the top blaze proportionately smaller. However, the trails are well signed and the paint blazes are frequent — about every 40 yards.

There are no trailside shelters, and backpackers are urged to arrange their hiking schedules so that nightfall will find them at a point where it will be convenient to use one of the 18 designated campsites in the forest. Where this is not feasible, so-called "throw down" camping is permissable — i.e., camping directly beside the trail. I had not heard this expression before but it is certainly very descriptive. Wood fires are permitted. No overnight camping is permitted within 1500 feet of either the scenic drives or the Allegheny Reservoir.

My visit to Allegheny was in mid-May, 1975, in company with Chuck Young, a co-worker of mine from Appalachian Outfitters in Oakton, Virginia. The forest was almost 325 miles from my hone, one of the longest distances I had to travel. We spent two full days in the forest, driving and hiking. If you are interested in bird watching, then mid-May is an ideal time to visit this forest. The migrating birds have already returned, they are in good voice, and the foliage is only partially advanced so that the birds are easy to spot and to study. In May, this forest is also distinguished by large patches of May Apple and bluets — a flower which I had previously associated with the southern Appalachians. And, in driving around adjacent to the forest you will see some of the biggest and thickest stands of bright yellow dandelions that you have ever laid eyes on. Makers of dandelion wine would have an unlimited source of raw material here.

In all, the forest has seven marked and signed trails that total 126 miles. But in our talks with district rangers Paul Brohn of Ridgway and Don Burge of Bradford, and later with Rod Larson, Recreation Specialist in the Supervisor's office at Warren, we learned of planned trail construction for the summer of 1975 — construction that would substantially increase the total trail mileage.

The Allegheny has hiking for everyone, from short family day hikes to longer day hikes, to a 5-7 day backpacking trip on the North Country Trail.

North Country Trail
Distance: 78 miles in May, 1975
Description: The National Trails System Act of 1968 (Public Law 90-543) established two long-distance scenic trails — the Appalachian in the east and the Pacific Crest in the west, as initial components of a nationwide system of long-distance trails. Some 12-14 other trails were placed in a study category with the proviso that they might later, by act of

Author relaxes at oil well.

Congress, be moved into an operations category. One of these study trails was the North Country Trail, which would tie into the A.T. in the northeastern United States, go across the northern states, and join the Lewis and Clark Trail in the west. In the Allegheny National Forest, some 78 miles of the North Country Trail has already been established.

We hiked bits and pieces of this trail as it winds its way south from the Willow Bay Recreation Area, located one mile south of the New York-Pennsylvania state line on the eastern shore of the Allegheny Reservoir. It follows a route south and west to a point 2 miles southeast of Guitonville, near the southern tip of the forest. The trail takes one through the oil well area of Pennsylvania, and we saw and photographed a number of these wells with their old rusting pumps and other oil-drilling apparatus. We followed the trail part way into the Tionesta Scenic Area, a 2,000-acre remnant of the original forest that once covered six million acres on the Allegheny Plateau of New York and Pennsylvania. The trail is marked with double white paint blazes.

Tanbark Trail
Distance: 28 miles
Description: This trail, marked with double blue paint blazes, begins at Tionesta Scenic Area, leads westward through Cherry Run and Henrys Mills, skirts the northern end of Minister Valley Trail, continues on to Hearts Content Scenic Area, and ends at the Allegheny River 8 miles north of Tidioute. Be certain to allow sufficient time to explore the Tionesta and Hearts Content Scenic Areas. If hiking from east to west it would be desirable to plan your hike to arrive at Hearts Content near the end of the day, to use the campground at that point, and to take the short but very beautiful loop trails into the scenic area. It contains a stand of virgin timber — white pine, hemlock, beech, and other hardwoods. It also has a special treat: a tiny stream with an ice cold spring that bubbles out of the ground with loud gurgling noises. Even if you do not plan to stay overnight it would be a shame to hike this close to the scenic area without partaking of its pleasures.

Minister Valley Trail
Distance: 6 miles
Description: Marked with double white paint blazes, this trail would be a pleasant end-of-day departure from the Tanbark Trail. It is a loop, which both begins and ends at different places on the Tanbark and wanders through the Minister Creek Recreation Area throughout its 6-mile length. There is a small campground at the recreation area (5 units).

Twin Lakes Trail
Distance: 6 miles
Description: This is a connecting trail marked with double white paint blazes, and runs between the North Country Trail and the Black Cherry Interpretive Trail. It can easily be located at its southern end, near the junction of Forest Service Roads 948 and 66. The other end begins at a junction point on the Black Cherry Trail. One can backpack, camp at Twin Lakes Campground, get in a swim and a hot shower at Twin Lakes. The shower costs a nominal 10-cents.

Tracy Ridge Trail
Distance: 4 miles
Description: I hiked all of this short trail beginning on Route 321 just north of Tracy Ridge Campground. That trail is marked with double white paint blazes and it skirts the campground. It does *not* go right through as the map would indicate. The trail goes mostly downhill towards the reservoir, hitting the Johnnycake Trail within 15 minutes from

*Mount Rogers National Recreation Area—looking west
into Mount Rogers scenic area. [Photo by U.S. Forest Service.]*

the beginning of your hike. Within sight of the reservoir you join the
North Country Trail. The junction point is marked with a confusing sign
which indicates that the North Country Trail goes south only. But if you
look close you will see the white paint blazes of the North Country
leading north to the Willow Bay Recreation Area, with 68 camp units.
The combination of Tracy Ridge and the swing north on the North
Country Trail makes for a very pleasant 7-8 mile hike.

Johnnycake Trail

Distance: 2 miles

Description: This short trail runs from the Handsome Lake Campground
(accessible only by boat) and joins the Tracy Ridge Trail. It is marked
with double white paint blazes.

Black Cherry Interpretive Trail
Description: This is really two trails, each being a short loop trail begin-
ning on the road across from the entrance to the Twin Lakes Recreation
Site in the extreme east side of the Forest, just south of the McKean-Elk
County Line. One loop is about .6 miles long, the other 1.3 miles long.
Each is marked with pedestal markers identifying trees and flowers in the
area. We hiked both loops and within the first 100 yards had spotted a
seldom seen bird, the Scarlet Tanager, and a seldom seen flower, the
Purple Trillium. The Twin Lakes overnight campground (60 camping
units) is located within the first loop. Entrance to the Twin Lakes Trail is
off the larger loop trail.

WESTERN PENNSYLVANIA

Ask the average American with what activity he associates the American
Youth Hostel movement, and he will reply, "inexpensive overnight accomodations for hikers and bikers." While that answer is generally correct, it is only partly correct in western Pennsylvania.

The Pittsburgh AYH Council does provide overnight lodging facilities
for bikers, hikers, and canoeists. But it has also developed and printed a
150-page, 60,000 word *Hiking Guide to Western Pennsylvania.* Not
content with that effort the Pittsburgh Council actually scouted, marked,
constructed, and now maintains the 140-mile Baker Trail. While I visited
a number of hiking trails in western Pennsylvania I could not visit them
all. For the rest, I relied heavily both on the AYH *Hiking Guide* and on
the information supplied to me by the two backpacking co-editors of the
Guide, Bruce Sundquist and Clifford C. Ham, both of whom reside in
the Pittsburgh area.

The Western Pennsylvania Guide contains descriptions of some 147
trails, and it has a wealth of other information, such as the sources of
various types of maps and literature and major organizations of interest
to hikers, on clothing and equipment for hiking, water purification, and
tips for backpacking the area. Cost of the guide book in 1975 was $2.00
and it can be obtained from: Pittsburgh Council, American Youth
Hostel, 6300 Fifth Avenue, Pittsburgh, Pennsylvania 15232.

Except for the Allegheny National Forest, there is not a great deal of
publicy owned land in this region. Most of the trails go through privately
owned land either entirely or in part. In fact, private land predominates
here more than in any other region in our six-state area.

Clark Run Trail
Distance: 1.8 miles
USGS Quad: Vintondale, Pennsylvania, 7½ minutes; Bureau of Forestry
Map, 1 inch equals .25 mile, free.
Description: Trail begins at parking area, Charles F. Lewis Natural Area,

in Gallitzin State Forest 5 miles west of Johnstown, Pennsylvania on State Route 403. From the parking area proceed up the south side of Clark Run, loop around the top along an old woods road, and return along the north side to the parking area. The entire trail is in the Conemaugh River Gorge. Although short in distance, this trail leads through a superb natural area with some outstanding examples of tuliptree, basswood, sugar maple and yellow birch. The trail is marked with 2 x 6 inch blazes, hot orange color.

The low point in elevation is 1280 feet at parking lot. High point is 1800 feet at the site of an old sawmill. Average elevation of the trail is 1500 feet. No camping is permitted in the Natural Area, but camping is permitted in the State Forest Land on Rager Mountain. This trail is for foot travel only. The map of the area, plus additional information may be obtained from the maintaining agency: Gallitzen State Forest, 131 Hillcrest Drive, Ebensburg, Pennsylvania 15931.

John P. Saylor Memorial Trail
Distance: 11.3 miles
USGS Quad: Ogletown and Windber, Pennsylvania; 7½ minutes. Pensylvania Bureau of Forestry Map 1 inch equals .5 mile, free.
Description: This trail is a memorial to John P. Saylor, an outstanding conservationist, who represented the 22nd Congressional District of Pennsylvania in the U.S. Congress from 1949 until his death in 1973. This is a circuit trail which begins and ends in the Babcock picnic area of the Gallitzin State Forest located .1 mile south of State Route 56, some 10 miles east of Johnstown, Pennsylvania. The trail is marked with 2 x 6 inch hot orange paint blazes, and at road intersections it is marked with the John P. Saylor Trail symbol. Trail elevation varies from a low point of 2180 feet to 2580 feet.

From the starting point, the hiker proceeds east on an old wagon road, which was the former Route 56 from Johnstown to Bedford. At 1.8 miles, you enter into the Clear Shade Wild Area. The wildlife in this area includes deer, turkey, grouse, smaller animals such as fox, beaver, muskrat, and many species of songbirds. Bear are seen occasionally. The area was originally logged between 1898 and 1913, and the hiker will see evidences of logging operations as he proceeds in a southwesterly direction throughout the Clear Shade area. More recent logging has been on a single tree selection basis. Main haul roads have been reseeded to grass and these will be seen during the course of the hike. Near the end of the hike in the Clear Shade area are the remains of an old railroad trestle constructed to maintain the proper grade for logging locomotives.

At 5.8 miles from starting point the hiker reaches the Crumb Road, T-R 816, which marks part of the southern boundary of the Wild Area. At this point, the trail makes almost a complete circle proceeding west, then north and then east, almost back to the Wild Area. At the latter point, 8.5 miles, the hiker passes the site of logging camp 59, used about 1900 by the Babcock Lumber Company. From here the Trail turns north towards the starting point. On the return route it passes near an area of deep rocky crevices and fissures known as Wolf Rocks. A well worn trail leads to the Wolf Rocks viewing point. Continuing north the trail reaches its end point at the picnic grounds in the recreation area, which was built and maintained by the Bureau of Forestry.

Water is available only from wet weather springs. Hikers are urged to carry their own. Backpack camping is permitted, trailer or vehicular camping is prohibited.

For a copy of map and additional information, write to: District Forester, 131 Hillcrest Drive, Ebensburg, Pennsylvania 15931.

Charleroi Interurban

Distance: 25 miles

USGS Quad: Monongahela, Hachett, Glassport, Bridgeville, Pennsylvania; 7½ minutes.

Description: This is one of a number of trails in the Pittsburgh area which follows the route of an abandoned interurban rail line. It is part of the Pittsburgh and Charleroi route of the Pittsburgh Railways Company, and the route is reported to be relatively intact and walkable. One can start at the village of Library, on State Route 88 about 10 miles south of Pittsburgh. From there the route goes generally southeast via Finleyville, Star Mine, Riverview, Monongahela, Black Diamond, Monessen Junction, and into Charleroi. Another spur runs west to Bentleyville and Ellsworth. The route is not clear on USGS maps and hikers will have to search for old trackway especially in towns.

Warrior Trail

Distance: 67 miles (from Greensboro on the Monongahela River in Pennsylvania to Cresaps Bottom on the Ohio River below Moundsville, West Virginia. On State Route 2.

USGS Quads: Masontown, Garards Fort, Oak Forest, Holbrook and New Freeport — of the foregoing are all 7½ minute maps of Pennsylvania; plus Cameron, Glen Easton, and Moundsville in West Virginia.

Description: This trail is but one of the activities of the Warrior Trail Association of Greene County, Pennsylvania, which was begun in 1965. The Association's primary interest seems to be in the fields of archaeology and Indian history. It has more than 150 members, monthly meetings attended by roughly half the membership, and in the 10 years of its existence it has established, marked, and now maintains this 67-mile trail along the high ridge route of a 5000 year old Indian trail. While most Indian trails crossed numerous waterways the Warrior Trail is unique because it does not cross a single stream.

The trail is marked at each mile with a creosoted round post with the words *Warrior Trail* and the mile number carved into it. Between the mile posts, there are a variety of marking devices: (1) routed unpainted wood signs reading Warrior Trail, (2) yellow signs generally at gate cross-

*Never too young to begin to learn to appreciate the joys
of backpacking on the Black Forest Trail of Central Pennsylvania.*

ings, (3) one-inch aluminum strips around trees and posts with the words
Warrior Trail, and (4) four-inch white painted aluminum arrows nailed to
trees and posts.

Unfortunately, both the white arrows and the aluminum strips suffer
heavily from vandals and souvenir hunters. Hence, we found the trail dific-
cult to follow in the two areas in which we hiked in September,
1975. Along with companions Sam Atkinson and Ed and Dan Hanlon, I
went north into Pennsylvania after a pleasant two-day stay at the late
Euell Gibbon's 8th annual Nature Wonder Weekend at North Bend State
Park in West Virginia. Even with help of an experienced trail hiker, who
showed us various points enroute where the trail crossed a road, darted
into a field, or went into a wooded area, we had our problems. Too many
of those little white markers had disappeared.

Leaving Greensboro, Pennsylvania, where we picked up the trail, we
proceeded into Waynesburg and purchased *The Warrior Trail Guide
Book*, with 10 maps included. We drove south to where the trail crosses
State Route 218, at milepoint 22, and hiked the trail for a mile west —
finding a single trail marker in this one mile stretch. We inspected the

very attractive new log shelter and then drove back to Waynesburg for a discussion with Jim Hennen, the local jeweler, who is an officer in the Association. Hennen and his wife work in the jewelry shop during the week and on the Warrior Trail on Sundays. We all agreed that painted blazes would provide a more permanently marked trail.

While it would be easy to criticize the association because of the less than adequate trail marking, who can really fault a volunteer organization that in less than 10 years has created a 67-mile trail, owns its own attractive clubhouse, has built three trailside shelters and produced a good guide book and maps?

Almost all of the trail is on private property, and in addition to the three trailside shelters, nine camping areas have been designated with permission of the owners.

The Warrior Trail Guide Book sells for $2 and the attractive trail patch sells for $1.25. For these two items and for further information, write to: Warrior Trail Association, Inc., County Office Building, Waynesburg, Pennsylvania 15370.

Baker Trail

Distance: 140 miles

USGS Quads: 7½ minute quads from south to north: Freeport, Leechburg, Whitesburg, Elderton, Rural Valley, Plumville, Dayton, Distant, Summerville, Corsica, Cooksburg, Marienville West, Mayburg, Kellettville, and Tylersburg.

Description: Hikers will find it much more practical and economical to buy the *Baker Trail Guidebook,* in which all of the above maps (slightly reduced in size) are reproduced with the trail and shelter identification prominently inserted. Total 1975 cost of the guidebook complete with text and maps was $1.00.

The 140 mile Baker Trail is a monumental contribution by the Pittsburgh Council, American Youth Hostels, Inc., to the hiking and biking fraternity. The Trail is described in condensed form in both the *AYH Hiking Guide to Western Pennsylvania* and in the *KTA Pennsylvania Hiking Trails.* It is described in detail in the 8½ x 11 inch *Baker Trail Guide Book,* 1974 Edition with its supplemental Bikeway Material Current as of the spring of 1975.

I hiked a bit of the Baker Trail in mid-May, 1975, with Chuck Young. This was in the Cook Forest State Park area. In mid-September, 1975 I hiked into the Cochrans Mills Shelter (shelter No. 3 from the south) and over part of the trail in that area. The trail is well identified with both 2 x 6 inch bright yellow blazes and by wooden signs reading "Baker Trail" which are placed along the trail itself and at some road crossings.

The hiker could probably hike the trail from one end to the other by simply following the paint blazes and the signs, but for those planning to use the overnight shelters, the guidebook is a must. Shelters are lo-

Little Crease shelter on Big-Blue Trail.
[Photo by Kevin H. Johnson.]

cated off the main trail and the trails leading to the shelters are not identified — either by signs or by paint blazes. Presumably this is to discourage visits by casual hikers who might engage in some equally casual vandalism. Even with the guidebook, I had difficulty finding the Cochrans Mills Shelter.

In all, there are eleven shelters on the trail, most of them being from 8 to 10 miles apart. Generally, each shelter has water, a latrine, a table, and fireplace. The toilets are only 32-inch square — seemingly built to discourage use by those of broad girth.

The guidebook lists points of interest along the trail, as well as grocery stores, parking areas, and State Park facilities. I visited the grocery store approximately one mile north of the Cochrans Mills Shelter and talked to H.A. King, who operates the store in the tiny village of Brick Church. His family had operated a general store on the same location for 103 years and he was a storehouse of information. He proudly displayed large black and white pictures taken sometime around the turn of the century. One showed the village of Cochrans Mills as it appeared before the area was inundated by the waters formed by the damming of Crooked Creek. He told me further that the shelter I had just visited was near the birthplace of Nellie Bly, the pen name of the American journalist, Elizabeth Cochrane (1867-1922).

I mention this incident to encourage hikers to take time out now and then to visit with those living near the hiking trail. Especially in western Pennsylvania, where many of the trails go over private property, it is a matter of courtesy to speak with the landowner. Many landowners give permission for the trail right-of-way because they like hikers and like to visit with them. Those hikers who engage in such visiting find that they develop a much stronger affinity for the trail and its people and that the hiking experience is much the richer.

In addition to the 11 shelters there are a number of primitive campsites to be found along the trail. At other places permission may be obtained from a landowner to camp in his fields or woods.

There is currently a gap of five miles between the north end of the Baker Trail and the North Country Trail in the Allegheny National Forest. Hikers desiring to bridge this gap may do so by using existing roads. A hiking trail is eventually expected to provide a link between the two trails.

The trail is open to all and no permissions or permits are needed. The Baker Trail is appropriate for short nature walks, day hikes, or extended backpacking trips. Among the interesting features along the trail are the 8,000-acre Cook Forest with its virgin hemlocks, white pines and other large trees; the Clarion River and Hemlock Island; Redbank Creek, Mahoning Dam and Reservoir; Russell Hill, Crooked Creek, and the bluffs overlooking the Allegheny River near Freeport. Even the bridges are interesting. There is a cable bridge, a covered bridge, a pagoda style bridge, and a zig-zag bridge; there are log bridges, and over some streams no bridges at all. And at some times of the year the "no bridge" situation can be most interesting!

In 1973 the Baker Trail area was scouted for a parallel bikeway. The details of this bikeway are included in the current edition of the Baker Trail Bikeway guidebook ($1.50; contains maps for both hiking and biking).

The Baker Trail guidebook ($1.00), a green and gold patch of the Baker Trail (75-cents), and up-to-date, free information may be obtained by writing to: American Youth Hostels, Inc., 6300 Fifth Avenue, Pittsburg, Pennsylvania 15232, or telephone on Thursday evenings only from 8 p.m. to 11 p.m., 412/362-8181.

Laurel Highlands Hiking Trail

Distance: 75 miles when completed; 57 miles completed as of September, 1975; remaining 18 miles to be completed in 1976.

Location: From Ohiopyle, Route 381 in Fayette County to Seward, Route 56 in Indiana County (5 miles from Johnstown, Pennsylvania).

USGS Quads: 7½ minute Quads from Ohiopyle: Kingwood, Mill Run, Seven Springs, Ohiopyle, Rachelwood, Boswell, Ligonier, Bakersville; 8½ x 13 inch map available free from Laurel Ridge State Park; 11 x 22 inch 3-color contour map available ($1.95 plus 25-cents for postage and tax) from Ligonier Mountain Outfitters, Route 30, Laughlintown, Pennsylvania 15655; pocket guide and map being prepared by the Commonwealth of Pennsylvania expected to be completed late in 1976.

Description: Laurel Ridge State Park, R.D. 3, Rockwood, Pennsylvania 15557; telephone 412/455-3744. Note: The Rockwood address is the *mailing* address. The Park office and maintenance buildings are located a mere 200 yards east of the trail on Route 653. Parking area and visitor center at that point.

Description: The temporary trail entrance begins at the village of Ohiopyle at a point some 300 yards east of the Wilderness Voyageur store (freeze dry food and other backpacking supplies and equipment available here). This first section ascends from a low of 1400 feet at Ohiopyle to a peak of 2712 feet at the 9 mile mark. The terrain from Ohiopyle to the 9 mile mark is very rugged and mountainous, with the 6 to 9 mile area being almost total ascent (not recommended for the beginning backpacker hiking south to north). After the 9 mile mark the trail levels out and remains around 2300 feet until the shelter area on Route 653. In general the first 18 miles is very rugged and should be attempted only by expert hikers who are certain they can hike the entire 18 miles until the new shelter area is completed at the 6.5 mile point. Camping is permitted only in shelter areas.

This first section of trail has many beautiful streams and is surrounded by much rhododendron and mountain laurel. There is an overlook at mile 2.3 with a spectacular view of the Youghiogheny River Gorge below.

Wildlife found on the trail includes deer, grouse, turkey, and a few bear. Rattlesnakes and black snakes may also be found. There are many other small birds and animals.

The 14-mile section from Route 653 north to Route 31 is a fairly easy section. Three overnight shelter areas are available at mile 18 (Route 653), at mile 24, and at mile 32 (Route 31). This section is highly recommended for the novice backpacker or the Sunday hiker. Approximately 2 miles north of Route 653 there is a very pretty overlook at mile 21. After passing the shelter area at mile 24 the trail continues north passing by the back slopes of the Seven Springs ski resort. The elevation of the entire section stays near 2700 feet.

In the summer of 1975 the 25 mile section of trail from Route 31 to Route 271 was completed. At the same time another shelter area was opened at mile 46.5 (just off U.S. Route 30). An additional shelter area at mile 38 is expected to be completed in 1976. The terrain in the first 15 miles of this section varies from 2400 to 2800 feet with several steep climbs. The Pennsylvania Turnpike is crossed at mile 36.8. North of the Route 30 shelter area the Trail rambles on for another 11 miles to Route 271. The elevation varies from 2500 to 2900 feet. The terrain is rugged and seems similar to the mountainous Ohiopyle section with its steep hills and deep valleys.

The final section of the trail from Route 271 to Route 56 near Johnstown is expected to be completed by the summer of 1976. It will include a shelter area at Route 271 (mile 57) and one at mile 66. It will also have a 30 car parking area at Route 56 near Seward, Pennsylvania (about 5 miles from Johnstown). This section is still under construction and is therefore not open to hiking at the present time. The preceding trail description is taken almost verbatim from information supplied to me by Robert J. Hufman, Superintendent of Laurel Ridge State Park.

All told, there will be six parking areas of 30 cars each located several hundred yards and out of sight of the trail. By winter, 1975, four of them were completed.

Each of the 8 shelter areas is complete with 5 adirondack shelters that are equipped with fireplaces, water pumps and sanitary facilities and hold from 4 to 6 people. Each area has space for 30 tents. There are streams along the trail which may be used for water at one's own risk, but there is safe drinking water at the shelter and parking areas.

The trail is very well marked with yellow blazes 1 inch wide by 5 inches long. Connector trails to parking and shelter areas are marked with blue blazes the same size. The time required to hike the trail varies greatly with the direction and section picked to hike, and also with the experience of the hiker. The 18 miles north from Ohiopyle to Route 653 averages about a hard 12 hours whereas the 14 miles from Route 653 to Route 31 can be done in less than 5 hours by a person who is a fairly fast hiker.

The Laurel Highlands Hiking Trail and its facilities are open year-round. The shelters are on a first come first served basis — no reservations are needed or taken. It is advisable to bring a tent along and not depend on getting a shelter — especially on weekends. No fire permits are required for the shelter areas. And, to repeat, *no camping is permitted anywhere but in the shelter areas.*

Food and lodging are available near the Trail at the following places: *Ohiopyle Area* — (Farmington and Uniontown). There are several stores in the trailhead area at Ohiopyle. *Farmington* — 9 miles south: Fort Necessity National Battlefield; Green Acres Motel; and Travelers Rest Motel. *Uniontown* — 9 miles on 40 west from Farmington: Mount Summit Inn. *Route 653, [Normalville and Somerset]* — Normalville, 6 miles west on 653: Dairy Bar Gas Station. *Somerset* (20 miles east on 653: Cobblers Motel; Highlander Motel; Holiday Inn; Maple Lane Motel; and McDonalds. *Route 31, Donegal, Bakersville and Somerset. Donegal* — 9 miles west on 31: The Maple Pot; Mom's Valley Inn; Donegal Motel; Holiday Inn; Sandman Motor Lodge. At Bakersville, 4 miles east on 31: Tall Timbers Restaurant and Gas Station; Bolands Dairy Bar and Oakhurst Tea Room.

Route 30, Ligonier and Jennerstown — Ligonier, 7 miles on 30 west: Gay Nineties Dairy Queen; Ligonier Towne House Restaurant; Holiday Inn. At Jennerstown, 4 miles on 30 east: Laurel Manor Motel and White Star Motel. *Route 271, Ligonier and Johnstown* — Ligonier, 12 miles on 271 south: and Johnstown, 5 miles on 271 north: Sheraton Inn; McDonald's; Holiday Inn; The Downtowner Motor Hotel. *Route 56, Seward and Johnstown* — Seward, 1 mile on 56 west and Johnstown, 7 miles on 56 east.

Comments: I visited the area in mid-September, 1975, hiking part of the trail at the Ohiopyle entrance, then driving north to inspect both the trail and its facilities on Route 653. I examined with considerable fascination the trailhead parking facilities, noting the spaces for 30 cars, the water pump, and the large wooden sign with its colored trail routes to assist the hiker in proceeding from the trailhead parking area to the main trail and to the shelter area. I next went to the visitor center, located perhaps 200 yards east of the trail intersection and from there walked to the shelter area. While I was greatly impressed with all aspects of the Laurel Highlands Hiking Trail, I was particularly captivated by its trailside shelter concepts. Each of the five shelters was of ingenious design with a wide 6 foot high stone fireplace directly in front of each shelter. The fireplace was so positioned that a shelter occupant could sit on the floor of the shelter and tend the cooking fire in the fireplace. The top of the fireplace chimney was tied into the shelter's overhanging roof.

Sturdy 1.5 inch eyebolts had been fastened into the shelter structure and into the masonry fireplace to make it easy for shelter occupants to

Shelter cluster in Laurel Ridge State Park, western Pennsylvania.
[Photo by Johnstown Tribune-Democrat.]

lash their tarps to the eyebolts and close in the shelter from rain, wind, and cold. Such a shelter, with a fire blazing merrily in the fireplace, could be a very pleasant haven on a cold night.

Each shelter cluster is out of sight and sound of both the trailhead parking area and of the highway from which it is serviced. Road access is by authorized park personnel only via a locked gate. But it is the concept of the shelter *cluster* that is really intriguing. Hiking trails have been receiving greatly increased use in recent years. As a consequence the single lone shelters spaced every 7 or 8 miles along major trails have suffered from overuse. In the Shenandoah National Park of Virginia this question was solved effectively from the Park's standpoint, but harshly from the hikers' view. In that park, all of the wooden sleeping bunks were torn out of the shelters in 1974 and the shelters declared out of bounds for overnight use. Backpackers were not permitted to sleep *inside* them, nor were they permitted to pitch their tents within sight of the shelters. This policy has been enforced with a vigor that many backpackers find highly disconcerting (especially when they are forced to move their tents in the dark of night!). The Laurel Highlands shelter areas, combining both shelters and cleaned out campsites, seems to be a much more desirable solution to the overuse problem.

I left the Laurel Highlands area convinced that I had examined a trail system that embodied all of today's most advanced concepts of trail design and construction. It could well become a model for future trail programs — both state and federal.

Sandy Beaver Trail

Distance: 23 miles

USGS Quads: West Point and East Liverpool North, Ohio; plus free map available from Columbiana Council, B.S.A., 24 North Park Avenue, Lisbon, Ohio 44432.

Description: This 23-mile trail begins at a point just east of East Liverpool, Ohio. The precise point is a historical marker on Ohio Route 39 on the boundary line between Ohio and Pennsylvania. From here the Trail proceeds north on a dirt road on the western side of Little Beaver Creek. At about milepoint 6 the trail passes through the Beaver Creek Church Camp (water, phone, toilet facilities). It goes past the restored Lost Lock at 8 miles and at 9 miles crosses the creek on the highway bridge (State Route 170) at Fredericktown. At this point the trail leaves the original towpath of the former Sandy Beaver Canal, goes west on an old bridle path and follows the creek on the north side for the rest of the hike.

Midpoint of the Trail is the Beaver Creek State Park where there is camping, water and toilets. In the region near the State Park there are ruins of old canal locks, restored buildings, a covered bridge and an operating grist mill.

West of the Beaver Creek State Park the trail follows the Dogwood Trail to Ohio Route 7. Continue to hike the north side of the creek. At

Bob King, a trailblazer in the literal sense of the word.
[Photo by John Amberson.]

Route 7, follow the highway to the intersection of Columbiana County Road 419 and Bear Hollow Road. West of Lusk Locks area there is considerable undergrowth. Trail ends at intersection with Road 901 near the village of Elkton.

This trail was established by the Order of the Arrow, Columbiana Council, B.S.A. The free map by the Columbiana Council contains a form on which a Scoutmaster or other leader can certify as to the number of Scouts and adults who have completed the entire hike. They then become eligible to receive the Sandy Beaver patch ($1.00 per patch). The map also contains a narrative of the trail describing points of interest along the route. Unfortunately it gives no mileages nor does the map (there are actually five small maps) contain any scale.

In addition to the hiking trail, there are 14 miles of excellent Class and Class II canoeing available from the park office (Beaver Creek State Park) to the Ohio River.

CENTRAL PENNSYLVANIA

Black Forest Trail [Lycoming and Potter Counties]
Distance: 42 miles
Map: Excellent five color map 30 x 24 inch available for $1.25. Send check payable to Tiadaghton Fire Fighters Association, c/o Bureau of Forestry, 423 E. Central Avenue, South Williamsport, Pennsylvania, 17701. The Pennsylvania Official Transportation Map shows this trail also.
Description: The name Black Forest is derived from the dense, dark (black) virgin coniferous forests. The trail is blazed with orange dots about three inches in diamter. Construction and maintenance was and is done by the Pennsylvania Bureau of Forestry, Tiadaghton District. A forester by the name of John Eastlake is credited with the conception and marking of the original route.

The 30 x 24 inch map identified above is something more than a map. It has some 24 pictures around its borders and the reverse of the map contains a wealth of detailed geologic, historical, and trail data, including a detailed trail log, showing by milepoint every significant feature, trail junction point and road intersection that the hiker will encounter. The trail was measured with a 165 foot tape, and mileage points are shown to the hundredth of a mile; conversions to kilometers are also shown. The map also notes the location of two blue blazed cross country ski trails, the George B Will Trail (6 miles) and the Santiero di Shay Trail (12.6 miles). Details of these trails, plus several lesser trails included on the reverse side of the map.

The trail officially begins just west of State Route 414, some 27 miles north of the city of Jersey Shore. Actual zero point is in a pine plantation .8 mile from the village of Slate Run. The only major highway crossed is State Route 44, which is reached at mile points 12.8 and 23.19. All the trail data on the reverse side of the map is shown in a counter clockwise direction, and it would be easier to hike it in that fashion if one plans to use the trail data on the reverse of the map. The two marked and signed ski trails, plus a number of other maintained trails make possible a variety of circle and side hike combinations. In addition there is both a north link at about mile point 13.5 and a south link at mile point 21.55 trail connecting the Black Forest Trail with the extensive Susquehannock Trail. The north link trail was constructed in 1975 and is not on either the Pennsylvania Official Transportation Map or the Black Forest Map. These links, providing access to the Susquehannock and thence to the Donut Hole Trail System, have tremendous hiking and backpacking opportunities.

There are no shelters on the Black Forest Trail (BFT), but symbols on the map show the location of frequent campsites and sources of drinking water. Lowest point of the trail is at 900 feet and the highest at 2100 feet. There are plenty of ups and down with fine vistas every few miles, as the trail winds up to heights overlooking Slate Run, Red Run, Morris Run, Big Dam Hollow, and others. In contrast to the up and down walking, the trail also provides less strenuous hiking on the pleasant grades of old railroad lines and lumber haul roads originally built in the early 1900's.

No fire or camping permits are required but hikers are expected to restrict wood fires to evening and early morning. They are also expected to leave all cans, bottles, and aluminum foil at home and to pack out everything they bring into the forest.

For those who feel uncomfortable without the USGS Quad maps, here are the ones for the Black Forest Trail: Lee Fire Tower, Cedar Run, and Slate Run, Pennsylvania 7½ minutes. But most hikers will find the BFS map more than adequate for their needs. Black Forest Trail patches are available for $1.00 each from the same source as the BFT map. Accommodations may be had at the Manor Hotel or the Black Forest Inn in Slate Run, Pennsylvania, or at the Cedar Run Inn at Cedar Run, Pennsylvania.

Susquehannock Trail System — Potter County
Distance: Circuit trail of 85 miles
Maps: A set of 19 reproduced USGS Quad maps with the trail route shown in heavy black lines is available from the Potter County Recreation, Inc., P.O. Box 245, Coudersport, Pennsylvania 16915. The price for the entire set in 1975 was $1.50 plus 25-cents postage. An 8½ x 13 inch reduced scale map of the entire trail system is also available from the same source. One can also obtain a 20 x 40 inch map of the STS available from Susquehannock Trail System, Secretary Betty Ahn, Route 6, Ulysses, R.D. 1, Pennsylvania 16948. Cost: $1.50 Postpaid.
Description: The Susquehannock Trail Club constructed and now maintains an 85-mile loop trail in north central Pennsylvania about 10 miles east of Coudersport. The loop trail links many old CCC fire trails, old logging roads, and railroad grades. It is marked on its northern end and southern end by 10 foot high wooden signs. Another sign has a complete map of the entire trail system. The Northern Gateway is on U.S. 6 in the vicinity of Denton Hill State Park, while the Southern Gateway is at Cross

Fork on State Route 144. Cross Fork is the only village crossed in the 85 mile loop; it has a motel, restaurant and grocery store.

A pleasant point from which to begin hiking this trail is the Susquehannock Lodge which is about 10 miles east of Coudersport and 3 miles east of the Denton Hill Susquehannock Trail sign on U.S. 6. The lodge, operated by Will and Betty Ahn, caters to hikers and provides meals, lodging, and even a generous stock of freeze dry foods. Both Will and Betty are members of the Trail Club and can provide much helpful advice and even car shuttle service for hiking parties. For reservations write to Susquehannock Lodge, Route 6 R.D., Ulysses, Pennsylvania 16948. Telephone: 814/435-2163.

I visited this trail in late September, 1975, checking out parts of it at the Southern Gateway, at the Ole Bull State Park where I spent the night, and at the Northern Gateway. Most of my hiking was done in the latter area in a steady rain after the area had already suffered through some 66 hours rain. The trail was a small river in places and elsewhere sizeable ponds had appeared. Even so, I had no trouble following the 2 x 6 inch international orange paint blazes. I was intrigued by the use of the double blaze to indicate a change in direction of the trail, with the top blaze canted a bit to indicate which way the turn should be made. In addition to the blazes, the trail is marked rather frequently with the orange STS symbol.

A detailed guidebook entitled *Big Susque Country* has a comprehensive topographic map, on which appears the location of springs (W) and telephones (T). This map as well as those described above, is obtainable from Potter County Recreation, Inc. The same organization will, on request, furnish a folder listing some two dozen inns, motels, cabins, campgrounds, and restaurants in the area. The guidebook describes the trail in a clockwise direction beginning at the Northern Gateway, but the hiking can begin at any convenient spot and proceed in either direction.

From the Gateway the trail goes east and south passing near Lyman Run State Park, then south to Cherry Springs Fire Tower, and through Ole Bull State Park, which is an excellent overnight camping spot. Approximately 4 miles south of Ole Bull the North Link (2 x 6 inch blue blazes) connects in 8 miles with the 42-mile Black Forest Trail. Another 4 miles south of the North Link there is the 6 mile long South Link connection with the Black Forest Trail, marked with 3 inch solid blue circles (nothing like a bit of variety in the blazing). These two links open up a variety of circuit hikes into the Black Forest Trail area. Shortly after the South Link intersection, the Susquehannock Trail turns west and in 10 miles reaches the village of Cross Forks (Southern Gateway). From there the trail bears generally north going through the Hammersley Run Wild Area, crossing the East Fork Road and reaching Patterson Park Picnic Area at State Route 44 before making the final leg north to the Lyman Run area and back to the Northern Gateway. The new Donut Hole Trail

System connects with the Susquehannock about 4 miles east of Cross Fork. From this trail connection, the hiker can go southwest through Kettle Creek State Park, cross Kettle Creek at that point and proceed south to State Route 120.

There are no shelters on the Susquehannock Trail System and no plans for building any. Hikers are permitted to camp anywhere on the trail and to build fires, using proper precautions. All of the trail is on state forest property.

There is an award and an emblem ($1.25) for hiking the entire 85 miles in one or more hikes. Write to Mrs. Betty Ahn at the Susquehannock Lodge for information as to requirements for obtaining the award.

Darlington Trail

Distance: 25 miles

USGS Quad: 7½ minute: Wertzville, Harrisburg East, Harrisburg, West Enders, Grantville, all in Pennsylvania.

KTA Map 4; PATC Map 1.

Description: This 25-mile trail, identified by 2 x 6 inch orange paint blazes, is bisected by the Susquehanna River. It provides a 65-mile circuit hike using the Horse-Shoe Trail and the A.T. as the other parts of the circuit. Named for the late Bishop Darlington, a hiking enthusiast, the Darlington Trail is maintained by the Susquehanna Appalachian Trail Club of Harrisburg.

The trail begins at Sterrets Gap on State Route 34 at the gas station and snack bar. From Sterrets Gap until its junction with the A.T. 1.7 miles east, the Darlington Trail and the Tuscarora Trail occupy the same route. The Darlington shelter is 0.1 mile north of the intersection of the three trails. From its junction with the A.T., the Darlington proceeds almost due east toward the Susquehanna, through Millers Gap and Lambs Gap enroute. At 12.5 miles there is a good view from the end of the ridge. From that point the trail turns south and descends steeply to reach U.S. Routes 11 and 15 at 13 miles. My daughter Sharon and I can vouch for the excellent restaurant at this point, the "Summerdale Junction." From the William Grove steam engine, outside the restaurant, right down to the last polished red lamp inside, the motif is that of an old time railroad station.

The new George Wade Bridge takes automobile traffic across the Susquehanna on Route 81, but the bridge is *verboten* for hikers — a strange commentary on the zeal with which our civilization promotes automobile traffic at the expense of the pedestrian. Be that as it may, the hiker *must* get across that bridge in some mechanized manner so that he can proceed to hike the 12.5 miles of the Darlington Trail on the east side of the river.

From the east side of the river, proceed north on U.S. Routes 22 and 322 until reaching State Route 39 (Linglestown Road). Follow 39 for 0.2 mile and at end of a railroad overpass, turn left on paved road. After reaching the top of the ridge on Blue Mountain (site of Darlington Monument), the trail turns almost due east. At 5 miles you will reach Pletz Pass, with side trail and road to Linglestown, and at 9.4 miles you will come to Heckets Gap and the Mt. Laurel Church. At 12 miles the yellow blazed Horse-Shoe Trail comes in on the left, and the two trails occupy the same route until reaching Manada Gap and the end of the Darlington Trail.

There is no detailed map of this area other than the USGS Quad and the sketch map that appears in the KTA *Pennsylvania Hiking Trails*.

Donut Hole Trail System

Distance: The main north-south trail running from State Route 120 north to junction with the Susquehannock Trail is 32 miles long. However, the side trails open up another 40-50 miles of hiking possibilities.

Maps: Set of four 11 x 16 inch maps of the "Donut Hole Trail System" (Sproul State Forest) issued free. Write to Department of Environmental Resources, P.O. Box 1467, Harrisburg, Pennsylvania 17120, and the District Forester, Star Route, Renovo, Pennsylvania 17764.

Description: Other than the large scale maps (2 inches equals 1 mile), and the information appearing in *Pennsylvania Hiking Trails*, there is precious little written information available on the trail. My information has been obtained from that source, plus knowledge gained from inspection of the trail at its southern end and at Kettle State Park and from correspondence and telephone conversation with personnel of the Sproul State Forest at Renovo, Pennsylvania. The Donut Hole Trail System is probably one of the lesser known trail systems in Pennsylvania, but it lies in such a beautiful part of the state that it should not be omitted from one's itinerary— either auto or hiking. The southern part of the area is bounded by State Route 120, an east-west road that goes closely beside the banks of two very impressive streams: the Sinnemahoning Creek and the West Branch of the Susquehanna.

Turning north off Route 120 at Westport, one follows a paved road known officially as Legislative Road 18003, but known locally as the Kettle Creek Road. It, too, stays close to the stream banks, affording the motorist beautiful views of the rushing waters. Some 6 miles north of Westport lies the Kettle Creek State Park with two extensive camping areas. Within the park, the A.R. Bush Dam creates a 1.5 mile lake clearly visible from the road.

In the southern end of the park there is a parking area for hikers only. Directly beside this is a large wooden sign on which is portrayed in color the various trails that make up the Donut Hole Trail System.

To hike the main trail from south to north one would proceed north off of Route 120 onto Montour Road for .3 mile. Montour Road is 28 miles southeast of Emporium on Route 120 and it is about 4-5 miles east of the village of Sinnemahoning. At the .3 mile point on Montour Road there is a trail to the right with a wooden sign reading "Bell Run Trail." I drove up Montour Road in a steady rain looking for a trail that I naively assumed would contain some reference to "Donut Hole." When I came upon the Bell Run sign (in my written notes it appears as Belle Hole Trail but we will ignore that minor inconsistency), I ignored it and charged up the mountain in low gear for another 2.5 miles in a futile search for the Donut Hole Trail.

Returning to the Bell Run (Belle Hole) trail sign, I consulted the KTA description and found that that was where I should have stopped in the first place. I sloshed up the orange blazed trail for a quarter mile, seeing rivulets which had been born of the 48-hour rain. The trail sign, which read Bell Run Trail gave no further information, nothing to indicate where the trail went or how far it was to any point of interest. *I mention these things to emphasize how important it is to obtain the maps before attempting to hike the Donut Hole Trail System.* In actuality the trail proceeds generally northwest for some 15 miles before crossing Kettle Creek at the lower campground in the Kettle Creek State Park. In making this 15-mile distance the hiker will be on some 11 different trails and roads.

Continuing on the trail north of Kettle Creek Park, it is 6 miles to the Tamarack Fire Tower and another 11 miles to the junction with the Susquehannock Trail System.

There are no shelters, but camping and fire building are permitted within the forest. Kettle Creek State Park would be an ideal central camping spot for those wishing to do day hiking only. More detailed information can be obtained by writing or visiting the Sproul Forest headquarters at Renovo, Pennsylvania.

Loyalsock

Distance: 57 miles

USGS Quads: Montoursville, Huntersville, Picture Rocks, Hillsgrove, Eagles Mere, and Laporte, Pennsylvania. 7½ minute maps. For those hiking the Loyalsock Trail (LT) a better arrangement is to buy the excellent 24-page *Guide to the Loyalsock Trail and Side Trails*, with the three Loyalsock maps included. Total price for guide and maps: $2.00 in 1975.

Description: Loyalsock—derived from an Indian word that means middle creek—is the name of one of the most beautiful trails in Pennsylvania, the joys of which first were introduced to me through the extensive color slide collection of George and Mary Spring, both working members of the Alpine Club. The Loyalsock has elevations from a low of 665 feet to a high of 2140 feet, with most of the trail being at the 1700 to 1900 foot elevation. The trail was laid out to take advantage of as many vista points, waterfalls, and other beauty spots as possible. There are eight main sections on the LT, each accessible from either end by automobile, a situation which makes day hiking and car shuttling very convenient. Side trails, loop trails, and lead-in trails are all identified by different colored metal disks. The total length, 57 miles, makes it especially suitable for Boy Scout groups working on their *50 Miler* hikes. Distances in the Guide are in hundredths of a mile, and measuring was done with a 52.8 foot chain. Even without benefit of the "new math" I was able to fiture out that 100 such chains would equal exactly 5280 feet or one mile.

There are no shelters in the LT system of trails, but camping is permitted and the guidebook identifies suggested campsites. Tent and trailer space and cabins are available from Millers Grocery, Forsville, Pennsylvania and also at Worlds End State Park. The park is crossed by the LT at milepoint 44.

Most experienced backpackers and trail maintaining organizations believe that a painted blaze is the most durable, reliable, vandal-proof and theft-proof manner of marking a trail. The Williamsport, Pennsylvania Alpine Club believes firmly in round metal disks nailed to trees with aluminum nails. The disks are three-inch can covers which are saved by club members, neighbors, and office associates. Painting sessions are arranged in which hundreds of can covers are painted on one side only and allowed to dry. At a later date they are painted on the other side (a must to prevent rust) and at a still later date the *LT* symbol or other symbols are painted in.

Embroidered LT patches are available to those who have hiked at least 10 miles of the trail. The guidebook and maps, the patch, and information on the Loyalsock Trail, may be obtained by writing to the LT Chairman, Williamsport Alpine Club, P.O. Box 501, Williamsport, Pennsylvania 17701.

The Alpine Club is an organization of between 40 and 50 members with a hard corps of perhaps 8 to 10 workers. The Loyalsock Trail system is an impressive example of what can be done by a small group of dedicated workers.

An actual size reprint of one page of the guidebook appears opposite.

Big Blue — Tuscarora Trail

In the early 1960's, the Appalachian Trail Conference, alarmed by the deteriorating condition of the A.T. in northern Virginia, authorized a long distance loop trail that would depart from the A.T. in the northern section of the Shenandoah National Park, swing west into the George Washington National Forest, then north through Hancock, Maryland (crossing the Potomac River at that point), and into Pennsylvania. In Pennsylvania the trail would follow the Tuscarora mountain ridge, then gradually swing north and east until rejoining the A.T. near the Darlington lean-to, approximately 12 miles south of the A.T. crossing of the Susquehanna River at Duncannon, Pennsylvania. Various names were suggested for this new trail but it was finally agreed that in Virginia and West Virginia, it would be called the Big Blue Trail and would be identified with blue blazes, whereas in Maryland and Pennsylvania it would be called the Tuscarora Trail and be marked with orange blazes.

Those who conceived this new trail felt that, at the very least, it

Mileage		Elevation
	Red X trail leads left to re-join LT at 3.38 m, and right is one mile to Pa. Highway 87.	
1.73	Spring and campsite. (Start to Crooked Riffles campsite 1.73 m. 2 hr.)	1540'
1.92	Trail takes left fork of woods road.	
	Road to right leads to dead end at proposed Vista in 1.5 m.	
1.95	Trail leaves road sharp left through oak woods with rough terrain.	
2.15	Crest of the Allegheny Ridge. Trail follows crest of ridge for 1.25 m. and in several places skirts the very edge of rock ledges affording fine views from outlooks.	1800'
3.38	Trail turns downhill on woods road.	1800'
	Red X trail comes in from left.	
3.51	Woods road intersection. Trail takes left fork.	
	Straight down road leads .90 m. to Kaiser Hollow on blue trail.	
3.60	Woods road intersection. Trail takes left fork.	1680'

4

would provide hikers with another side trail off the A.T. of some 200 miles into some very interesting country. It would also provide insurance for the A.T. so that if the situation in northern Virginia became intolerable, the Trail could be rerouted over the Big Blue-Tuscarora. The new loop also presented the opportunity for hikers to take an almost 400-mile circuit hike utilizing the Big Blue-Tuscarora for the major part of the circuit and the A.T. for the remainder.

In the following pages we will describe that part of the new trail that exists in Pennsylvania and Maryland, approximately 105 miles. The remaining 150 miles will be described under the headings for the other two states of Virginia and West Virginia. My daughter Sharon and I explored the Maryland-Pennsylvania part of the trail from south to north by car and foot in early June, 1975, at a time when the mountain laurel were just coming into blossom and when the air was heavy with the fragrance of wild azalea and black locust flowers. The guiding spirit behind the Tuscarora Trail since the first mile of trail was marked in 1968 and is hard working: Albert McDonald, of Keystone Trails Associates, 10781 Helmer Drive, Philadelphia, Pennsylvania 19154.

And, while the entire trail is generally referred to in conversation as the Big Blue-Tuscarora I will, since we are discussing trails in Pennsylvania, hereafter refer to it simply as the Tuscarora Trail. The book, *Pennsylvania Hiking Trails*, published by KTA, has eight pages of maps and eight pages of narrative description of the trail showing its route from *north* to *south*. For convenience I will describe the Tuscarora Trail in the same north to south manner as has been done in the KTA publication.

Tuscarora Trail

Section 1: distance, 9 miles; elevation, minimum 583 feet, maximum 1350 feet; USGS Quads: 7½ minute Shermans Dale, Landisburg, or 15 minutes New Bloomfield, Loysville.

The northern terminus at A.T. is .1 mile south of the Darlington lean-to. Nearest approach by car is at Sterretts Gap on State Route 34, just north of its intersection with State Route 944. From the A.T., the trail goes generally west and for the first 1.7 miles you will follow the orange blazes of both the Tuscarora and the Darlington Trail. At Sterretts Gap, where there is a gas station and snack bar, you leave the Darlington and continue on the Tuscarora westward through private property and nearby wild life refuges, reaching maximum elevation of 1350 feet at milepoint 6.6. Begin your gradual descent following Polecat Road for some two miles and reaching the end of Section 1 on State Route 74 at elevation 583 feet.

Section 2: distance, 10.5 miles; elevation minimum 583 feet, maximum 1850 feet; USGS Quads: 15 minutes Loysville or 7½ minutes Landisburg and Andersonburg.

Section begins at elevation 583 feet at a gas station on State Route 74 near the intersection with Polecat Road. Park cars at 0.6 milepoint west of State Route 74. At 3 miles you reach the high point of the section — 1850 feet on Barkley Ridge. McClure's Gap is 3.5 miles and Berry's Gap is 5.7 miles. At 7.1 miles a side trail to the right leads to Trout Run and into Kennedy Valley. At 9.4 miles reach the intersection of Flat Rock Trail (to the left) and the Warner Trail (to the right). At 9.7 miles there is excellent spring at sharp turn. At 10.5 miles reach State Route 233, the end of section. To continue on Tuscarora Trail turn right along State Route 233 for 100 yards, then left into State House Trail. Ahead 500 feet on Route 233 is the Park Superintendent Office on your left and a telephone booth on your right. To reach the park campground, continue on Route 233 another one-fourth mile.

Section 3: distance, 9 miles; elevation, minimum 750 feet, maximum 2000 feet; USGS Quads: 15 minutes Loysville and Shippensburg or 7½ minutes Andersonburg.

The section begins at elevation 750 feet on State Route 233 at a point 500 feet south of the park Superintendent's office in Col. Denning State Park. The trail follows the State House Trail for .3 miles, then bears left with a steady climb for the first mile, then an even steeper climb for the next half-mile until reaching the ridge (1600 feet) that separates Perry and Cumberland Counties. At 9 miles the trail reaches the "ramp road" (incline not passable by car) at an elevation of 2000 feet.

Section 4: distance, 18 miles; elevation, minimum, 815 feet, maximum 2200 feet; USGS Quads: 15 minutes Shippensburg, or 7½ minutes Newburg, Doylesburg and Shade Gap.

The section begins at the "ramp road" and promptly crosses Cowpens Road. At 2.5 miles pass the Sherman Mountain Fire Tower; at 6.1 miles find shelter on your right, and a spring on your left. The trail turns southwest and follows the ridge in that same direction for another 8 or 9 miles. At 17.5 miles one reaches the end of Knob Mountain and begins descending, reaching State Highway 641 at 18 miles.

Section 5: distance, 9.3 miles; elevations, minimum 815 feet, maximum 1900 feet; USGS Quads, 7½ minutes Shade Gap, Fannettsburg, Burnt Cabins; 15 minutes Orbisonia quad (out of print).

This section begins at State Highway 641. Turn left and go south for .2 mile and then turn right on a dirt road that is passable by automobile. Reach State Route 75 at .9 mile and turn right on this paved road. At 1.1 mile turn left off the highway, and from that point on you follow a series of roads and lanes, gaining elevation, and hiking generally in a southwesterly direction. At 4.4 miles you reach elevation 1900 feet and turn left on crest of the Tuscarora Mountain. At 6.4 miles, cross over the Tuscarora Tunnel of Pennsylvania Turnpike. At 9.3 miles, having descended to 1537 feet you reach the Fannettsburg-Burnt Cabins road and the end of the section. Turn right to continue on trail.

Section 6: distance, 12.5 miles; elevation, minimum 1050 feet, maximum

On the Big Blue-Tuscarora Trail
are Fred Blackburn [left] and Al McDonald.

2458 feet; USGS Quads, 7½ minutes Fannettsburg, Burnt Cabins, McConnellsburg, plus the 15 minute Orbisonia quad, which is out of print.

This section begins on Fannettsburg-Burnt Cabins hardtop. Turn right and at 100 yards turn left into woods' road alongside of Tuscarora Mountain. Then proceed in a southwesterly direction for 5.5 miles until reaching the parking lot and refreshment area in Cowans Gap State Park. From the lot the trail bears left into a picnic area then begins to climb steadily to the top of the ridge. We found the 4 mile walk from the parking area to the lookout tower (elevation 2458 feet) to be a most pleasant one, scaring up one deer and drinking in the beauty of the wild azalea and the mountain laurel on the way. There are several good viewpoints along here; the one from the lookout tower is especially rewarding. From the tower it is another 3 miles to Tuscarora Summit, on the south side of U.S. Route 30 to C. & O. Canal, Hancock, Maryland.

Section 7: distance, 34.2 miles; elevation, minimum 380 feet, maximum 2120 feet; USGS Quads, 7½ minutes — McConnellsburg, Mercersburg, Pennsylvania; Big Cove Tannery, Cherry Run, Maryland; and Hancock, West Virginia; PATC Map K is expected to be ready in 1976.

The section begins at U.S. Route 30. Cross the highway and proceed south on a woods road that parallels the ridgetop to the west. At .4 mile you enter the State Forest and continue south crossing State Route 16 at 2 miles. Cross the jeep road at 3.8 miles and at 7.7 miles a blue blazed loop trail leads to a spring at elevation 1300 feet. The spring is 645 feet below the trail. At 8.7 miles you reach the south junction of the blue loop trail and at 9.6 miles a yellow blazed trail goes east for 2.4 miles to State Route 456.

At 15.2 miles you reach the State Game Land gate, a state barn and public road, and at 18.3 miles the trail crosses into Maryland and comes within 30 yards of one of the historical stone Mason-Dixon markers put in place in colonial days by the two English surveyors, Charles Mason and Jeremiah Dixon, who surveyed the boundary between Maryland and Pennsylvania to settle a border dispute.

At 21 miles reach the junction with the paved Moorseville Road and at 22.1 miles cross the bridges over Licking Creek. At 22.6 miles reach the Pecktonville Road with the County Picnic Park adjacent to the north. Then in rapid succession the hiker reaches Road Y at 23.5 miles, the Licking Creek Road and U.S. 40 at 24.4 miles, the dirt road under Interstate 70 at 25.9, the railroad crossing at 26.1 and finally at 26.5 miles the junction of the dirt road and the Chesapeake and Ohio Canal towpath — with the Potomac River on the left — reaching Lock #52 and the Tonoloway aqueduct at 33.0 miles. At 34.2 miles, reach the end of the Tuscarora Trail at the bridge on U.S. Route 522 which crosses the Potomac River at Hancock, Maryland. South of this point the hiker will be on the Big Blue Trail, which extends for approximately 150 miles through West Virginia and Virginia all the way to its junction with the A.T. in the northern section of the Shenandoah National Park

The Tuscarora Trail is well blazed with fresh orange blazes (2 x 6 inch in A.T. fashion). The blazing at road intersections is particularly well done and we had no trouble picking up the trail in a number of places when we were checking it out by car.

There are no shelters along this trail except for the rather uninviting Darlington shelter at the eastern terminus of the trail and another shelter in Section 4. There are public campgrounds at the Col. Denning and Cowans Gap State Park.

Mid-State Trail
(Near Pennsylvania State University)
Rothrock & Bald Eagle State Forests
in Huntingdon, Centre, and Mifflin Counties

Mid-State — "Metric System Trail"
Distance: 89 kilometers (55 miles)
USGS Quad: 7½ minute, Alexandria, Franklinville, Pine Grove Mills, McAlevy's Fort, State College, Barrville, Centre Hall, Burnham, Spring Mills, and Coburn; Mid-State Trail Maps 1-12. Note: The USGS maps do not show the route of the Mid-State Trail. *The Mid-State Trail* (hereafter referred to by initials MST) guidebook maps *do* show the route of the MST and of prominent side trails. The 35-page pocket size guide and set of 12 maps cost $1.25 postpaid in 1975. A best buy!
Description: Guidebook distances for most hiking trails in the United States are still expressed in miles. A few show metric conversions but generally less prominently than the mileage information. The MST completed in 1972, went the kilometer route with the publication of its second guide book. Even in the description of its trail markings the MST guidebook sticks to the metric. A.T. guidebooks will say that the A.T. is marked with paint blazes that are 2 inches wide and 6 inches high. The MST guide book states that "The main trail is paint blazed with orange rectangles of 5 cm x 15 cm (2" x 6"). See what I mean? (By pure serendipity the letters MST also stand for Metric System Trail).

The MST is narrated in its guide book in a southwest to northeast direction. A special feature of the trail is its many overlooks. The views are varied with farms and woods on one side and heavily wooded ridges and valleys on the other.

The entrance to the trail is at Colerain Picnic Area, 1.9 miles northeast of Spruce Creek village on State Route 45. Turn across Spruce Creek at Kerm's Spruce Creek Inn and Mobile Station. The sign for the picnic area is visible once you have crossed the creek, but is not visible from State Route 45. The water pump marking the start of the MST is visible to the left from this sign near a picnic shelter. From this starting point, the trail proceeds generally northeast and for its entire length of 89 kilometers it runs parallel to and anywhere from 5 to 15 kilometers south of State Route 45.

Throughout its length the trail leads through or near a number of state parks (blue blazed side-trails provide access to the parks), across streams, across two major highways (State Route 26 and U.S. 322), to campsites and springs, and eventually to the end of the trail at Poe Paddy Picnic Area. There are no shelters on the trail, but public campground facilities are available at the four state parks on or near the trail. The guidebook indicates other points where campsites are available. Fires are permitted except during the high fire danger months of April, May, October and November.

This rather newly completed trail was built by the Penn State Outing Club and is maintained by the same organization. The guidebook (Fourth Edition 1975/1976) lists a number of planned changes in the route and extensions of the trail scheduled for the future. Those planning to do extensive hiking on this trail are advised to contact the maintaining organization for information on changes that have taken place since the issuance of the guidebook and maps. To purchase guidebook and maps, the MST patch (available after hiking 20 kilometers), contact: Hiking Division, Penn State Outing Club, 4 Intramural Building, University Park, Pennsylvania 16802.

The Forbes Road Historic Trail [Fulton County]

Distance: 29 miles

USGS Quads: 7½ minutes, Burnt Cabins, Hustontown, Wells Tannery, Pennsylvania; plus a set of seven sketch-maps available from Scout Service Center, Hagerstown, Maryland.

Description: This trail traces a portion of the route of the historic "Forbes Road," an overland trail first cleared by the British General John Forbes during the French and Indian War. The original Forbes Road was cut through virgin wilderness to enable a military expedition to move west and drive the French and their Indian allies from the Ohio River. The detailed history of this 1755 military road, plus the route (7 sketch maps) is contained in a Hiker's Guide available from: Mason-Dixon Council, B.S.A., P.O. Box 2133, Hagerstown, Maryland 21740. Cost of the guide is 50-cents plus postage.

Although the trail can be hiked in either direction and from various entry points, we will describe the route from east to west. It begins at the north parking area in Cowans Gap State Park. From there it proceeds north, paralleling somewhat the Tuscarora Trail with some five short connector trails between the two. Forbes Trail goes north to a point just beyond the Pennsylvania Turnpike, where it turns left (west) on U.S. 522 and follows that highway until reaching the halfway point of the trail at Fort Littleton. The Mason-Dixon Council Camp Sinoquipe is located slightly more than a mile north of Fort Littleton. Those desiring to camp here should obtain permission in advance from the Council. There is no charge for tent campers, but there is a $10 charge for the use of a cabin. Each cabin will accomodate 25 people.

From Fort Littleton, the trail continues west along State Route 475, crossing the Pennsylvania Turnpike three times before it reaches the end of the trail near the intersection of the Pennsylvania Turnpike, U.S. Route 30, and the Bedford County line. Throughout its 29 miles the trail takes the hiker over country roads, jeep trails, a telephone cable line, and a few miles on the paved U.S. Route 522.

Upon completion of the hike the Forbes Road Trail emblem may be purchased for 60-cents.

EASTERN PENNSYLVANIA

French Creek State Park and
Hopewell Village National Historic Site

Distance: 43 miles divided among seven different trails

USGS Quad: Elverson, 7½ minutes; Large scale map $1.25, available from Brandywine Valley Outing Club, Box 7033, Wilmington, Delaware 19803.

Description: This 8,000-acre state park is situated in the densely populated southeastern corner of Pennsylvania. The Hopewell Village National Historic Site, which is maintained by the National Park Service, is located within the park. The restored village includes the big stone furnace, a charcoal house, blacksmith shop, tenant houses, water wheel, and the ironmaster's "big house." There is an attractive visitor center with a well informed ranger on duty. Maps and books relating to the area and to the iron making industry are on sale at the center.

I visited here in early October, 1975, and was greatly impressed with the trail system and with the Hopewell Village. There are both group and family campgrounds in the park which would make it an ideal place for a series of day hikes to see the Village and to explore the network of trails.

The large scale map (16 x 20 inch) shows all the trails clearly, and the reverse side of the map contains a description of each — where it begins, how it is marked — everything except the distance! For one trail, the Horse-Shoe Trail, the distance is shown. Some 8 miles of the total 121 miles of that trail goes through the park. It is the best maintained and easiest to follow of any of the seven. The Horse-Shoe Trail, described in detail elsewhere in this book, enters the park in the south, proceeds past the family campground and the fire tower (spectacular views from the top), and the dam at Scott's Run Lake; then it proceeds in a northwesterly direction across Six-Penny Creek and leaves the park at a beautiful spring. *The Horse-Shoe Trail Guidebook* can be purchased at the visitor center in the Hopewell Village.

The other six trails, whose mileage totals 35 miles, are: Boone Trail, Turtle Trail, Raccoon Trail, Lenape Trail, Buzzard's Trail and Fire Trail.

Of these, the Boone and Lenape trails are the most prominent. For overnight accomodations (other than the campgrounds), there is Shirey's Youth Hostel at Geigertown, Pennsylvania 19523, on the western border of the park.

Repairing the bridge across Kettle Creek are Ken Bassler and Sam Harris.

The John J. Tyler Arboretum

At first blush it may seem inconsistent to single out this 700-acre arboretum for a description of its hiking trails. But I was informed by hikers who have visited the arboretum that it *must* be included in any book describing hiking trails in Pennsylvania. It is located four miles from Media, Delaware County, Pennsylvania, and is situated on land that was granted by William Penn to Thomas Minshall in 1681. The land remained in the possession of Minshall's descendants for seven generations until 1945, when it was bequeathed as an arboretum for use of the public.

Two brothers, Minshall and Jacob Painter, descendants of Thomas Minshall, began planting a wide variety of trees and shrubs on the land as far back as 1830. Many are rare trees and some, such as the Cedar of Lebanon, now 15 feet in circumference, have grown to very large size. There are areas of rhododendron, lilacs (50 varieties), daffodils (30,000 bulbs planted), daylilies, dogwood, holly, and a host of other plants and shrubs.

And the arboretum contains 20 miles of broad walking trails, one of which, the Wilderness Trail, is blazed and winds for 10 miles throughout the area. Admission to the arboretum is free. An information brochure and a map showing all of the trails may be obtained by writing to: John J. Tyler (Painter) Arboretum, P.O. Box 216, 515 Painter Road, Lima, Pennsylvania 19060. Telephone: 215/LO6-5431.

The Delaware and Lehigh Canal Towpath Trail

Distance: 60 miles

USGS Quad: 7½ Minutes: Lembertville, Stockton, Lumberville, Frenchtown, Riegelsville and Easton. A free map of the northernmost 12.5 miles of hiking is available from Hugh Moore Park; sketch maps of the entire 60 miles are available with the book *A Wayfarer's Guide to the Delaware Canal.*

Description: This towpath trail extends the length of the 60-mile Delaware Canal, plus 3 miles beyond along the Lehigh Canal. The two rivers and the two canals come together at Easton and near the Hugh Moore Park's Canal Museum is located the confluence. Both canals were built in the early 1800's during the great canal building boom that took place after the opening of the Erie Canal in 1825.

This was the last trail that I examined on my scouting trips to the mid-Atlantic states. I visited this particular trail on a warm sunny mid-October day in 1975, stopping at four places as far south as Durham Furnace at the junction of State Routes 611 and 32. There are many inviting places to stop, places with parking areas, restored locks, picnic tables, and footbridges that enable one to cross the canal. Hiking on the towpath beside the beautiful Delaware River is quite pleasant, but I suspect it would be unpleasantly warm during summer middays, as there is not too much shade.

Those planning to hike the towpath should by all means write in advance for the free map, the explanatory material, camping reservation forms, locations of campgrounds, and the certification forms for those who have hiked the 12.5 miles of the northernmost part of the canal and who wish to purchase the patch to which they are thus entitled. Write to: Hugh Moore Park, 200 South Delaware Drive, P.O. Box 877, Easton, Pennsylvania 18042.

The material which will be received contains a price list and order blank for the 19 canal-oriented books the Museum sells. The book, *A Wayfarer's Guide*, by Willis Rivinus, with the maps of the entire 60-mile canal, costs $1.50 plus 25-cents. To this you need to add 9-cents tax.

The area at the extreme southern end of the canal (Bristol, Morrisville, Yardley) is heavily industrialized. Most hikers will prefer to start further north, at Washington Crossing State Park, where there is a historical museum.

At New Hope, situated at approximately the midpoint of the canal, is a mule-drawn excursion barge that takes passengers 5.5 miles up the canal on every day but Monday, afternoons only. Flyers with details and exact hours are available at Pennsylvania visitor centers.

The section of the trail that is most heavily used, especially by Boy Scout groups, is the 12.5 miles north of Durham Furnace. The Park Commission requests hiking groups to register in advance, giving both the numbers in the party and dates. The registration forms are enclosed with the free map and price list furnished upon request. Trail data for the northernmost 12.5 miles follows:

Miles   South to North — Delaware Canal

0.0 *Durham Furnace* at junction of Pennsylvania State Route 611 and 212

1.1 *Riegelsville.*

3.8 *Ground Hog Lock #22-23.* Picnic tables, restrooms, water, parking, overnight camping (for Scout Units only).

4.4 *Raubsville.* Restored Lockhouse is Visitor Information Center for Roosevelt State Park (summer months).

5.4 *Brown's Crossing Bridge.*

9.3 *Canal Museum.* Restrooms, soda, water, picnic tables, parking Lehigh Canal (Begin Hugh Moore Park)

10.0 *Outlet Lock — Section 8.* Remains of Collector's Office

11.5 *Primitive Overnight Camping Area.*

12.5 *Locktender's House.* By Guard Lock No. 8 and Chain Dam.

Horse-Shoe Trail

Distance: 124 miles

USGS Quad: Valley Forge Section (eastern end) 43.0 miles; junction of Pennsylvania Route 252 and Pennsylvania Route 23 to Plowville (Pennsylvania Route 10). USGS 7½ minute Quads: Valley Forge, Malvern, Downingtown, Pottstown, Elverson, and Morgantown; Horse-She Trail Guide Book, Maps 1 and 2. Reading Section (central) Plowville (Pennsylvania Route 10) to Mount Gretna (Pennsylvania Route 117) 43 miles. USGS 7½ minute Quads: Morgantown, Terre Hill, Sinking Spring, Ephrata, Womelsdorf, Richland, Lititz, Manheim, Lebanon; *Horse-Shoe Trail Guide Book,* Maps 2 and 3. Stony Mountain Section (western end) from Mount Gretna (Pennsylvania Route 117) to Junction with A.T. on Stony Mountain: 38 miles. USGS 7½ minute Quads: Lebanon, Palmyra, Hershey, Grantville; *Horse-Shoe Trail Guide Book,* Maps 3 and 4.

In addition to the above maps, the trail appears on the Pennsylvania

A specially built wood pile, used by a collier in the manufacturing of charcoal. [Photo by Kevin H. Johnson.]

Official Highway Map. A glance at that map will show that it runs from east to west just north of and parallel to the Pennsylvania Turnpike. As it nears Hershey, the trail begins veering north and goes almost due north until joining the A.T. on Stony Mountain.

Description: As you may have guessed from its name, this trail is for hikers *and* horseback riders. Motorized vehicles of any kind are not welcome on this trail, most of which runs over private property. The trail is marked with yellow paint blazes and at some road intersections it is further identified by yellow painted horseshoes nailed to trees. White blazed trails lead to hostels.

In company with my daughter Sharon, I checked out the western and central sections of the trail in early June. We hiked small distances on it and, since much trail mileage is on quiet country roads, we were able to follow a good deal of it by car. In early October I hiked over much of the trail that goes through both the French Creek and Valley Forge State Parks. In French Creek I met backpacker Stan Horzempa, from Chester, Pennsylvania, who had just hiked over 70 miles of the trail and was un-enthusiastic about it — too much road walking and inadequate camping facilities and lack of drinking water. Next day I met the two hiking sisters from Wilmington, Mary King and Maggi Donovan. They had hiked the entire 124 miles and thought it was terrific, but they had day-hiked the entire distance and conceded that the backpacker would have problems on the Horse-Shoe Trail.

The exact beginning point for the trail is in Valley Forge State Park at the stone bridge over Valley Creek near intersection of State Routes 252 and 23. One could start there without benefit of a map and begin hiking because the trail is well marked. However, anyone planning to do any extensive hiking on it is advised to purchase the 33-page 4 x 6 inch *Guide to the Horse-Shoe Trail in Pennsylvania*. It has four fold-over maps included. Cost of entire package is $2.00 and it may be obtained by writing to: Mrs. Robert L. Chalfant, Secretary, Horse-Shoe Trail Club, Inc., 1325 Jericho Road, Abington, Pennsylvania 19001.

The Guide lists the locations of the four youth hostels near the trail. Hikers must possess AYH passes to use the hostels. The Guide gives much history of the trail, especially in the Valley Forge area where Washington and the Continental Army spent the winter of 1777-1778. Location of overnight campgrounds as well as eating places and motels also are included. I purchased my copy of the Guide at the Hopewell Village Visitor Center in French Creek State Park.

Other Trails

The Commonwealth of Pennsylvania has substantial holdings of state game lands — 262 parcels distributed totalling 1,666,429 acres. A free index map showing their location throughout the state can be obtained by writing to: Pennsylvania Game Commission, P.O. Box 1567, Harrisburg, Pennsylvania 17120.

On the reverse side of the index map is a description, price, and order form for the two types of maps that are available. One is 17 x 22 inches and shows all game lands within a particular county. The other, from a new series first issued in 1975, is an 8½ x 13 inch affair called a *Sportsmen's Recreation Map*. There is one such map for each of the 262 game land parcels. They are multi-colored and are printed on slick paper and, they show hiking trails, service roads, and parking areas, among other things. Of the two, the *Sportsmen's Recreation Map* will be more suitable for those desiring hiking trail information.

State game lands are open to hikers and hunters but are generally closed to motor vehicles. Snowmobiles are permitted to use trails marked with orange diamonds between January 15 and April 15.

The Keystone Trails Association has singled out certain game lands

that have trails and has described them in its *Pennsylvania Hiking Trails*.
Neither overnight camping nor fires are permitted on state game lands.

DELAWARE

Copies of the Official Map of Delaware and maps and information on State Parks, State Forests and recreation may be obtained by writing or visiting:

>Division of Parks and Recreation
>Edward Tatnall Building
>Dover, Delaware 19901
>Telephone: 302/678-4401

Delaware

Delaware, our First State, is also one of our smallest and hiking trails here are almost non-existent. The only one of note I found is the Brandywine Trail and even there, more than half the mileage lies in Pennsylvania, but there are two other trails in the offing. One of them, the Brandywine Battlefield Trail, approximately five miles long, will begin at the Brandywine River Museum and is expected to be completed in time for major Bicentennial activities.

The other projected trail will be approximately 205 miles long and is described in this chapter. Most of it has been marked, some of it already blazed, and permissions from almost all of the private landowners has been obtained. The completion of this trail is the pet project of Bob Yost, the energetic president of the 400-member Wilmington Trail Club. The trail is expected to be completed in 1977.

Early in March each year, members of the club go over each mile of the Brandywine Trail; they remove all blowdowns and repaint the 2 x 6-inch blazes that identify the trail. The annual end-to-end hike is held two weeks later. Anywhere from 40 to 70 members gather at 6 a.m. at Ludwigs Corner, in Pennsylvania, and set their sights on the end of the trail 36 miles to the south in Wilmington. Other club members cheer them on from various vantage points along the route with beverages and snacks. About half who start the hike actually finish it, and since daylight hours in March are still rather limited, the hikers who do finish generally walk the last few miles in darkness. The club has conducted hikes in various parts of the United States and overseas, and a few of their hardiest hikers even participate in the 100-kilometer hike on the C. & O. canal in the Washington, D.C. area.

Brandywine Trail

Distance: 37.5 miles

USGS Quads: 7½ minute, Pottstown, Downingtown, Unionville, West Chester, Pennsylvania; Wilmington, North, Delaware.

Description: This trail begins .5 miles east of State Route 100, near the intersection with Birch Run Road approximately 15 miles south of Pottstown, Pennsylvania. It ends near the Hagley Museum in Wilmington. The trail is maintained by the Wilmington Trail Club. I visited the area in early October, 1975, and hiked the last 15 miles in an all day steady rain with three active members of the Club, Turner Darden, Mary King and her sister Maggi Donovan. The experience left me considerably humbled as to my hiking prowess, even though I had hiked the Appalachian Trail from south to north in 1970, over its 2000 mile length.

First, Turner Darden, the male member of the trio was an experienced hiker who had hiked over many areas of the United States and abroad. But it was the two ladies who had the most humbling effect upon me.

They both decided in 1970 that they would take up hiking. Both are married; Maggi is the mother of five children. They hiked extensively with the Wilmington Trail Club and in 1973 went to Switzerland with 23 other members of the club for a walking tour of the Swiss Alps. Overweight people take note: on this trip Maggi lost 20 pounds in 9 days! A year or so later they arranged another such trip with a group of five people and each year since joining the club, the two have participated in the annual one-day 36 mile walk of the entire Brandywine Trail, which takes place in March.

But it was their 1975 Chesapeake and Ohio Canal hike (see chapter on Maryland for description of the C. & O. Canal) that really deflated my ego. This hike begins in Georgetown in the District of Columbia; it takes place in April. Each hiker is expected to do 100 kilometers within a 24-hour period. For those of you not yet familiar with the metric system, 100 kilometers is about 62 miles! Maggi and Mary completed the entire hike, finishing up at about 1 a.m. the next day — within a 22-hour period. Both women plan to repeat the performance in 1976 and they extended a warm invitation to me to join them. I begged off giving, as a weak excuse, the infirmities of old age. They then suggested that perhaps I could hike with them the last 15 or 20 miles or so, and this I have tentatively agreed to do.

Now for details of the Brandywine Trail. It is marked with the conventional A.T. 2 x 6 inch white paint blazes. It begins at Horse-Shoe Trail Road near the village of Ludwigs Corner on State Route 100 some 15 miles south of Pottstown, Pennsylvania. From there it goes generally south over country roads and wooded trails until nearing the village of Lenape. From Lenape, the point where I was introduced to the trail, it follows paved roads for 2 miles and railroad tracks (rerouting of this section is planned) for perhaps another two miles. Near the end of the tracks is a blue blazed trail to the left leading for approximately .3 mile to the Brandywine River Museum, with its collections of Wyeth paintings.

After the railroad walking, the trail swerves over to the banks of the Brandywine River, where the hiker passes under towering sycamore trees, goes by a number of impressive estate homes, and eventually reaches a point directly across from the first stone buildings used in the powder-making activities of the early DuPont enterprises. The trail was generally in excellent shape and extremely well marked. The one exception was a half-mile stretch near the end where paint blazes were sparse and the trail was a tangled mass of waist high grass and weeds.

One should not plan a hike on the Brandywine Trail without allowing sufficient time to visit many points of interest close by. The Hagley Foundation and the Eleutherian Mills have walking and bus excursions which show the DuPont's early powder plants, plus dioramas and models of early flour mills, textile mills and iron ore industries. One can visit the 200-room Winterthur Mureum, which is a former Du Pont home on nine levels with many exquisite examples of early United States furniture. There is also a restored Town Hall, the downtown Brandywine Village restoration, and the Longwood Gardens.

One important restriction applies to the Brandywine Trail. The Pennsylvania part of it is open to all. South of Chadds Ford, however, the trail goes through many private estates and permission for use is to members of the Wilmington Trail Club only, or to groups or individuals escorted by members of the Club. If you wish to hike on the Delaware section of the trail, you need to make advance arrangements with the: Wilmington Trail Club, P.O. Box 1184, Wilmington, Delaware 19803.

THE BRANDYWINE — SUSQUEHANNA TRAIL [Proposed]

The Wilmington Trail Club, with the help of several other clubs in the Keystone Trails Association, is currently engaged in building a 205-mile trail, beginning at the Horse-Shoe Trail in West Vincent Township, (15 miles south of Pottstown, Pennsylvania) and ending at the Appalachian Trail, near Whiskey Spring Road, a few miles from Mount Holly Springs, Pennsylvania.

The proposed trail will utilize the present Brandywine Trail from Horse-Shoe Trail Road. It will pass through the newly-formed Marsh Creek State Park, where trail elevations afford a magnificent view of the new Marsh Creek Reservoir, to Chadds Ford, Pennsylvania. Several re-routings are planned to eliminate much of the hard roads presently in use.

At Chadds Ford the trail will assume a southwesterly course through the farm, mushroom, and Quaker area around Kennet Square, Pennsylvania. There will be some road walking in this section to the lovely White Clay Creek Valley, near Landenberg, Pennsylvania, and then south, winding along the White Clay to Newark, Delaware. From Newark it will proceed west into northeastern Maryland, traversing Elk Neck State Forest, a section of wildlife sanctuary, and much public hunting ground.

At Perryville, Maryland, one will have to drive across U.S. Route 40 bridge over the Susquehanna River to Havre de Grace. No pedestrian traffic is allowed on the bridge.

Hiking north from Havre de Grace, one will encounter unique terrain running along the Susquehanna River for the next 90 miles. Although farms have crept rather close to the Susquehanna, the deep gorges cut by the river and its tributaries remain in a true wilderness state. Hiking this section will be rather strenuous and awe-inspiring. One may hike for days and, aside from passing an occasional road or cabin, would never imagine that one is so close to Philadelphia or Baltimore.

About five miles northwest of U.S. Route 30 (Wrightsville, Pennsylvania), at Codorus Furnace, the trail will proceed west through farm-lands (more road walking) on its way to the small but mighty Conewago Mountains north of York, Pennsylvania. From the Conewago's west it is a short 30 miles over wooded hills and mountains to the A.T.

Camping areas will be set up approximately one days journey apart and blue blazed side trails are being planned, but there will be no shelters. In some areas water may be a problem, since one may have to carry a one-day supply or prevail upon the local inhabitants.

Towns, parks, forests, and points of interest which the trail will traverse or by-pass are listed as follows in a clockwise direction of travel: Marsh Creek State Park, Downingtown, Pennsylvania; Battlefield of the Brandywine; Brandywine River Museum; Chadds Ford, Pennsylvania; White Clay Creek State Park, Newark, Delaware; Rittenhouse Park; Iron Hill County Park; Elkton, Maryland; Elk Neck State Forest, Perryville, Maryland; Havre de Grace, Maryland; Susquehanna State Park; Conowingo Dam; Peach Bottom Atomic Power Plant; P.O. & L's Otter Creek Recreation Area; Safe Harbor Dam, Wrightsville, Pennsylvania; Codorus Furnace; Conewago Mountains; Game Lands #242; Gifford Pinchot State Park; Round Top Ski Area, Dillsburg, Pennsylvania; Long Mountain.

The trail will be marked with 2 x 6 inch orange paint blazes. Further information may be obtained from: Wilmington Trail Club, P.O. Box 1184, Wilmington, Delaware 19803.

1. APPALACHIAN TRAIL
2. DELAWARE WATER GAP NATIONAL RECREATION AREA
3. SOUTHERN NEW JERSEY
4. NORTHERN NEW JERSEY

New Jersey

For the New Jersey Official Highway Map and for information on New Jersey's State Forests, Parks, Recreation Areas, Natural Areas and Historic Sites, write for the *Year 'Round Guide — New Jersey*. This may be obtained from:

> Bureau of Parks
> P.O. Box 1420
> Trenton, New Jersey 08625
> Telephone: 609/292-2797

For information on State Forests only, write to:

> Bureau of Forestry
> P.O. Box 2808
> Trenton, New Jersey 08625
> Telephone: 609/292-2520

The Appalachian Trail in New Jersey

From Pennsylvania the Appalachian Trail crosses the Delaware River on the Interstate 80 highway bridge. It goes through the Delaware Gap National Recreation Area, climbs up past Sunfish Pond, and proceeds northeast on the Kittatinny Range. The trail dips briefly into New York near Unionville, then back south into New Jersey, until reaching the area of Greenwood Lake where it goes north into New York to stay. The trail in this area receives tremendous summer-time use. And the hiker coming all the way from Georgia now, for the first time, begins to see lakes and ponds from his vantage point on the trail. Approximately 65 miles of the trail goes through the northwestern corner of New Jersey. Elevations are seldom above 1500 feet, the high point on the Kittatinny Range being 1690 feet.

Delaware Water Gap
National Recreation Area

This 40-mile mountain range parallels the Delaware River from the Delaware Water Gap in the south to Port Jervis to the north. It consists of three distinct sections: (1) The Delaware Water Gap area and Worthington State Forest; (2) The Stokes State Forest; and (3) High Point State Park. The Appalachian Trail crosses over from Pennsylvania to New Jersey via the I-80 bridge at the Water Gap and proceeds north to the New York line along the Kittatinny Range.

Two of the most spectacular river gorges in the eastern United States are the Potomac Gorge at Harpers Ferry, West Virginia (where the Shenandoah and Potomac Rivers and Virginia, West Virgina and Maryland come together) and the Delaware Water Gap, Pennsylvania, where the Delaware River separates Pennsylvania and New Jersey. The 2,000-mile A.T. crosses through both of these gaps. At Harpers Ferry, the trail is so laid out as to afford hikers the best possible views from *both* the Virginia-West Virginia and the Maryland sides of the river. But at the Delaware Water Gap the trail permits views from only the Pennsylvania side.

Once the trail crosses the Delaware River it scoots away as though it were ashamed to have people view the Gap from the New Jersey side. In doing so it ignores an already existing trail to the top. There are many who feel the trail should be rerouted over the top of 1552 foot Mount Tammany, which overlooks the Gap. From the river's edge it is but 3.75 miles to another outstanding attraction in this area — a beautiful glacial lake which bears the name "Sunfish Pond." I have hiked the A.T. and the

Mount Tammany Trails in this area and it would have been rather easy for me to have described the network of trails. Yet it seemed only proper that the privilege of describing the trail system in the Delaware Water Gap be reserved to a man who has worked so hard for the past ten years to protect it. That man is Casey Kays of Hackettstown, New Jersey.

Kays first laid eyes on Sunfish Pond on August 13, 1961 and promptly fell in love with the place. In 1965 he was horrified to learn that a public utility planned to convert this beautiful little pond into a pump storage area as part of a system for generating electricity. Sunfish Pond . . . a pump storage area? Casey resolved to fight.

His weapons were few. He was a factory worker with a high school education, but he owned a typewriter and he knew how to use it. Even so it was a mismatch — something like a featherweight getting into the ring with Muhammed Ali. Sympathetic conservationists knew it was a hopeless cause. Everyone knew it was hopeless — except Casey himself and a handful of other leading members of the Lenni Lenape League that Casey had helped to organize in 1966. He wrote letters, letters, and more letters — over 2000 in all. He wrote articles for the newspapers. He helped organize hikes and pilgrimages to dramatize the plight of his beloved Sunfish Pond. He button-holed political figures and obtained their support. Gradually the tide of battle began to change. The utility company began to make concessions.

Eventually it threw in the towel and Sunfish Pond and 68 surrounding acres were returned (deeded back) to the State of New Jersey. A modern day David and Goliath encounter had ended with David emerging as the victor. Sunfish Pond is now a National Natural Landmark, with a plaque at the lakesite. However, Casey states the fight goes on, at present to have the state reacquire the remaining 370 acres of the former Worthington State Forest east of the Pond, which contains its main watershed. Casey's slogan today is: *"Help Save ALL Of Sunfish Pond!"*

Such was the situation when I breezed into the Delaware Water Gap on a bright blue October day in 1975. I stopped at the Visitor Center of the National Park Service National Recreation Area, discussed the trails with Ranger Sue Harrison, and then put in a long distance call to Casey Kays. He readily agreed to describe the trails in the area, and here is his description, plus a picture of Casey taken in front of Sunfish Pond.

Trails to the Top of Mount Tammany

"From the famous Delaware Water Gap (New Jersey side of the Gap), there are three trails leading to the top of Mount Tammany, 1552 feet above sea level and 1265 feet above the normal surface of the Delaware River. (Figures from the United States Army Corps of Engineers.) Named after the Lenni Lenape Indian chief, 'Tamenund,' this is the dividing point in the Appalachian Mountain range between New Jersey and Pennsylvania's Mount Minsi, (1463 feet above sea level) which was named after the Minsi tribe of the Wolf Clan of the Lenni Lenape (also

Casey Kays of Hackettstown, New Jersey, who led the environmentalist's fight to save Sunfish Pond. [Photo by Gail Houston, National Park Service.]

known as the Delawares).

Many years ago this beautiful region of the Upper Delaware River Valley was the home of the Minsi tribe, more commonly associated with the Minisink Flats about 25 miles north of the Gap.

There is also a fourth trail (yellow) from the National Park Service main headquarters located along Highway Route 80, 1/2 mile south of the Gap. All but one of these four trails are indicated on sketch maps that can be secured from the National Park Service Information Center at the Gap or from the New Jersey Worthington State Forest headquarters located just off River Road about 4 miles north of the Delaware Water Gap toll bridge.

The trail not shown on the sketch map begins by the shoulder of the highway, .3 mile from the parking area in the Gap, and leads up the sheer cliffs to the summit. This particular trail to the very scenic top of Mount Tammany is a real challenge and breathtaking in more than one way. It is for the adventureous hiker and provides a number of excellent lookouts for one who is willing to exert himself. However, caution must be taken, and this trail should not be attempted *unless ideal weather conditions exist.*

The red trail begins from the parking area at the Gap, where you can fill your canteen from a nearby spring. This trail is 1.5 miles to the top.

The blue trail follows the Appalachian Trail for about a half-mile alongside of Dunnfield Creek and Gorge, before it diverts to the right, as the A.T. continues on to Sunfish Pond. A short distance further, the blue trail crosses Dunnfield Creek, swings to the left and then soon swings to the right, up a very steep and rocky trail. Then it goes along the crest to the face of the escarpment. This trail offers excellent views of the Water Gap, the River Valley, and the Big Pocono section of Pennsylvania.

Both the blue trail and the yellow trail are approximately 2.1 miles long. Average hiking time to the top is about 1.5 hours.

From the top of Mount Tammany (if you walk down a short distance) an excellent view of the Indianhead rock profile can be seen and photographed. I personally like to think of it as guarding this ancient waterway, carved by the Delaware River through the eons of time."

Casey Kays

Southern New Jersey

Batona Trail
Distance: 29.8 miles
USGS Quads: 7½ Minutes; Medford Lakes, Indian Mills Chatsworth, Hammonton, Atsion, Jenkins, Green Bank, and Oswego. All these cover the Wharton State Forest area to the south; 15 minutes: Pemberton, Egg Harbor. Plus an 8 x 16 inch map containing mileage table and "Particu-

Indianhead profile on Mount Tammany overlooking the Delaware Water Gap. [Photo by Casey Kays.]

lars" available for 35-cents in coin from: Morris Bardock, 1233 Princess
Avenue, Camden, New Jersey 08103. Telephone: 609/WO 4-5089.
Description: This trail, in a very interesting section of New Jersey, begins
in one state forest (Wharton) and ends in another to the north (Lebanon).
It goes over a sizeable stretch of private land and has a public campground at roughly the midpoint and another about 7 miles from the
northern end. The Carranza monument, also near midpoint, was erected
in memory of Emilie Carranza, a Mexican pilot, whose plane crashed at
that point in 1928.

I spent the better part of a day in mid-October, 1975 hiking over the
northern, central, and southern parts of this trail, but I am indebted to
Morris Bardock, of the Batona Hiking Club of Philadelphia, for supply-
ing much of the detailed information. In case you have not already
guessed it, the word "Batona" is derived from three words: Back to
Nature. This is the club that created the trail and does the maintenance,
trail clearing, paint blazing, and preparation and distribution of the
maps.

The southern part of the trail, the 100,000-acre Pine Barrens Wilderness, was offered to the State of New Jersey in 1912 for $1,000,000 but
the offer was rejected by the voters. Some 42 years later the state purchased the entire tract and named it the Wharton State Forest. The
Wharton family had owned the property since 1876. The pine barrens are
also — and equally — famous for canoeing. The area is very accessible to
those living in southern New Jersey, as well as those living in Delaware
and eastern Pennsylvania.

The trail goes over land that is rather flat but extremely interesting.
Elevation averages 50 to 60 feet. The people in south Jersey take some
kidding about the lack of elevation. The fire tower is located on the high
point — Apple Pie Hill, with a dizzying elevation of 205 feet. On the extreme northern end of the trail, the forest growth is young oak, 15 to 20
feet high. In the pine barrens it is almost all pine, again mostly 15 to 20
feet high. Here the hiker may encounter deer, beaver, squirrels and an
abundance of bird life. The streams, being cedar water, appear to be
brown in color. The trees do not provide too much shade and hiking in
mid-day in the summer could be on the warm side and somewhat
buggy. Insect repellant is advised.

There are several paved roads that cross the trail and it could be
day-hiked by starting in various points. Backpackers should allow at
least two days for hiking and exploring in this interesting area. At least a
few hours should be allowed for exploring the historic Batsto village at
the southern end of the trail. Now a museum, it was once a thriving
industrial community of a thousand people. Restored buildings include
the grist mill, saw mill, iron furnace site and the town mansion, among
many others. Admission: $1 for adults. Open year round.

Camping facilities are available at both Lebanon and Wharton state forests. Primitive camping permits are required, which may be obtained at the State Forest offices. There are water pumps at the campsites, but water should be carried. The trail is blazed in pale pink.

Maps and folders of the two state forests may be obtained by writing to: Bureau of Parks, P.O. Box 1420, Trenton, New Jersey 08625. Or, by writing to or visiting, Lebanon State Forest, New Lisbon, New Jersey 08064, (office located on State Route 72 approximately .5 mile south of intersection with State Route 70); and Wharton State Forest, Batsto R.D. 1, Hammonton, New Jersey 08037 (office located at Batsto Village).

Those wishing to hike with members of the Batona Club may obtain the Clubs six-month schedule of hiking, camping and canoeing trips by writing to: Laura Cramer, 6244-A Mulberry Street, Philadelphia, Pennsylvania 19135.

Northern New Jersey

Contrasted with southern New Jersey which has only one significant trail (Batona Trail), northern New Jersey has many beautiful hiking trails, and if the northern Jew Jerseyite cannot find enough trails in his own state to satisfy his hiking appetite, he need only proceed a few miles north or east into New York to enjoy the many trails available there.

The New York-New Jersey Trail Conference, organized in 1923, is a federation of some 47 organizations, each of which maintains some portion of the 700-mile network of trails in the two state area for which the Conference is responsible. These trails are described in *The New York Walk Book*, published jointly by the Conference and by the American Geographical Society. The book has been around a long time, the first edition was printed in 1923, with revisions in 1934, 1951 and 1971.

Upon close examination I found that the 300-page book is arranged in an orderly fashion, has a good set of maps, and contains much interesting historical information. The hard cover book sells for $9.95; the soft cover sells for $5.95. Both can be purchased at book stores, outdoor stores or directly from: New York-New Jersey Trail Conference, GPO Box 2250, New York, New York 10001.

The set of colored maps in the back of the book are at a scale of one-inch to the mile — a little small for field use. Recognizing this fact, the Conference in 1974 began issuing separate maps, which are available from the Conference at a cost of $1.00 each. Write for free index of those maps already in print.

In addition to the Conference maps, there is another set of maps developed and sold through commercial sources. These are the *Hikers Region Map*. This set of maps, each one 11 x 17 inch in size, covers the hiking trails in the Greater New York City area and beyond. And the word "beyond" includes such areas as Mount Greylock in Massachusetts, the Poconos in Pennsylvania, the Delaware Water Gap, and an area around Great Barrington, Massachusetts. The maps sell for 50-cents each, and one can obtain the complete index of available maps by sending a first class postage stamp and address to: Walking News, Inc., P.O. Box 352, New York, New York 10013.

Before my invasion of northern New Jersey, I felt it desirable to obtain some expert counsel. So it was that on a Saturday night in early October I spent two hours around the dining room table of Jack Coriell, near Summerville, New Jersey. Coriell, a trail supervisor of the New York-New Jersey Trail Conference was well prepared for my visit. The table contained road maps, *The New York-New Jersey Trail Guide of the Appalachian Trail*, plus the separate Conference maps. Together we mapped out areas that I might visit.

The trail descriptions that follow are but a sampling of the many that are described in the *New York Walk Book*. The book index lists some 30 individual trails in New Jersey, but then it goes on to list and describe many more under more general headings, such as trails within state parks, state forests, wildlife refuges, and reservations. There are perhaps 100 or more trails in all for northern New Jersey.

New Jersey Highlands Area

Three trails — Allis, Sterling Ridge, and Hewitt-Butler — ae described below, in that order, because together they provide a north-south trail of some 28 miles from a junction with the A.T. in the north to the village of Butler in the south. For all trails described in this area, refer to USGS Quads: Wanaque and Greenwood Lake, New York-New Jersey, 7½ minute, and to Hikers Region Maps 37A and 37B; also New York-New Jersey Trail Conference Wyanokie Area Map.

Allis Trail
Distance: 2 miles
Description: Trail marked with 2 x 3-inch blue blazes. Begins on State Route 210, about 2 miles west of Sterling Forest Gardens and approximately 2 miles east of village of Greenwood Lake. After a mile of road walking south, it connects the Appalachian Trail with the Sterling Ridge Trail.

Sterling Ridge Trail
Distance: 8.4 miles
Description: The trail is marked with 2 x 3 inch blue blazes. On the north the trail begins at State Route 210 near the summit of Tuxedo Mountain. From there it proceeds south past the Sterling Fire Tower and southwest of Big Beech Mountain. There are good views in all directions from the fire tower. The trail ascends Big Beech Mountain. Shortly before reaching the end at Hewitt, it proceeds within sight of the iron works and two 25-foot water wheels, after first crossing the Wanaque River on an iron bridge.

Hewitt-Butler Trail

Distance: 18 miles

Description: Marked with 2 x 3 inch blue blazes, this trail extends the entire length of the Wyanokie region from Hewitt south to the village of Butler. At its northern terminus the trail begins on Route 511 at the junction with East Shore Road (Note: In all my driving on the east side of the Wanaque Reservoir, I never did see the "511" sign; apparently the route is identified with its better known name of "Greenwood Lake Road").

From Hewitt the trail proceeds southwest, crossing the Horse Pond Mountain Trail and then the Burnt Meadow Road. It ascends to the top of and then follows the top of Long Hill for some 2 miles. After leaving Long Hill it ascends to Tip-Top Point, and shortly thereafter to Manaticut Point, with fine views. It then descends steeply, and crosses West Brook Road, after which it ascends to an easterly view which includes the New York City skyline. Next, the trail crosses the three Pine Paddies from which there are excellent views of the Wanaque Reservoir and Wyanokie High Point. From here it proceeds past a brook onto the Snake Den Road in vicinity of the AEU (American Ethical Union) Camp. The trail can be reached by car at this point, which is the way I reached it. I parked my car at the AEU parking area and hiked on the Hewitt-Butler Trail, the red-blazed Wyanokie Circular Trail, and the yellow-blazed Mine Trail, getting a small sample of each. The variety of colors and the fairly frequent intersections of these trails could be confusing. Fortunately the Trail Conference people had all trails clearly blazed, so I had no uncertainty at any intersection.

Leaving the Snake Den Road and entering Norvin Green State Forest, the trail proceeds south near the crest of Wyanokie High Point, and after leaving the Forest, it goes west before crossing Otter Hole Road (limited parking) and entering the woods to pick up the Torne Trail and make a steep ascent of Torne Mountain. In the 4 miles between Snake Den Road and Torne Mountain the Hewitt-Butler Trail intersects seven other trails.

Leaving the summit of Torne, the trail goes past the upper end of Torne Trail and proceeds to South Torne and Osio Rock. It then descends steeply and follows an old road through the valley before arriving at Star Lake. The trail continues past Cold Spring Lake to Macopin Road and from there continues on auto roads for an additional mile to the center of Butler (as of November, 1975 the trail had been worked on only as far as Cold Spring Lake. Parking problems exist at the southern end).

Wyanokie Circular Trail

Distance: 8.7 miles

Description: Blazes are red on white. To reach this trail, cross the Wanaque Reservoir on West Brook Road. The second road to the left is Snake Den Road. Turn left (south) for .7 mile to the AEU Camp and park. A parking fee may be charged. Begin hiking east on Ellen Avenue,

passing between houses before entering woods and intersecting the
Mine Trail (yellow). The trail passes the Green Mountain Club open
shelter and then ascends steeply to Wyanokie High Point (1032 feet)
where there are excellent views, including New York City's famed skyline. On the way down the trail intersects a number of other trails (more
colors!) and reaches the Stone Hunting House cave some 4.1 miles from
the starting point. After crossing two brooks and passing another cave, it
makes Black Rock (5.4 miles) with a view of Kitchell Lake. Descending,
the trail follows Snake Den wood road to Boy Scout Lake and then traverses Saddle Mountain, where it follows the Hewitt-Butler Trail over
two brooks and the three Pine Paddies, each with different views of the
Wyanokies. From there the trail crosses a brook, turns left away from
the Hewitt-Butler Trail and reaches Snake Den Road. It follows this road
for .6 mile past the AEU Camp back to the starting point.

Mine Trail

Distance: 5.4 miles

Description: Blazes are yellow on white. This trail also starts at the AEU
Camp (see directions for Wyanokie Trail). Both trails leave the AEU
Camp after entering the woods, the Mine Trail branches right to Wyanokie Falls, then turns back and crosses Wyanokie Circular Trail, turns left
and ascends Ball Mountain, named for two large boulders shaped like
giant balls. There are excellent views from this point. The trail continues
along a ridge before descending to Roomy Mine, which is open for 75
feet. Use flashlight; it's dark in there. After passing the flooded Blue
Mine, the Trail passes the Green Mountain Club open shelter and then
follows a low route to Snake Den Road (2.3 miles from starting point).
Leaving Snake Den Road, it proceeds in northwest direction, crossing
other trails, until reaching Boy Scout Lake. It follows the lake overflow
to West Brook Road, which is the road that bisects the reservoir. After
crossing the road, it ascends to Tip-Top Point on the Hewitt-Butler Trail,
which it follows to Manaticut Point.

Note: In the description of the several trails above, the reader will
have noticed certain points, such as Green Mountain Club shelter, three
Pine Paddies, and Boy Scout Lake mentioned on two or more occasions.
There are many good trails in this beautiful area, some of them reach
the same points, and sometimes two trails occupy the same route for
short distances. But with the above narrative, plus Hikers Region Maps
37A and 37B, there should be little difficulty in locating the starting
point and following all of these trails. If more detail is desired consult
the New York Walk Book.

Stonetown Circular Trail

Distance: 9.5 miles

Description: Blazes: red triangle on white. To reach the trail, cross the
Wanaque Reservoir from east to west and take the first road right,
Stonetown Road. Proceed north for a scant mile and park on the left at a
fire station. This trail goes over a number of peaks involving the equiva-

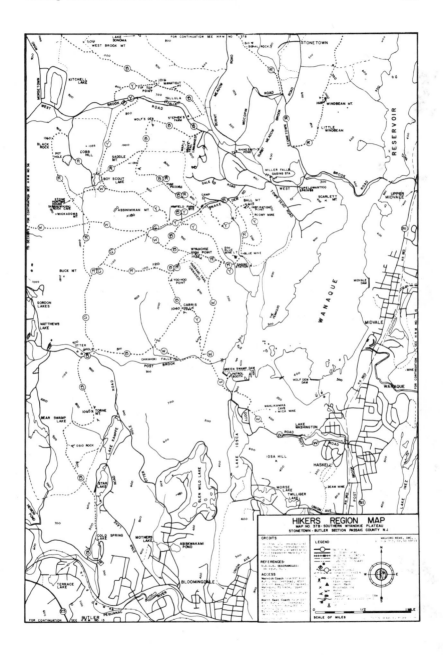

HIKERS REGION MAP
MAP NO. 37B-SOUTHERN WYANOKIE PLATEAU
STONETOWN-BUTLER SECTION PASSAIC COUNTY N.J.

lent of a 2500-foot climb and it is considered strenuous. Driving time at each end of the hike plus the 9.5 miles of up and down hiking makes for a full day's activity.

From fire station, retrace the route south on road for .5 mile and turn left into the woods. The trail begins immediately ascending Windbeam Mountain, a climb of about 600 feet. It proceeds in a counter clockwise direction for its entire length. Fine views are visible from a lookout point on the way up and from a fire tower on top (elevation 1026 feet).

The trail proceeds north, climbing Bear Mountain and Board Mountain with beautiful views of the Wanaque reservoir. Next it turns left (west), descends, and follows White Road reaching Stonetown Road at a point 2 miles north of a fire station. Turning south, it follows Stonetown Road for .3 mile before turning right off the road and beginning the ascent of Harrison Mountain and the southern terminus of Horse Pond Mountain Trail.

Turning south it descends, crossing Sawmill Brook on a bridge on Burnt Meadows Road (6.2 miles from starting point). It then follows the road south for .3 mile before turning left to climb Tory Rocks. From here the trail winds south and ascends Signal Rock with view of the Ramapos, Windbeam, and Bear mountains. Descending and continuing south, the trail parallels Stonetown Road to Magee Road and turns left to the fire station on Stonetown Road.

KITTATINNY MOUNTAIN RANGE
Stokes State Forest

The Stokes State Forest is located some 14 miles north of the National Recreation Area at Delaware Water Gap, described in previous pages. The forest is bisected by U.S. Route 206. For information write to Superintendent, Stokes State Forest, Branchville, New Jersey 07826. Park headquarters are on the north side of U.S. 206 about 1.5 miles west of Culvers Lake. On the last night of my scouting trip in New Jersey (October 1975), I camped overnight in the Stokes Shotwell Camping Area, visited the Park Office promptly the next morning, and then hiked part of three different trails in the Stony Lake Day Use Area.

There are 18 marked and measured trails in this Forest including the Appalachian Trail. Total mileage — 34 including 9.3 miles of the A.T. Excluding the A.T. all of the other trails are in the 1, 2 and 3 mile category. The ones I hiked over all appeared to have received substantial use, were well blazed, and traversed beautiful forest growth.

At the Park Office ask for the Forest map and the "Trail Guide for Stokes State Forest." This is a most helpful brochure which gives the name of each trail, its length, the color with which it is marked, the time required to hike, and even a symbol to indicate the ease of hiking. It also has a three or four sentence description of each trail. This inexpensive six-page information-packed handout was one of the most helpful that I encountered in my odyssey through the six mid-Atlantic states. My compliments to those who conceived it.

I will not attempt to describe each of the 18 trails in the Stokes Forest. It is important to realize, however, that most of the state parks and state forests do have a system of marked trails and their number is rapidly increasing. Most of them have devised, sometimes I suspect out of sheer desperation, some type of handout to satisfy the increasing number of park and forest visitors who wish to do some hiking. If the hiking enthusiast is persistent he can generally flush out one of these handouts to make his hiking more enjoyable.

Appendix I

Hiking Clubs in the Mid-Atlantic States

(Most of these clubs conduct regularly scheduled hikes. Newcomers are welcome.)

REGIONAL ORGANIZATIONS

Sierra Club: National Office at 530 Bush St., San Francisco, CA 94108

Addresses in Mid Atlantic States:

New Jersey	360 Nassau St., Princeton 08540
Pennsylvania:	C/O Harold Lockwood
	2015 Land Title Building
	Philadelphia, PA 19110

Other Mid Atlantic States:

Sierra Club, Potomac Chapter
324 C Street, S.E.
Washington, D.C. 20003
Phone: 202/547-1144

Appalachian Mountain Club: headquarters at 5 Joy Street, Boston, MA.
(AMC has chapters in New Jersey and Pennsylvania)

New York—New Jersey Trail Conference, GPO Box 2250, New York, NY 10001
(There are some 45 local hiking clubs that are affiliated with the Conference. The Conference will provide the names and addresses of these hiking clubs.)

Appalachian Trail Conference, P.O. Box 236, Harpers Ferry, WV 25425
(The ATC will provide a listing of names and addresses of hiking clubs in the 14-state Appalachian Trail area, these clubs being the ones that maintain section sof the A.T. or make financial contributions.)

Keystone Trails Association, RD 1, Box 91, Ramich Road, Temple PA 19560

(KTA is a confederation of some 35 hiking organizations located in Pennsylvania and Delaware. Names and addresses of all these clubs are shown in the trail guide *Pennsylvania Hiking Trails*. A listing of the names and addresses of these clubs will be furnished upon request.)

Potomac Appalachian Trail Club (District of Columbia, Maryland, Virginia and West Virginia)
1718 N Street, NW
Washington, D.C. 20036
Phone: 202/638-5306

HIKING CLUBS IN VIRGINIA

Mt. Rogers Appalachian Trail Club, 29 Shadow Grove Circle, Bristol, VA 24201

Virginia Tech Outing Club, Dept. of Civil Eng., Virginia Tech., Blacksburg, VA 24061

Roanoke Appalachian Trail Club, 1201 3rd St. SW, Roanoke, VA 24016

Tidewater Appalachian Trail Club, P.O. Box 62044, Virginia Beach, VA 23462

Old Dominion Appalachian Trail Club, Box 25283, Richmond, VA 23260

University of Virginia Outing Club, Box 101-X, Newcomb Hall, Charlottesville, VA 22903

HIKING CLUBS IN MARYLAND

Mountain Club of Maryland, 6608 Carroll Hts. Road, Skyesville, MD 21784

Maryland Appalachian Trail Club, Rt. 9 Box 84, Hagerstown, MD 21740

Terrapin Trail Club, Student Union Bldg., Univ. of Md., College Park MD 20742

HIKING CLUBS IN WEST VIRGINIA

West Virginia Highlands Conservancy, Box 711, Webster Springs, WV 26288

West Virginia Scenic Trails Assoc., Inc., P.O. Box 4042, Charleston, WV 25304

HIKING CLUBS IN DELAWARE

Wilmington Trail Club, Box 1184, Wilmington, DE 19899

Brandywine Valley Outing Club, P.O. Box 7033, Wilmington, DE 19803

HIKING CLUBS IN DISTRICT OF COLUMBIA

Wanderbirds Hiking Club, C/O Frank Shelburne, 2020 F St., NW, Washington, DC 20006

American Youth Hostels, Potomac Area Council, 1520 16th St. NW, Suite A, Washington, DC 20036

Appendix II
Recommended Additional Reading

The Appalachians, Maurice Brooks; Houghton, Mifflin Co., Boston

Appalachian Hiker, Adventure of a Lifetime, Edward B. Garvey; Appalachian Books, Oakton, VA 22124

The Appalachian Trail, Wilderness on the Doorstep, Ann and Myron Sutton; J.B. Lippincott Company, Philadelphia and New York

Guide to the Appalachian Trail in Central and Southwestern Virginia: Appalachian Trail Conference, Harpers Ferry WV 25425

Guide to Trails in the Shenandoah National Park, Helen and Dana Dalrymple; Potomac Appalachian Trail Club, Washington, DC 20036

Skyland, The Heart of the Shenandoah National Park, George Freeman Pollock; Chesapeake Book Company

Potomac Trail Book, Robert Shosteck; Potomac Books, Inc., Washington, DC

The Baltimore Trail Book, Suzanne Meyer Mittenhal; Sierra Club, Baltimore, MD

Guide to the Appalachian Trail from the Susquehanna River to the Shenandoah National Park; Potomac Appalachian Trail Club, Washington, DC 20036

Hiking Guide to the Monongahela National Forest and Vicinity, Bruce Sundquist; West Virginia Highlands Conservancy, Webster Springs, WV 26288

184 Miles of Adventure, Hikers Guide to the C. & O. Canal: BSA, Baltimore Area Council, 701 Wyman Park Drive, Baltimore, MD 21211

Towpath Guide to the C. & O. Canal (4 Volumes), Thomas F. Hahn; American Canal and Transportation Center, Glen Echo, MD

Guide to the Appalachian Trail in Pennsylvania, Keystone Trails Assoc.; Appalachian Trail Conference, Harpers Ferry, WV 25425

Hiking Guide to Western Pennsylvania; Bruce Sundquist and Clifford Ham; American Youth Hostels—Pittsburgh, PA Council

Pennsylvania Hiking Trails, Madeline Fleming; Keystone Trails Assoc., Appalachian Trail Conference, Harpers Ferry, WB 25425

Guide to the Appalachian Trail in New York and New Jersey (7th Edition); New York—New Jersey Trail Conference, GPO Box 2250, New York, NY 10001

New York Walk Book, New York—New Jersey Trail Conference and the American Geographical Society; Doubleday/Natural History Press, Garden City, NY

Backpacker Magazine (Published bi-monthly), 28 West 44th St., New
    York, NY 10036

Wilderness Camping Magazine (Published bi-monthly), 1597 Union St.,
    Schenectady, NY 12309

Appendix III
Acknowledgements

So many people and organizations came forward to help out on this writing assignment that it became almost like a crusade. At the risk of overlooking some of these helpful individuals, I list those which my always faulty memory brings to mind. I am most grateful to all who provided assistance.

Ed Garvey, January, 1976

VIRGINIA

The staff of the Jefferson National Forest and particularly the Mt. Rogers National Recreation Area, Mike Penfold, Charlie Blankenship, Bernie Schruender, Roger Eubanks; the staff of the George Washington National Forest, Joe Hudick, Charlie Huppuch, Bob Grace, Mel Anhold; the staff of the Shenandoah National Park; Ben Bolen, Commissioner of Parks; Kevin Johnson, Rita Cloutier, Dedie Bauer, Kevin Couch, Malcolm Eckhardt, Chuck Young, Frank Whitten, Tom Floyd; Ann and Myron Sutton.

WEST VIRGINIA

The West Virginia Department of Commerce; the staff of the Monongahela National Forest, John Ballantyne, Jim Bruce, Harry Mahoney, Lee Scharr, Roger Bucklew, Gary Lytle; Bruce Bond, Arthur Foley, Bob Burrell; Marty Conway, Superintendent, Harpers Ferry National Historical Park; the staff of the Appalachian Trail Conference.

MARYLAND

Sierra Club, Baltimore Chapter; American Youth Hostels, Potomac Chapter; Gus Crews, Carleton Gooden, and Grant and Ione Conway, Thomas Hahn, Fred Blackburn.

PENNSYLVANIA

The Commonwealth of Pennsylvania, including the Travel Development Bureau, the Game Commission, the Bureau of State Parks, the Bureau of Forestry; Rod Larson and the staff of the Allegheny National Forest; Bob Hufman, Superintendent of Laurel Ridge State Park; American Youth Hostels, Pittsburgh Council, Bruce Sundquist, Cliff Ham; Keystone Trails Association, Maurice Forrester, Madeline Fleming, Henry Finerfrock family, James Hennen, Ernest Downey, Wil and Betty Ahn, George and Mary Spring, John eastlake, Stan Horzempa, Al McDonald, Henry Knauber.

DELAWARE

Bob Yost, Turner Darden, Ralph Newman, Mary King, Maggi Donovan, Mel Brinton.

NEW JERSEY

The State of New Jersey Bureau of Parks and the Bureau of Forestry; the New York—New Jersey Trail Conference, Jack Coriell, Casey Kays, Harry Nees, Morris Bardock.

Index of Trails